EasyWriter

SIXTH EDITION

EasyWriter

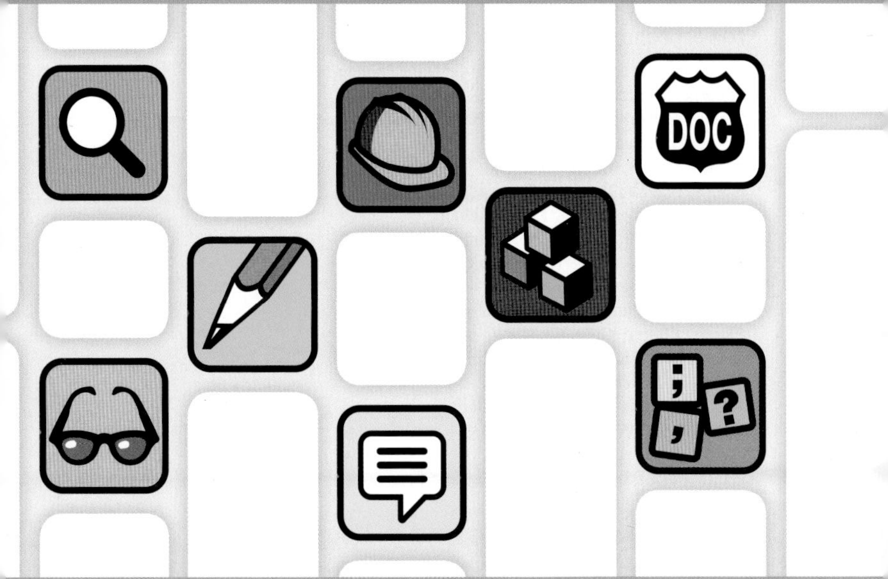

Andrea A. Lunsford
STANFORD UNIVERSITY

Coverage for multilingual writers with
Paul Kei Matsuda ARIZONA STATE UNIVERSITY
Christine M. Tardy UNIVERSITY OF ARIZONA

Boston | New York

FOR BEDFORD/ST. MARTIN'S

Vice President, Editorial, Macmillan Learning Humanities: Edwin Hill
Editorial Director, English: Karen S. Henry
Senior Publisher for Composition, Business and Technical Writing, Developmental Writing: Leasa Burton
Executive Editor: Carolyn Lengel
Associate Editor: Jonathan Douglas
Senior Production Editor: Ryan Sullivan
Senior Media Producer: Allison Hart
Senior Production Supervisor: Jennifer Wetzel
Marketing Manager: Emily Rowin
Copy Editor: Wendy Polhemus-Annibell
Indexer: Kirsten Kite
Senior Photo Editor: Martha Friedman
Senior Art Director: Anna Palchik
Text Design: Claire Seng-Niemoeller
Cover Design: William Boardman
Composition: Jouve
Printing and Binding: RR Donnelley and Sons

Printed in China.

1 0 9 8 7

f e d c b

For information, write: Bedford/St. Martin's, 75 Arlington Street, Boston, MA 02116 (617-399-4000)

ISBN 978-1-319-05076-4

ACKNOWLEDGMENTS

Art acknowledgments and copyrights appear on the same page as the art selections they cover.

How to Use This Book

Chances are that you're called on to write and do research often, maybe even every day. Whenever you have questions about writing and research, *EasyWriter* offers quick and reliable answers.

Finding Help in the Book

Brief Contents. Under the front cover flap is a brief table of contents. If you're looking for advice on a specific topic, just flip to the chapter. The tabs at the top of each page tell you where you are.

Model Student Projects. If you're looking for examples of different writing projects, the guide inside the front cover lists models of real student writing in the print book and digital resources.

The Top Twenty. On page 1 is advice on the twenty most common problems teachers are likely to identify in academic writing by first-year students. The Top Twenty provides examples and brief explanations to guide you toward recognizing, understanding, and editing these common errors. Cross-references point to other places in the book where you'll find more detailed information.

Media References. Turn to the back cover for information on all the digital resources—online videos of student writers, exercises, adaptive quizzing, student writing models, and more. Cross-references at the bottom of a page direct you to media content related to that section of the book.

Documentation Navigation. Each documentation section has its own color-tabbed pages; look for directories within each section to find models for citing your sources. Color-coded source maps walk you through the process of citing sources.

Glossary/Index. The index lists everything that's covered in the book. You can find information by looking up a topic, or, if you're not sure what your topic is called, by looking up the word you need help with. The index doubles as a glossary that defines important terms. Any **boldface term** you see in the print book is defined in the index.

Revision Symbols. The list of symbols on the last book page can help you learn more about any markings an instructor or a reviewer may make on your draft.

Glossary of Usage. This glossary, which appears right before the index, gives help with commonly confused words.

Page Navigation Help

The descriptions below correspond to the numbered elements on the sample pages on the next page.

1. **Guides at the top of every page.** Headers tell you what **chapter** or **section** you're in, the **chapter number** and **section letter**, and the **page number**. **Icons** that indicate the name of the section (building blocks for Grammar, for example) also appear at the top of the page.
2. **"Multilingual" icons.** Help for speakers of all kinds of English, and from all educational backgrounds, is identified with a "Multilingual" icon. A directory to all content for multilingual writers appears on p. 389.
3. **Hand-edited examples.** **Example sentences** are hand-edited in orange, allowing you to see an error or nonstandard usage and its revision at a glance. Orange pointers and boldface type make examples easy to spot on the page.
4. **Cross-references to digital resources.** Cross-references at the bottom of a page point you to video, quizzing, student writing models, and more.
5. **Boxed tips.** Many chapters include quick-reference **Checklist** boxes with an overview of important information, and **For Multilingual Writers** boxes appear throughout the book.

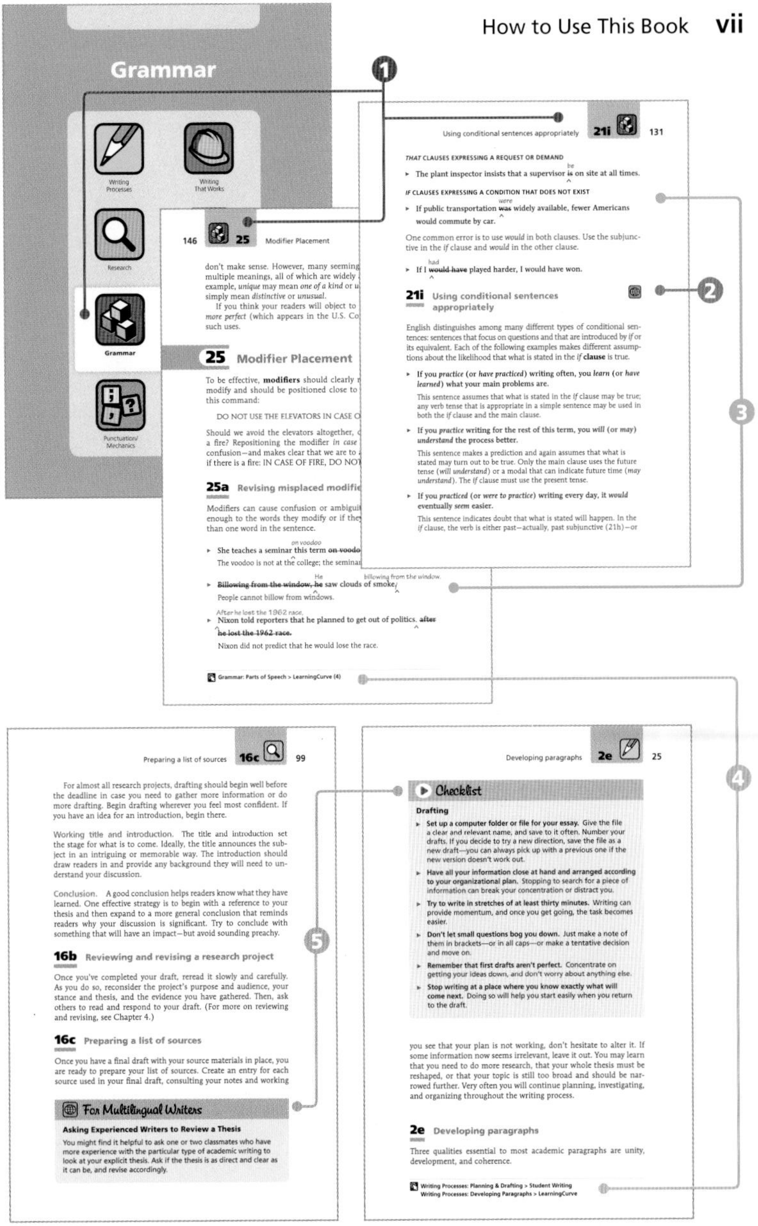
Grammar
Writing Processes
Writing That Works
Research
Grammar
Punctuation/ Mechanics
1
2
3
4
5
Using conditional sentences appropriately 21i 131
THAT CLAUSES EXPRESSING A REQUEST OR DEMAND
The plant inspector insists that a supervisor is be on site at all times.
IF CLAUSES EXPRESSING A CONDITION THAT DOES NOT EXIST
If public transportation was were widely available, fewer Americans would commute by car.
One common error is to use would in both clauses. Use the subjunctive in the if clause and would in the other clause.
If I would have had played harder, I would have won.
21i Using conditional sentences appropriately
English distinguishes among many different types of conditional sentences: sentences that focus on questions and that are introduced by if or its equivalent. Each of the following examples makes different assumptions about the likelihood that what is stated in the if clause is true.
If you practice (or have practiced) writing often, you learn (or have learned) what your main problems are.
This sentence assumes that what is stated in the if clause may be true; any verb tense that is appropriate in a simple sentence may be used in both the if clause and the main clause.
If you practice writing for the rest of this term, you will (or may) understand the process better.
This sentence makes a prediction and again assumes that what is stated may turn out to be true. Only the main clause uses the future tense (will understand) or a modal that can indicate future time (may understand). The if clause must use the present tense.
If you practiced (or were to practice) writing every day, it would eventually seem easier.
This sentence indicates doubt that what is stated will happen. In the if clause, the verb is either past—actually, past subjunctive (21h)—or
146 25 Modifier Placement
don't make sense. However, many seeming
multiple meanings, all of which are widely
example, unique may mean one of a kind or u
simply mean distinctive or unusual.
If you think your readers will object to
more perfect (which appears in the U.S. Co
such uses.
25 Modifier Placement
To be effective, modifiers should clearly
modify and should be positioned close to
this command:
DO NOT USE THE ELEVATORS IN CASE O
Should we avoid the elevators altogether,
a fire? Repositioning the modifier in case
confusion—and makes clear that we are to
if there is a fire: IN CASE OF FIRE, DO NOT
25a Revising misplaced modifie
Modifiers can cause confusion or ambigui
enough to the words they modify or if the
than one word in the sentence.
She teaches a seminar on voodoo this term on voodo
The voodoo is not at the college; the semina
He Billowing from the window, he saw clouds of smoke billowing from the window.
People cannot billow from windows.
After he lost the 1962 race, Nixon told reporters that he planned to get out of politics. after he lost the 1962 race.
Nixon did not predict that he would lose the race.
Grammar: Parts of Speech > LearningCurve (4)
Preparing a list of sources 16c 99
For almost all research projects, drafting should begin well before the deadline in case you need to gather more information or do more drafting. Begin drafting wherever you feel most confident. If you have an idea for an introduction, begin there.
Working title and introduction. The title and introduction set the stage for what is to come. Ideally, the title announces the subject in an intriguing or memorable way. The introduction should draw readers in and provide any background they will need to understand your discussion.
Conclusion. A good conclusion helps readers know what they have learned. One effective strategy is to begin with a reference to your thesis and then expand to a more general conclusion that reminds readers why your discussion is significant. Try to conclude with something that will have an impact—but avoid sounding preachy.
16b Reviewing and revising a research project
Once you've completed your draft, reread it slowly and carefully. As you do so, reconsider the project's purpose and audience, your stance and thesis, and the evidence you have gathered. Then, ask others to read and respond to your draft. (For more on reviewing and revising, see Chapter 4.)
16c Preparing a list of sources
Once you have a final draft with your source materials in place, you are ready to prepare your list of sources. Create an entry for each source used in your final draft, consulting your notes and working
For Multilingual Writers
Asking Experienced Writers to Review a Thesis
You might find it helpful to ask one or two classmates who have more experience with the particular type of academic writing to look at your explicit thesis. Ask if the thesis is as direct and clear as it can be, and revise accordingly.
Developing paragraphs 2e 25
Checklist
Drafting
Set up a computer folder or file for your essay. Give the file a clear and relevant name, and save to it often. Number your drafts. If you decide to try a new direction, save the file as a new draft—you can always pick up with a previous one if the new version doesn't work out.
Have all your information close at hand and arranged according to your organizational plan. Stopping to search for a piece of information can break your concentration or distract you.
Try to write in stretches of at least thirty minutes. Writing can provide momentum, and once you get going, the task becomes easier.
Don't let small questions bog you down. Just make a note of them in brackets—or in all caps—or make a tentative decision and move on.
Remember that first drafts aren't perfect. Concentrate on getting your ideas down, and don't worry about anything else.
Stop writing at a place where you know exactly what will come next. Doing so will help you start easily when you return to the draft.
you see that your plan is not working, don't hesitate to alter it. If some information now seems irrelevant, leave it out. You may learn that you need to do more research, that your whole thesis must be reshaped, or that your topic is still too broad and should be narrowed further. Very often you will continue planning, investigating, and organizing throughout the writing process.
2e Developing paragraphs
Three qualities essential to most academic paragraphs are unity, development, and coherence.
Writing Processes: Planning & Drafting > Student Writing
Writing Processes: Developing Paragraphs > LearningCurve

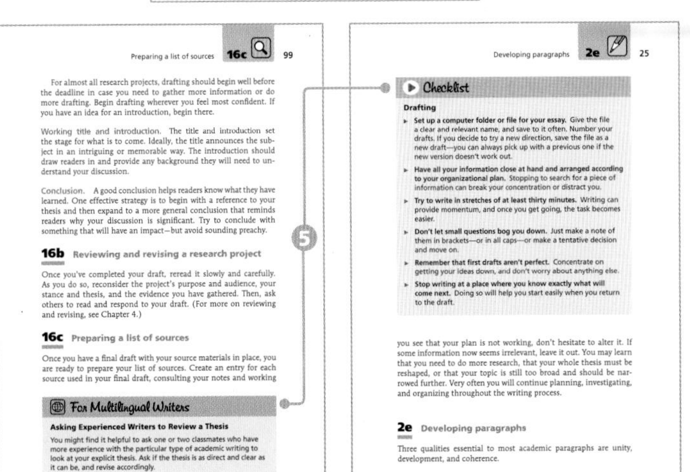

EasyWriter

The Top Twenty

Surface errors—grammar, punctuation, word choice, and other small-scale matters—don't always disturb readers. Whether your instructor marks an error in any particular assignment will depend on personal judgments about how serious and distracting it is and about what you should be focusing on in the draft. In addition, not all surface errors are consistently viewed as errors: some of the patterns identified in research for this book are considered errors by some instructors but stylistic options by others. Such differing opinions don't mean that there is no such thing as correctness in writing—only that *correctness always depends on some context*, on whether the choices a writer makes seem appropriate to readers.

Research reveals a number of changes that have occurred in student writing over the past thirty years. First, writing assignments in first-year composition classes now focus less on personal narrative and much more on research essays and argument. As a result, students are now writing longer essays than they did in the 1980s and working much more often with sources, both print and nonprint. Thus it's no surprise that students today are struggling with the conventions for using and citing sources.

What else has changed? For starters, wrong-word errors are *by far the most common* errors among first-year student writers today. Thirty years ago, spelling errors were most common by a factor of more than three to one. The use of spell checkers has reduced the number of spelling errors in student writing—but spell checkers' suggestions may also be responsible for some (or many) of the wrong words students are using.

All writers want to be considered competent and careful. You know that your instructors usually judge you by your control of the conventions you have agreed to use, although the conventions change from time to time. To help you in producing academic writing that is conventionally correct, you should become familiar with the twenty most common error patterns among U.S. college students today, listed here in order of frequency. A brief explanation and examples of each error are provided in the following sections, and each error pattern is cross-referenced to other places in this book where you can find more detailed information and examples.

Checklist

The Top Twenty

1. Wrong word
2. Missing comma after an introductory element
3. Incomplete or missing documentation
4. Vague pronoun reference
5. Spelling (including homonyms)
6. Mechanical error with a quotation
7. Unnecessary comma
8. Unnecessary or missing capitalization
9. Missing word
10. Faulty sentence structure
11. Missing comma with a nonrestrictive element
12. Unnecessary shift in verb tense
13. Missing comma in a compound sentence
14. Unnecessary or missing apostrophe (including *its/it's*)
15. Fused (run-on) sentence
16. Comma splice
17. Lack of pronoun-antecedent agreement
18. Poorly integrated quotation
19. Unnecessary or missing hyphen
20. Sentence fragment

1 Wrong word

▸ Religious texts, for them, take ~~prescience~~ *precedence* over other kinds of sources.

Prescience means "foresight," and *precedence* means "priority."

▸ **The child suffered from a severe ~~allegory~~ allergy to peanuts.**

Allegory is a spell checker's replacement for a misspelling of *allergy*.

▸ **The panel discussed the ethical implications ~~on~~ of the situation.**

Wrong-word errors can involve using a word with the wrong shade of meaning, using a word with a completely wrong meaning, or using a wrong **preposition** or another wrong word in an idiom. Selecting a word from a thesaurus without knowing its meaning or allowing a spell checker to correct spelling automatically can lead to wrong-word errors, so use these tools with care. If you have trouble with prepositions and idioms, memorize the standard usage. (See Chapter 20 on word choice and Chapter 27 on prepositions and idioms.)

2 Missing comma after an introductory element

▸ **Determined to get the job done, we worked all weekend.**

▸ **Although the research study was flawed, the results may still be useful.**

Readers usually need a small pause—signaled by a comma—between an introductory word, **phrase**, or **clause** and the main part of the **sentence**. Use a comma after every introductory element. When the introductory element is very short, you don't always need a comma, but including it is never wrong. (See 35a.)

3 Incomplete or missing documentation

▸ **Satrapi says, "When we're afraid, we lose all sense of analysis and reflection~~."~~" (263).**

The page number of the print source for this quotation must be included.

- **According to one source, James Joyce wrote two of the five best**
  ("100 Best").
  novels of all time. ^

  The source mentioned should be identified (this online source has no author or page numbers).

Cite each source you refer to in the text, following the guidelines of the documentation style you are using. (The preceding examples follow MLA style—see Chapter 45; for other styles, see Chapters 46–48.) Omitting documentation can result in charges of plagiarism. (See Chapter 15.)

4 Vague pronoun reference

POSSIBLE REFERENCE TO MORE THAN ONE WORD

- **Transmitting radio signals by satellite is a way of overcoming the**
  the airwaves
  problem of scarce airwaves and limiting how ~~they~~ are used. ^

  In the original sentence, *they* could refer to the signals or to the airwaves.

REFERENCE IMPLIED BUT NOT STATED

  a policy
- **The company prohibited smoking, ~~which~~ many employees** ^
  appreciated.

  What does *which* refer to? The editing clarifies what employees appreciated.

A **pronoun** should refer clearly to the word or words it replaces (called the *antecedent*) elsewhere in the sentence or in a previous sentence. If more than one word could be the antecedent, or if no specific antecedent is present, edit to make the meaning clear. (See Chapter 26.)

5 Spelling (including homonyms)

  Reagan
- **Ronald ~~Regan~~ won the election in a landslide.** ^

  Everywhere
- **~~Every where~~ we went, we saw crowds of tourists.** ^

The most common misspellings today are those that spell checkers cannot identify. The categories that spell checkers are most likely to miss include homonyms, compound words incorrectly spelled as separate words, and proper **nouns**, particularly names. After you run the spell checker, proofread carefully for errors such as these—and be sure to run the spell checker to catch other kinds of spelling mistakes.

6 Mechanical error with a quotation

▸ **"I grew up the victim of a disconcerting confusion,"/ Rodriguez says (249).**

The comma should be placed *inside* the quotation marks.

Follow conventions when using quotation marks with commas (35h), colons, and other punctuation. Always use quotation marks in pairs, and follow the guidelines of your documentation style for block quotations. Use quotation marks for titles of short works (39b), but use italics for titles of long works (43a).

7 Unnecessary comma

BEFORE CONJUNCTIONS IN COMPOUND CONSTRUCTIONS THAT ARE NOT COMPOUND SENTENCES

▸ **This conclusion applies to the United States/ and to the rest of the world.**

No comma is needed before *and* because it is joining two phrases that modify the same verb, *applies*.

WITH RESTRICTIVE ELEMENTS

▸ **Many parents/ of gifted children/ do not want them to skip a grade.**

No comma is needed to set off the restrictive phrase *of gifted children*, which is necessary to indicate which parents the sentence is talking about.

Do not use commas to set off **restrictive elements** that are necessary to the meaning of the words they modify. Do not use a comma before a **coordinating conjunction** (*and, but, for, nor, or, so, yet*) when the conjunction does not join parts of a compound sentence (error 13). Do not use a comma before the first or after the last item in a series, between a **subject** and **verb**, between a verb and its **object** or object/complement, or between a **preposition** and its object. (See 35i.)

8 Unnecessary or missing capitalization

▸ **Some ~~Traditional~~ traditional Chinese ~~Medicines~~ medicines containing ~~Ephedra~~ ephedra remain legal.**

Capitalize proper nouns and proper adjectives, the first words of sentences, and important words in titles, along with certain words indicating directions and family relationships. Do not capitalize most other words. When in doubt, check a dictionary. (See Chapter 41.)

9 Missing word

▸ **The site foreman discriminated against women and promoted men with less experience.**

Proofread carefully for omitted words, including prepositions (27a), parts of two-part verbs (27b), and correlative **conjunctions**. Be particularly careful not to omit words from quotations.

10 Faulty sentence structure

▸ **~~The information which high~~ High school athletes are presented with ~~mainly includes~~ information on what credits ~~needed~~ they need to graduate,**

~~and thinking about the college~~ which ~~athletes are trying~~ colleges to try to play for, and how to apply.

A sentence that starts with one kind of structure and then changes to another kind can confuse readers. Make sure that each sentence contains a subject and a verb, that subjects and **predicates** make sense together (30b), and that comparisons have clear meanings (30d). When you join elements (such as subjects or verb phrases) with a coordinating conjunction, make sure that the elements have parallel structures (see Chapter 33).

11 Missing comma with a nonrestrictive element

▸ **Marina, who was the president of the club, was first to speak.**

The clause *who was the president of the club* does not affect the basic meaning of the sentence: Marina was first to speak.

A **nonrestrictive element** gives information not essential to the basic meaning of the sentence. Use commas to set off a nonrestrictive element (35c).

12 Unnecessary shift in verb tense

▸ **Priya was watching the great blue heron. Then she ~~slips~~ slipped and ~~falls~~ fell into the swamp.**

Verbs that shift from one **tense** to another with no clear reason can confuse readers (34a).

13 Missing comma in a compound sentence

▸ **Meredith waited for Samir, and her sister grew impatient.**

Without the comma, a reader may think at first that Meredith waited for both Samir and her sister.

A compound sentence consists of two or more parts that could each stand alone as a sentence. When the parts are joined by a coordinating conjunction, use a comma before the conjunction to indicate a pause between the two thoughts (35b).

14 Unnecessary or missing apostrophe (including *its/it's*)

- Overambitious parents can be very harmful to a ~~childs~~ child's well-being.
- The library is having ~~it's~~ its annual fund-raiser. ~~Its~~ It's for a good cause.

To make a noun **possessive**, add an apostrophe and an *-s* (*Ed's book*) or an apostrophe alone (*the boys' gym*). Do *not* use an apostrophe in the possessive **pronouns** *ours*, *yours*, and *hers*. Use *its* to mean *belonging to it*; use *it's* to mean *it is* or *it has*. (See Chapter 38.)

15 Fused (run-on) sentence

- Klee's paintings seem simple, but they are very sophisticated.
- ~~She~~ Although she doubted the value of meditation, she decided to try it once.

A **fused sentence** (also called a *run-on*) joins clauses that could each stand alone as a sentence with no punctuation or words to link them. Fused sentences must either be divided into separate sentences or joined by adding words or punctuation. (See Chapter 28.)

16 Comma splice

- I was strongly attracted to her, for she was beautiful and funny.
- We hated the meat loaf~~,~~ that the cafeteria served ~~it~~ every Friday.

A **comma splice** occurs when only a comma separates clauses that could each stand alone as a sentence. To correct a comma splice, you can insert a semicolon or period, connect the clauses with a word such as *and* or *because*, or restructure the sentence. (See Chapter 28.)

17 Lack of pronoun-antecedent agreement

► ~~Every student~~ [All students] must provide their own ~~uniform.~~ [uniforms.]

► Each of the puppies thrived in ~~their~~ [its] new home.

Pronouns must agree with their antecedents in gender (male or female) and in number (singular or plural). Many **indefinite pronouns**, such as *everyone* and *each*, are always singular. When a singular antecedent can refer to a man or a woman, either rewrite the sentence to make the antecedent plural or to eliminate the pronoun, or use *his or her*, *he or she*, and so on. When antecedents are joined by *or* or *nor*, the pronoun must agree with the closer antecedent. A collective **noun** such as *team* can be either singular or plural, depending on whether the members are seen as a group or as individuals. (See 26b.)

18 Poorly integrated quotation

► A 1970s study of what makes food appetizing [showed how color affects taste:] "Once it became apparent that the steak was actually blue and the fries were green, some people became ill" (Schlosser 565).

► [According to Lars Eighner,] "Dumpster diving has serious drawbacks as a way of life" (~~Eighner~~ 383). Finding edible food is especially tricky.

Quotations should all fit smoothly into the surrounding sentence structure. They should be linked clearly to the writing around them (usually with a signal phrase) rather than dropped abruptly into the writing. (See 15a.)

19 Unnecessary or missing hyphen

- This paper looks at fictional and real life examples.

  A compound adjective modifying a noun that follows it requires a hyphen.

- The buyers want to fix-up the house and resell it.

  A two-word verb should not be hyphenated.

A compound **adjective** that appears before a noun needs a hyphen. However, be careful not to hyphenate two-word verbs or word groups that serve as subject complements. (See Chapter 44.)

20 Sentence fragment

NO SUBJECT

- Marie Antoinette spent huge sums of money on herself and her favorites. ~~And~~ Her extravagance helped bring on the French Revolution.

NO COMPLETE VERB

- The old aluminum boat was sitting on its trailer.

BEGINNING WITH A SUBORDINATING WORD

- We returned to the drugstore~~.~~, ~~Where~~ where we waited for our buddies.

A **sentence fragment** is part of a sentence that is written as if it were a complete sentence. Reading your draft out loud, backwards, sentence by sentence, will help you spot sentence fragments. (See Chapter 29.)

Checklist

Taking a Writing Inventory

One way to learn from your mistakes is to take a writing inventory. It can help you think critically and analytically about how to improve your writing skills.

1. Collect two or three pieces of your writing to which either your instructor or other students have responded.
2. Read through these writings, adding your own comments about their strengths and weaknesses. How do your comments compare with those of others?
3. Group all the comments into three categories—*broad content issues* (use of evidence and sources, attention to purpose and audience, and overall impression), *organization and presentation* (overall and paragraph-level organization, sentence structure and style, and design and formatting), and *surface errors* (problems with spelling, grammar, punctuation, and mechanics).
4. Make an inventory of your own strengths in each category.
5. Study your errors. Mark every instructor and peer comment that suggests or calls for an improvement, and put all these comments in a list. Consult the relevant part of this book or speak with your instructor if you don't understand a comment.
6. Make a list of the top problem areas you need to work on. How can you make improvements? Then note at least two strengths that you can build on in your writing. Record your findings in a writing log that you can add to as the class proceeds.

Taking a Writing Inventory

Writing Processes

Writing Processes

Writing That Works

Research

Language

Grammar

Style

Punctuation/ Mechanics

Documentation

1 A Writer's Choices

You send a text message to your best friend confirming weekend plans. Later on, you put together an analysis of cost-cutting possibilities for the manager of the company you're interning for. And later still, just before calling it a day, you pull out the notes you took on your biology experiment and write up the lab report that is due tomorrow. In between, you do a lot of other writing as well—notes, lists, blog entries, Facebook status updates, tweets, and so on.

These are the kinds of writing most of us do every day, more or less easily, yet each demands that we make various important choices. In your text message, you probably use a kind of shorthand, not bothering to write complete sentences or even entire words. For your boss, however, you probably choose to be more formal, writing complete sentences and appropriate punctuation. And for your lab report, you probably choose to follow the format your instructor has demonstrated. In each case, the choices you make are based on your **rhetorical situation**—the entire context in which your writing takes place.

1a Moving between informal and formal writing

Students are doing more writing and reading today than ever before, and much of it is online—on Facebook, Twitter, Tumblr, Snapchat, and other social media sites. Writing on social networking sites is generally informal and allows almost instant feedback; anticipating audience responses can make online writers very savvy about analyzing audiences and about using an appropriate style and tone for the occasion.

Student Stephanie Parker tweeted:

> Rain's over, going to Trader Joe's for some healthy stuff to fight this cold . . . suggestions?

Student Erin McLaughlin posted on Facebook:

> Help send one of my Ghanian friends to college. The smallest contribution helps! http://www.indiegogo.com/teachaman

In these two short messages, Stephanie and Erin show a keen awareness of audience and two common purposes for social writing—to ask for information (healthy food suggestions for Stephanie) and to give information (about a cause Erin supports). Erin is asking her audience to help a friend from Ghana go to college, and since most of her friends are also college students, she assures them that they don't need to have a lot of money to make a difference. The link goes to a site about a group effort to raise enough funds to send a young man, Jey, to the University of Ghana.

Like Stephanie and Erin, you are probably adept at informal social writing across a range of genres and media. You may not think very hard about your audience for a tweet or Facebook post, or about your purpose for writing in such spaces, but you are probably more skilled than you give yourself credit for when it comes to making appropriate choices for varying kinds of informal writing.

Because social media writing is so common, it's easy to fall into the habit of writing very informally. But remember the importance of a writer's choices: don't forget to adjust style and voice for different occasions and readers.

In the writing you do from now on, you'll need to be able to move easily back and forth between informal and formal situations. So take time to look closely at some of your informal social media writing: What do you assume about your audience? What is your purpose? How do you represent yourself online? What do the photos you post and your likes and dislikes say about you? Do you come across as the person you want others to see you as? How do you establish your credibility? Why do you write the way you do in these situations? Analyzing the choices you make in an informal writing context will help you develop the ability to make good choices in other contexts as well.

1b Email and other "in-between" writing

When writing some academic and professional messages, including emails to instructors, you may find yourself somewhere in the middle of the spectrum between "informal" and "formal" writing. On these occasions, lean toward following the conventions of academic English, and be careful not to offend or irritate your audience. For email especially, this will mean stating your purpose clearly and succinctly in the subject line and using a formal greeting (*Dear Professor Banks* rather than *Hey!*).

In addition, you will want to keep your messages as clear and concise as possible and sign off with your name. Make sure you have proofread the message and that you've addressed your intended audience. Finally, make sure that the username on the account you use for formal messages does not present a poor impression. If your username is Party2Nite, consider changing it, or use your school account for academic and professional communication. And remember: such messages are permanent and always findable.

1c Meeting expectations for academic writing

Expectations about academic writing vary considerably from field to field (see Chapter 10), but becoming familiar with widespread conventions will prepare you well for writing in most academic contexts.

Authority. Most instructors expect you to begin to establish your own authority—to become a constructive critic who can analyze and interpret the works of others.

To establish authority, assume that your opinions count (as long as they are informed rather than tossed out with little thought) and that your audience expects you to present them in a fair, well-reasoned manner. Show your familiarity with the ideas and works of others, both from the assigned course reading and from good points your instructor and classmates have made.

Directness and clarity. Research for this book confirms that readers depend on writers to organize and present their material—using sections, paragraphs, sentences, arguments, details, and source citations—to aid understanding. Good academic writing offers a clear **thesis**, prepares readers for what is coming next, provides definitions, and includes topic sentences.

Writing Processes: Expectations for College Writing > Video Prompts (2)

To achieve directness in your writing, try the following strategies:

- State your main point early and clearly. Academic writing may call for an explicit **claim** or thesis (2b and 8d).
- Avoid overqualifying your statements. Instead of writing *I think the facts reveal*, come right out and say *The facts reveal*.
- Avoid unnecessary digressions. If you use an anecdote or example from personal experience, be sure it relates directly to the point you are making.
- Use appropriate evidence and authorities of various kinds to support each point you make (2c). Carefully document all of your sources, including visuals and media.
- Make explicit links between ideas (2e). The first sentence of a new paragraph should reach back to the paragraph before and then look forward to what comes next.
- Follow clear, easy-to-follow organizational patterns.

Checklist

U.S. Academic Style

- Consider your purpose and audience carefully, making sure that your topic is appropriate to both. (1d–f)
- State your **claim** or **thesis** explicitly, and support it with evidence and authorities of various kinds. (2b)
- Carefully document all of your sources, including visual ones. (Chapters 45–48)
- Make explicit links between ideas. (2e)
- Use the appropriate level of formality. (20a)
- Use conventional formats for academic genres. (Chapter 10)
- Use conventional grammar, spelling, punctuation, and mechanics. (Chapters 21–44)
- Use an easy-to-read type size and typeface and conventional margins. For print projects, double-space text. (3a)

1d Considering the assignment and purpose

For the writing you do that isn't connected to a class or work assignment, you may have a clear purpose in mind. Even so, analyzing exactly what you want to accomplish and why can help you communicate more effectively.

An academic assignment may explain why, for whom, and about what you are supposed to write, or it may seem to come out of the blue. Comprehending the assignment is crucial to your success, so make every effort to understand what your instructor expects.

- What is the primary purpose of your writing—to persuade? to explain? to entertain? something else?
- What purpose did the person who gave you the assignment want to achieve—to test your understanding? to evaluate your thinking and writing abilities? to encourage you to think outside the box?
- What, exactly, does the assignment ask you to do? Look for words such as *analyze*, *explain*, *prove*, and *survey*. Remember that these words may differ in meaning from discipline to discipline and from job to job.

1e Choosing a topic

Experienced writers say that the best way to choose a topic is to let it choose you. Look to topics that compel, puzzle, or pose a problem for you: these are likely to engage your interests and hence produce your best writing.

- Can you focus the topic enough to write about it effectively in the time and space available?
- What do you know about the topic? What else do you need to learn?
- What seems most important about it?
- What do you expect to conclude about the topic? (Remember, you may change your mind.)

For information on exploring a topic, see 2a.

Writing Processes: Rhetorical Situations > Storyboards

1f Reaching appropriate audiences

Every communicator can benefit from thinking carefully about who the audience is, what the audience already knows or thinks, and what the audience needs and expects to find out. One of the characteristics of an effective communicator is the ability to write for a variety of audiences, using language, style, and evidence appropriate to particular readers, listeners, or viewers. Even if your text can theoretically reach people all over the world, focus your analysis on those you most want or need to reach and those who are likely to take an interest.

- What audience do you most want to reach—people who are already sympathetic to your views? people who disagree with you? members of a group you belong to? members of a group you don't belong to?
- In what ways are the members of your audience different from you? from one another?
- What assumptions can you legitimately make about your audience? What might they value—brevity, originality, deference, honesty, wit? How can you appeal to their values?
- What sorts of information and evidence will your audience find most compelling—quotations from experts? personal experiences? statistics? images?
- What responses do you want as a result of what you write? How can you make clear what you want to happen? (For more on audience, see 17c.)

1g Considering stance and tone

Knowing your own stance—where you are coming from—can help you think about ways to get your readers to understand and perhaps share your views. What is your overall attitude toward the topic—approval? disapproval? curiosity? What social, political, religious, or other factors account for your attitude? You should also be aware of any preconceptions about your topic that may affect your stance.

Your purpose, audience, and stance will help to determine the tone your writing should take. Should it be humorous? serious?

impassioned? Think about ways to show that you are knowledgeable and trustworthy. Remember, too, that visual and audio elements can influence the tone of your writing as much as the words you choose.

1h Considering time, genre, medium, and format

Many other elements of your context for a particular writing project will shape the final outcome.

- How much time will you have for the project? Do you need to do research or learn unfamiliar technology? Allow time for revision and editing.
- What genre does your text call for—a report? a review? an argument essay? a lab report? a blog post? Study examples if you are unfamiliar with the conventions of the genre.
- In what medium will the text appear—on the open Internet? on a password-protected website? in a print essay? in a presentation? Will you use images, video, or audio?
- What kind of organization should you use?
- How will you document your sources? Will your audience expect a particular documentation style (see Chapters 45–48)? Should you embed links?

1i Collaborating

Writers often work together to come up with ideas, to respond to one another's drafts, or to coauthor texts. Here are some strategies for working with others:

- Establish ground rules for the collaboration. Be sure every writer has an equal opportunity—and responsibility—to contribute.
- Exchange contact information, and plan face-to-face meetings (if any).
- Pay close attention to each writer's views. Expect disagreement, and remember that the goal is to argue through all possibilities.
- If you are preparing a document collaboratively, divide up the drafting duties and set reasonable deadlines. Work together to iron out

Writing Processes: Working with Others > Tutorial
Writing Processes: Working with Others > Video Prompt

the final draft, aiming for consistency of tone. Proofread together, and have one person make corrections.

- Give credit where credit is due. In team projects, acknowledge all members' contributions as well as any help you receive from outsiders.

2 Exploring, Planning, and Drafting

One student defines drafting as the time in a writing project "when the rubber meets the road." As you explore your topic, decide on a thesis, organize materials to support that central idea, and sketch out a plan, you have already begun the drafting process.

2a Exploring a topic

Among the most important parts of the writing process are choosing a topic (1e), exploring what you know about it, and determining what you need to find out. The following strategies can help you explore your topic:

- Brainstorm. Try out ideas, alone or with another person. Jot down key words and phrases about the topic, and see what they prompt you to think about next.
- Freewrite without stopping for ten minutes or so to see what insights or ideas you come up with. You can also "freespeak" by recording your thoughts on your phone or other device.
- Draw or make word pictures about your topic.
- Try clustering—writing your topic on a sheet of paper, then writing related thoughts near the topic idea. Circle each idea or phrase, and draw lines to show how ideas are connected.
- Ask questions about the topic: *What is it? What caused it? What is it like or unlike? What larger system is the topic a part of? What do people say about it?* Or choose the journalist's questions: *Who? What? When? Where? Why? How?*
- Browse sources to find out what others say about the topic.

Writing Processes: Prewriting > Video Prompts (3)

2b Developing a working thesis

Academic and professional writing in the United States often contains an explicit **thesis statement**. You should establish a working thesis early in your writing process. Your final thesis may be very different from the working thesis you begin with. Even so, a working thesis focuses your thinking and research, and helps keep you on track.

A working thesis should have two parts: a topic, which indicates the subject matter the writing is about, and a comment, which makes an important point about the topic.

- **In the graphic novel *Fun Home*, images and words combine to make meanings that are more subtle than either words alone or images alone could convey.**

A successful working thesis has three characteristics:

1. It is potentially *interesting* to the intended audience.
2. It is as *specific* as possible.
3. It limits the topic enough to make it *manageable*.

You can evaluate a working thesis by checking it against each of these characteristics, as in the following examples:

- **Graphic novels combine words and images.**

INTERESTING? The topic of graphic novels could be interesting, but this draft of a working thesis has no real comment attached to it—instead, it states a bare fact, and the only place to go from here is to more bare facts.

- **In graphic novels, words and images convey interesting meanings.**

SPECIFIC? This thesis is not specific. What are "interesting meanings," exactly? How are they conveyed?

Writing Processes: Prewriting > Storyboards

 For Multilingual Writers

Stating a Thesis

In some cultures, it is considered rude to state an opinion outright. In the United States, however, academic and business practices require writers to make key positions explicitly clear.

▸ **Graphic novels have evolved in recent decades to become an important literary genre.**

MANAGEABLE? This thesis would not be manageable for a short-term project because it would require research on several decades of history and on hundreds of texts from all over the world.

2c Gathering evidence and doing research

What kinds of evidence will be most persuasive to your audience and most effective in the field you are working in—historical precedents? expert testimony? statistical data? experimental results? personal anecdotes? Knowing what kinds of evidence count most in a particular field or with particular audiences will help you make appropriate choices.

If the evidence you need calls for research, determine what research you need to do:

- Make a list of what you already know about your topic.
- Keep track of where information comes from so you can return to your sources later.
- What else do you need to know, and where are you likely to find good sources of information? Consider library resources, authoritative online sources, field research, and so on.

(For more on research, see Chapters 13–16.)

2d Planning and drafting

Sketch out a rough plan for organizing your writing. You can simply begin with your thesis; review your notes, research materials, and media; and list all the evidence you have to support the thesis. An informal way to organize your ideas is to figure out what belongs in your introduction, body paragraphs, and conclusion. You may also want—or be required—to make a formal outline, which can help you see exactly how the parts of your writing fit together.

Thesis statement

- I. First main idea
    - A. First subordinate idea
        1. First supporting detail or point
        2. Second supporting detail
        3. Third supporting detail
    - B. Second subordinate idea
        1. First supporting detail
        2. Second supporting detail
- II. Second main idea
    - A. First subordinate idea
        1. First supporting detail
        2. Second supporting detail
    - B. Second subordinate idea
        1. First supporting detail
        2. Second supporting detail
            - a. First supporting detail
            - b. Second supporting detail

The technique of storyboarding—working out a narrative or argument in visual form—can also be a good way to come up with an organizational plan. You can create your own storyboard by using note cards or sticky notes, taking advantage of different colors to keep track of threads of argument, subtopics, and so on. Move the cards and notes around, trying out different arrangements, until you find an organization that works well for your writing situation.

No matter how good your planning, investigating, and organizing have been, chances are you will need to do more work as you draft. The first principle of successful drafting is to be flexible. If

Writing Processes: Planning & Drafting > Video Prompts (3)

 Checklist

Drafting

- **Set up a computer folder or file for your essay.** Give the file a clear and relevant name, and save to it often. Number your drafts. If you decide to try a new direction, save the file as a new draft—you can always pick up with a previous one if the new version doesn't work out.
- **Have all your information close at hand and arranged according to your organizational plan.** Stopping to search for a piece of information can break your concentration or distract you.
- **Try to write in stretches of at least thirty minutes.** Writing can provide momentum, and once you get going, the task becomes easier.
- **Don't let small questions bog you down.** Just make a note of them in brackets—or in all caps—or make a tentative decision and move on.
- **Remember that first drafts aren't perfect.** Concentrate on getting your ideas down, and don't worry about anything else.
- **Stop writing at a place where you know exactly what will come next.** Doing so will help you start easily when you return to the draft.

you see that your plan is not working, don't hesitate to alter it. If some information now seems irrelevant, leave it out. You may learn that you need to do more research, that your whole thesis must be reshaped, or that your topic is still too broad and should be narrowed further. Very often you will continue planning, investigating, and organizing throughout the writing process.

2e Developing paragraphs

Three qualities essential to most academic paragraphs are unity, development, and coherence.

Writing Processes: Planning & Drafting > Student Writing
Writing Processes: Developing Paragraphs > LearningCurve

Unity. An effective paragraph focuses on one main idea. You can achieve unity by stating the main idea clearly in one sentence—the **topic sentence**—and relating all other sentences in the paragraph to that idea. Like a thesis (see 2b), the topic sentence includes a topic and a comment on that topic. A topic sentence often begins a paragraph, but it may come at the end—or be implied rather than stated directly.

Development. In addition to being unified, a good paragraph holds readers' interest and explores its topic fully, using whatever details, evidence, and examples are necessary. Without such development, a paragraph may seem lifeless and abstract.

Most good academic writing backs up general ideas with specifics. Shifting between the general and the specific is especially important at the paragraph level. If a paragraph contains nothing but specific details, its meaning may not be clear to readers—but if a paragraph makes only general statements, it may seem boring or unconvincing.

Coherence. A paragraph has coherence—or flows—if its details fit together in a way that readers can easily follow. The following methods can help you achieve paragraph coherence:

- A general-to-specific or specific-to-general *organization* helps readers move from one point to another.
- Repetition of key words or phrases links sentences and suggests that the words or phrases are important.
- Parallel structures help make writing more coherent (see Chapter 33).
- **Transitions** such as *for example* and *however* help readers follow the progression of one idea to the next.

The same methods that you use to create coherent paragraphs can be used to link paragraphs so that a whole piece of writing flows smoothly. You can create links to previous paragraphs by repeating or paraphrasing key words and phrases and by using parallelism and transitions.

The following sample paragraph from David Craig's research project (45e), which identifies a topic and a comment on the topic and then offers detailed evidence in support of the point, achieves

 Checklist

Strong Paragraphs

Most readers of English have certain expectations about how paragraphs work:

- Paragraphs begin and end with information that is important for the reader.
- The opening sentence is often the topic sentence that tells what the paragraph is about.
- The middle of the paragraph develops the idea.
- The end may sum up the paragraph's contents, closing the discussion of an idea and anticipating the paragraph that follows.
- A paragraph makes sense as a whole; the words and sentences are clearly related.
- A paragraph relates to other paragraphs around it.

coherence with a general-to-specific organization, repetition of key content related to digital communication and teenagers, and transitions that relate this paragraph to the preceding one and relate sentences to one another.

Based on the preceding statistics, parents and educators appear to be right about the decline in youth literacy. And this trend coincides with another phenomenon: digital communication is rising among the young. According to the Pew Internet & American Life Project, 85 percent of those aged twelve to seventeen at least occasionally write text messages, instant messages, or comments on social networking sites (Lenhart et al.). In 2001, the most conservative estimate based on Pew numbers showed that American youths spent, at a minimum, nearly three million hours per day on messaging services (Lenhart and Lewis 20). These numbers are now exploding thanks to texting, which was "the dominant daily mode of

Transition from preceding paragraph

Topic sentence

Supporting evidence

Sentence-to-sentence transition

communication" for teens in 2012 (Lenhart), and messaging on popular social networking sites such as Facebook and Tumblr.

3 Making Design Decisions

In a time when millions of messages are vying for attention, effective design is especially important: the strongest message may not get through to its audience if it is presented and designed in an ineffective, bland way. You will want to understand and use effective design to make sure you get—and keep—your audience's attention.

3a Design principles

In designer Robin Williams's *Non-Designer's Design Book*, she identifies four simple principles that are a good starting point for making any print or digital text more effective.

Contrast. Begin with a focal point—a dominant visual or text that readers should look at first—and structure the flow of other information from that point. Use color, boldface or large type, white space, and so on to set off the focal point.

Alignment. Horizontal or vertical alignment of words and visuals gives a text a cleaner, more organized look. In general, wherever you begin aligning elements—on the top or bottom, on the right or left, or in the center—stick with it throughout the text.

Repetition. Readers are guided in large part by the repetition of key words or design elements. Use color, type, style, and other visual elements consistently throughout a document.

Proximity. Parts of a text that are related should be physically close together (*proximate* to each other).

3b Appropriate formats

Think about the most appropriate way to format a document to make it inviting and readable for your intended audience.

White space. Empty space, called "white space," guides the reader's eyes to parts of a page or screen. Consider white space at the page level (margins), paragraph level (spacing between paragraphs or sections), and sentence level (space between lines and between sentences). You can also use white space around particular content, such as a graphic or list, to make it stand out.

Color. Choose colors that relate to the purpose(s) of your text and its intended audience.

- Use color to draw attention to elements you want to emphasize—such as headings, bullets, boxes, or visuals—and be consistent in using color throughout your text.
- For academic work, keep the number of colors fairly small to avoid a jumbled or confused look.
- Make sure the colors you choose are readable in the format you're using. A color that looks clear onscreen may be less legible in print or projected on a screen.

Paper. For print documents, choose paper that is an appropriate size and color for your purpose. A printed essay, poster, and brochure will probably call for different sizes and types of paper. For academic papers, put your last name and the page number in the upper-right-hand corner of each page unless your instructor requires a different formatting style.

Type. Choose an easy-to-read type size and typeface, and be consistent in the styles and sizes of type used throughout your project. For most college writing, 11- or 12-point type is standard. And although unusual fonts may seem attractive at first glance, readers may find them distracting and hard to read over long stretches of material.

Spacing. Final drafts of any printed academic writing should be double-spaced, with the first line of paragraphs indented one-half inch. Other documents, such as memos, letters, and web texts, are usually single-spaced, with a blank line between paragraphs and no paragraph indentation. Some kinds of documents, such as newsletters, may call for multiple columns of text.

Headings. Consider organizing your text with headings that will aid comprehension. Some kinds of reports have standard headings (such as *Abstract*) that readers expect.

- Distinguish levels of headings using indents along with type. For example, you might center main headings and align lower-level headings at the left margin.
- Look for the most succinct and informative way to word your headings. You can state the topic in a single word (*Toxicity*); in a noun phrase (*Levels of Toxicity*) or gerund phrase (*Measuring Toxicity*); in a question to be answered in the text (*How Can Toxicity Be Measured?*); or in an imperative that tells readers what to do (*Measure the Toxicity*). Use the structure consistently for all headings of the same level.

3c Visuals and media

Choose visuals and media that will help make a point more vividly and succinctly than words alone. In some cases, visuals may even be your primary text. Consider carefully what you want visuals, audio, or video to do for your writing. What will your audience want or need you to show? Choose visuals and media that will enhance your credibility, allow you to make your points more emphatically, and clarify your overall text. (See the series of figures on pp. 31–32 for advice on which visuals to use in particular situations.)

Effective media content can come from many sources—your own drawings or recordings you make, as well as audio or video materials created by others. If your document will be on the web, you can insert clips that readers can watch and listen to as they read your text. Such inserts can make powerful appeals: if you are writing about the ongoing migrant crisis in Europe, for example, a link to a video clip of people barely surviving in border "camps" may make the point better than you can do in words. Include such links as you would other visuals, making sure to provide a caption as well as a lead-in to the clip and a commentary after it if appropriate. And remember: if you are using media created by someone else, be sure to give appropriate credit and to get permission before making it available to the public as part of your work.

Position and identification of visuals and media. Position visuals alongside or after the text that refers to them. In academic and other formal writing, number your visuals (number tables separately from other visuals), and provide informative captions. In some instances, you may need to give readers additional data such as source information in the caption.

Fig. 1. College Enrollment for Men and Women by Age, 2015 (in millions)

Table 1. Refugee Population by Country or Territory of Origin: 2011-2015, UNHCR, 2016

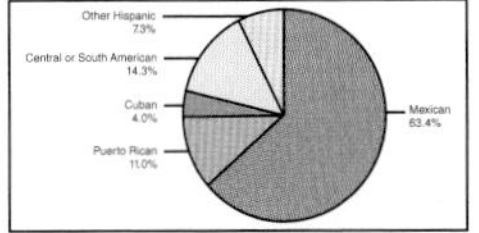

Use *pie charts* to compare parts to the whole.

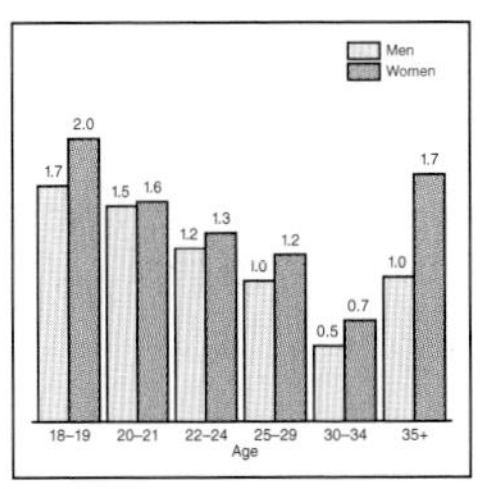

Use *bar graphs* and *line graphs* to compare one element with another, to compare elements over time, or to show correlations and frequency.

Table 10: Commuter Rail Schedule: Reading/Haverhill Line, Boston 2004

	Train 223	Train 227	Train 231
North Station	3:00 pm	4:36 pm	5:15 pm
Reading	3:38 pm	4:54 pm	5:42 pm
Haverhill	4:04 pm	5:31 pm	6:21 pm

Use *tables* to draw attention to detailed numerical information.

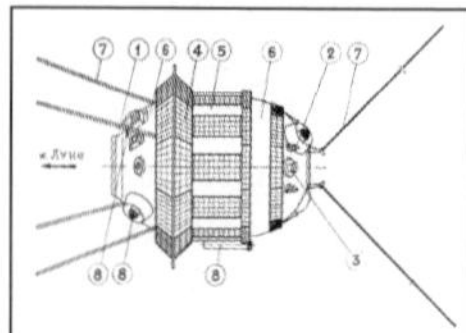

Use *diagrams* to illustrate textual information or to point out details of objects or places described.

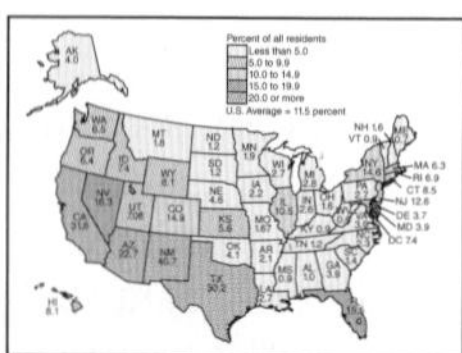

Use *maps* to show geographical locations and to emphasize spatial relationships.

Use *cartoons* to illustrate a point dramatically or comically.

Use *photographs* or *illustrations* to show particular people, places, objects, and situations described in the text or to help readers find or understand types of content.

Use *links to audio or video material* to help readers see and hear the point you are making.

3d Manipulation of visuals and media

Technical tools available today make it relatively easy to manipulate media. As you would with any source material, carefully assess any visuals and video or audio files you find for effectiveness, appropriateness, and validity.

- Check the context in which the content appears. Is it part of an official government, school, or library site?
- Is the information you find about the visual or media source believable?
- If the visual is a chart, graph, or diagram, are the numbers and labels in it explained? Are the sources of the data given? Will the visual representation help readers make sense of the information, or could it mislead them?
- Is biographical and contact information for the designer, artist, or photographer given?

Checklist

Using Visuals and Media Effectively

- Use visuals and media files as a part of your text, not just as decoration.
- Tell the audience explicitly what the visual or media file demonstrates, especially if it presents complex information. Do not assume readers will "read" the material the way you do; your commentary on it is important.
- Number and title all visuals. Number tables and figures separately.
- Refer to each visual or media file before it actually appears in your text.
- Follow established conventions for documenting sources, and ask permission for use if someone else controls the rights. (15b)
- Get responses to your visuals and media in an early draft. If readers can't follow them or are distracted by them, revise accordingly.
- If you alter a visual or media file, be sure to do so ethically.

Designing and Performing Writing: Communicating in Other Media > Tutorials (2)

At times, you may make certain changes to visuals and media that you use, such as cropping an image to show the most important detail, enhancing sound quality, or brightening a dark image. To ensure that your alterations to images are ethical, follow these guidelines:

- Never mislead readers. Show things as accurately as possible.
- Tell your audience what changes you have made.
- Include all relevant information about the original visual or media file, including the source.
- Make sure you have identified the sources of all still and moving images, audio files, and so on.

4 Reviewing, Revising, and Editing

After giving yourself—and your draft—a rest, make time to review your work (by yourself or with others) and to revise and edit. Becoming an astute critic of your own writing will pay off as you get better and better at taking a hard look at your drafts, revising them thoughtfully, and editing them with care.

4a Reviewing

Reviewing calls for reading your draft with a critical eye and asking others to look over your work. Ask classmates or your instructor to respond to your draft, answering questions like these:

- What do you see as the major point, claim, or thesis?
- How convincing is the evidence? What can I do to support my thesis more fully?
- What points are unclear? How can I clarify them?
- How easy is it to follow my organization? How can I improve?
- What can I do to make my draft more interesting?

Writing Processes: Reviewing & Revising > Storyboards (3)
Writing Processes: Reviewing & Revising > Practice
Writing Processes: Reviewing & Revising > Video Prompts (3)

4b Revising

Revising means using others' comments along with your own analysis of the draft to make sure it is as complete, clear, and effective as possible. These questions can help you revise:

- How does the draft accomplish its purpose?
- Does the title tell what the draft is about?
- Is the thesis clearly stated, and does it contain a topic and a comment?
- How does the introduction catch readers' attention?
- Will the draft interest and appeal to its audience?
- How does the draft indicate your stance on the topic?
- What are the main points that illustrate or support the thesis? Are they clear? Do you need to add material to the points or add new points?
- Are the ideas presented in an order that will make sense to readers?
- Are the points clearly linked by logical transitions?
- Have you documented your research appropriately?
- How are visuals, media, and research sources (if any) integrated into your draft? Have you commented on their significance?
- How does the draft conclude? Is the conclusion memorable?

4c Editing

Once you are satisfied with your revised draft's big picture, edit your writing to make sure that every detail is as correct as you can make it for the readers you plan to share it with (5a).

- Read your draft aloud to make sure it flows smoothly and to find typos or other mistakes.
- Are your sentences varied in length and in pattern or type?
- Have you used active verbs and effective language?
- Are all sentences complete and correct?
- Have you used the spell checker—and double-checked its recommendations?

Writing Processes: Editing & Proofreading > Student Writing

- Have you chosen an effective design and used white space, headings, and color appropriately?
- Have you proofread one last time, going word for word?

(For more on troubleshooting your writing, see "The Top Twenty" on pp. 1–11.)

5 Sharing and Reflecting on Your Writing

Once you have completed a piece of writing, think about sharing it. You've worked hard on a topic that's important to you, and there's a good chance others will care about it, too. Sharing and talking about a piece of writing that you've finished is also a good step toward reflecting back over the entire writing experience and assessing what you learned from it.

5a Sharing with audiences

Chances are, you have already shared some of your writing with family, friends, and others online (1a). So why not go ahead and share what you've written with others you think will be interested? You might just hear back from them. Making your work more available to readers can engage other audiences and start a conversation.

- Can you find other interested readers through social media sites like Facebook or Twitter?
- Should you keep a blog to share your writing, using a free site such as Blogger?
- Would your work find audiences on YouTube, Instagram, or other visual platforms?
- Could you submit your writing to student publications or organizations on your campus?

You can also share your ideas by joining conversations started by others. You might contribute to Wikipedia or other wikis; comment on online newspaper or magazine articles, editorials, or videos; write reviews for books and other products on Amazon; post to fan fiction sites; or find other public sites where you can participate in producing content and responding to work others have written. As a writer today, you have nearly limitless possibilities for interaction with other readers and writers.

5b Reflecting on your own work

Thinking back on what you've learned helps make that learning stick. Whether or not your instructor requires you to write a formal reflection on a writing course or piece of writing, make time to think about what you have learned from the experience.

Your development as a writer. The following questions can help you think critically about your writing:

- What lessons have you learned from the writing? How will they help you with future writing projects?
- What aspects of your writing give you the most confidence? What needs additional work, and what can you do to improve?
- What confused you during this writing? How did you resolve your questions?
- How has this piece of writing helped you clarify your thinking or extend your understanding?
- Identify a favorite passage of your writing. What pleases you about it? Can you apply what you learn from this analysis to other writing situations?
- How would you describe your development as a writer?

Writing Processes: Reflecting to Learn > Student Writing
Academic, Professional, and Public Writing: Portfolios > Student Writing

Writing That Works

Writing Processes

Writing That Works

Research

Language

Grammar

Style

Punctuation/
Mechanics

Documentation

6 Learning from Low-Stakes Writing

Professor Peter Elbow differentiates between "high-stakes writing"—which you do for formal graded assignments and examinations—and "low-stakes writing"—informal writing that is often ungraded but that helps you think about, learn, and remember course material and stay engaged with your classes. So one very good way to put your writing to work is to use it as a way to learn!

6a The value of low-stakes writing

Sometimes referred to as "writing to learn," low-stakes writing is powerful because it gives you a chance to figure out what you know and don't know about a topic, and can help you watch your own mind at work—all without having to be judged or graded. Research shows that reflecting on your own thinking, writing, and learning style can contribute significantly to your development as a knowledgeable and critical thinker. Your instructor may assign such low-stakes writing throughout the term; if so, take advantage of it. If not, do some informal writing yourself and see how it helps improve your understanding of course material—and your grades!

6b Types of low-stakes assignments

Quickwrites. A good way to get mental gears going, quickwrites are prompts—usually open-ended questions about a topic of study—to which writers respond in short bursts of two to eight minutes. Instructors often use quickwrites to get class discussion started and focused, but you can use them on your own to get your thinking about a subject down on paper (or screen).

Freewrites. Like quickwrites, freewrites ask you to write about a topic without stopping, usually for ten minutes. Freewrites let you explore your thinking without worrying about correctness, grades, and so on.

Thought pieces. Some instructors assign thought pieces—pieces of writing that sum up background information and your own opinions and analyses of a subject. They can help you see how much you know—and how much more you need to know—about your topic.

Reading responses. These may be the most frequently assigned type of low-stakes writing. In reading responses, you sum up your understanding of an assigned reading and evaluate its effectiveness. Whether or not your instructor assigns such responses, you will profit by setting up a reading log and recording your responses and critical evaluations there.

Class discussion forums. Many instructors set up forums online—on a local course management system, a class blog or wiki, or a class page on Facebook or other social media site—as a space to continue dialogues from the classroom. Active participation in these forums will allow you to get your views out there for others to respond to and help you understand the viewpoints of others.

 Checklist

Participating in Class Blogs, Wikis, and Other Forums

- Take seriously these opportunities to put your writing to work. Engaging with others about the course material and summing up your views in writing will help you internalize the information.
- Be polite and professional when writing to a class blog, wiki, or other forum.
- Avoid unnecessary criticism of others; the point of these activities is to have productive exchanges about what you are learning. Rather than criticize, simply ask for clarification or offer what you take to be correct information.
- If others seem to be criticizing you, give them the benefit of the doubt and reply with courtesy and patience.
- For email threads, decide whether to reply off-list to the sender of a message or to the whole group, and be careful to use REPLY or REPLY ALL accordingly to avoid potential confusion.
- Remember that many class forums, blogs, wikis, and email lists are archived, so more people than you think may be reading your messages.

7 Analyzing and Reading Critically

Reading critically is an important aspect of putting your writing to work because what you write will always be in response to what others have said. Critical reading is crucial today, when information is coming at you so fast that it's tempting to skim. Although skimming is an important tool, high-stakes reading requires you to read carefully, asking questions about the meaning of the text, the author's purpose, and why the text is convincing (or not).

7a Previewing

Find out all you can about a text before beginning to look closely at it, considering its context, author, subject, genre, and design.

- Where have you encountered the work? Are you encountering it in its original context? What can you infer from the original or current context of the work about its intended audience and purpose?
- What information can you find about the author, creator, or sponsor of the text? What purpose, expertise, and possible agenda might you expect this person to have?
- What do you know about the subject of the text? What opinions do you have about it, and why? What more do you want to learn about it?
- What does the title (or caption or other heading) indicate?
- What role does the medium play in achieving the purpose and connecting to the audience?
- What is the genre of the text—and what can it tell you about the intended audience or purpose?
- How is the text presented? What do you notice about its design and general appearance?

7b Annotating

As you read a text for the first time, mark it up or take notes, highlighting the author's main ideas and key terms. Consider the text's content, author, intended audience, genre, and design.

Critical Thinking & Argument: Reading Critically > Storyboards

- What do you find confusing or unclear about the text? Where can you look for more information?
- What key terms and ideas—or key patterns—do you see? What key images stick in your mind?
- What sources or other works does this text refer to?
- Which points do you agree with? Which do you disagree with? Why?
- Do the authors or creators present themselves as you anticipated?
- For what audience was this text created? Are you part of its intended audience?
- What underlying assumptions can you identify in the text?
- Are the medium and genre appropriate for the topic, audience, and purpose?
- Is the design appropriate for the subject and genre?
- Does the composition serve a purpose—for instance, does the layout help you see what is more and less important in the text?
- How effectively do words, images, sound, and other media work together?
- How would you describe the style of the text? What contributes to this impression—word choice? references to research or popular culture? formatting? color? something else?
- Talk back to the text throughout, noting where you agree and disagree—and why. Jot down questions you'd like to ask the writer.

7c Summarizing

Try to summarize the contents of the text in your own words. A summary *briefly* captures the main ideas of a text and omits information that is less important for the reader. Try to identify the key points in the text, find the essential evidence supporting those points, and then explain the contents concisely and fairly, so that a reader unfamiliar with the original text can make sense of it all. Deciding what to leave out can make summarizing a tricky task. To test your understanding—and to avoid unintentional plagiarism—put the text aside while you write your summary.

7d Analyzing

You can learn many good lessons about how to make appropriate and effective choices in your own writing by studying the choices other writers have made. You may want to begin the process of analysis by asking additional questions about the text.

- What are the main points in this text? Are they implied or explicitly stated? What major claim is made?
- Which points do you agree with? Which do you disagree with? Why?

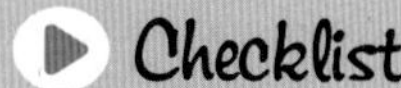

Analyzing a Text

- What cultural contexts—the time and place the argument was written; the economic, social, and political events surrounding the argument; and so on—inform the text? What do they tell about where the writer, creator, or sponsor is coming from and what choices he or she has had to make?
- What is the main issue of the text?
- What emotional, ethical, or logical appeals has the writer chosen to use in the text? Are the appeals reasonable and fair?
- What strategies has the writer chosen to establish credibility?
- What sources does the author use to inform the text? How current and reliable are they? Are some perspectives left out, and if so, how does this exclusion affect the argument?
- What claim does the text make, and how solid is the supporting evidence?
- How has the writer or creator chosen visuals and design to support the main ideas of the text? How well do words and images work together to make a point?
- What overall impression does the text create? Are you favorably impressed—or not?

Critical Thinking & Argument: Reading Critically > Student Writing (6)
Critical Thinking & Argument: Analyzing Arguments > LearningCurve (2)

- Does anything in the text surprise you? Why, or why not?
- What kinds of examples does the text use? What other kinds of evidence does the text offer to support its claims? What other examples or evidence should have been included?
- Are opposing viewpoints included and treated fairly?
- How trustworthy are the sources the text cites or refers to?
- What assumptions does the text make? Are those assumptions valid? Why, or why not?
- Do the authors or creators achieve their purpose? Why, or why not?
- What intrigues, puzzles, or irritates you about the text? Why?
- What else would you like to know?

7e Student rhetorical analysis

For a class assignment, Milena Ateyea was asked to analyze the choices former Harvard president Derek Bok made in a brief text arguing that colleges should seek to persuade rather than censor students who use speech or symbols that offend others. In analyzing "Protecting Freedom of Expression on the Campus," Milena focuses on Bok's choice of particular emotional, ethical, and logical appeals.

Critical Thinking & Argument: Analyzing Arguments > Student Writing
Critical Thinking & Argument: Reading Critically > Tutorial
Critical Thinking & Argument: Analyzing Arguments > Tutorials (2)

STUDENT WRITING

Title suggests mixed response to Bok

Connects article to her own experience to build credibility (ethical appeal)

Brief overview of Bok's argument

Identifies Bok's central claim

Links Bok's claim to strategies he uses to support it

Direct quotations show appeals to emotion through vivid description

Bok establishes common ground between two positions

Emphasizes Bok's credibility (ethical appeal)

A Curse and a Blessing

When Derek Bok's essay "Protecting Freedom of Expression on the Campus" was first published in the *Boston Globe*, I had just come to America to escape the oppressive Communist regime in Bulgaria. Perhaps my background explains why I support Bok's argument that we should not put arbitrary limits on freedom of expression. Bok wrote the essay in response to a public display of Confederate flags and a swastika at Harvard, a situation that created a heated controversy among the students. As Bok notes, universities have struggled to achieve a balance between maintaining students' right of free speech and avoiding racist attacks. When choices must be made, however, Bok argues for preserving freedom of expression.

In order to support his claim and bridge the controversy, Bok chooses a variety of rhetorical strategies. The author first immerses the reader in the controversy by vividly describing the incident: two Harvard students had hung Confederate flags in public view, thereby "upsetting students who equate the Confederacy with slavery" (69). Another student, protesting the flags, decided to display an even more offensive symbol—the swastika. These actions provoked heated discussions among students. Some students believed that school officials should remove the offensive symbols, whereas others suggested that the symbols "are a form of free speech and should be protected" (69). Bok chooses ways to establish common ground between the factions: he regrets the actions of the offenders but does not believe we should prohibit such actions just because we disagree with them.

The author earns the reader's respect because of his knowledge and through his logical presentation of the issue. In partial support of his position, Bok chooses a U.S. Supreme Court ruling, which reminds us that "the display of swastikas or Confederate flags clearly falls within the protection of the free-speech clause of the First Amendment" (70). The author also emphasizes the danger of

STUDENT WRITING

the slippery slope of censorship when he warns the reader, "If we begin to forbid flags, it is only a short step to prohibiting offensive speakers" (70). Overall, however, Bok's choice of appeals lacks the kinds of evidence that statistics, interviews with students, and other representative examples of controversial conduct could provide. Thus, his essay may not be strong enough to persuade all readers to make the leap from this specific situation to his general conclusion.

Links Bok's credibility to use of logical appeals

Comments critically on kinds of evidence Bok's argument lacks

Throughout, Bok chooses to imply his personal feelings rather than state them directly. As a lawyer who was president of Harvard for twenty years, Bok knows how to present his opinions respectfully without offending the feelings of the students. However, qualifying phrases like "I suspect that" and "Under the Supreme Court's rulings, as I read them" could weaken the effectiveness of his position. Furthermore, Bok's attempt to be fair to all seems to dilute the strength of his proposed solution. He suggests that one should either ignore the insensitive deeds in the hope that students might change their behavior, or talk to the offending students to help them comprehend how their behavior is affecting other students.

Reiterates Bok's credibility

Identifies qualifying phrases that may weaken claim

Analyzes weaknesses of Bok's proposed solution

Nevertheless, although Bok's proposed solution to the controversy does not appear at first reading to be very strong, it may ultimately be effective. His rhetorical choices leave enough flexibility to withstand various tests, and Bok's solution is general enough that it can change with the times and adapt to community standards.

Raises possibility that Bok's imperfect solution may work

In writing this essay, Bok faced a challenging task: to write a short response to a specific situation that represents a very broad and controversial issue. Some people may find that freedom of expression is both a curse and a blessing because of the difficulties it creates. As one who has lived under a regime that permitted very limited, censored expression, I am all too aware that I could not have written this response when I lived in Bulgaria. As a result, like Derek Bok, I believe that freedom of expression is a blessing, in spite of any temporary problems associated with it.

Summarizes Bok's task

Ties conclusion back to title

Returns to own experience, which argues for accepting Bok's solution

STUDENT WRITING

Work Cited

Bok, Derek. "Protecting Freedom of Expression on the Campus." *Current Issues and Enduring Questions*, edited by Sylvan Barnet and Hugo Bedau, 10th ed., Bedford/St. Martin's, 2014, pp. 69-71. Originally published in *The Boston Globe*, 25 May 1991.

8 Building Arguments

Research conducted for this book shows that argument is the most frequently assigned genre in first- and second-year writing classes. Learning how to respond successfully to such assignments and compose your own arguments will serve you well in college and beyond.

8a Identifying basic appeals in an argument

Emotional appeals. Emotional appeals stir our emotions and remind us of deeply held values. In analyzing any text, look carefully to see how the writer has chosen to use emotional appeals to rouse the audience's emotions.

Ethical appeals. Ethical appeals support the credibility, moral character, and goodwill of the argument's creator. To identify these appeals, ask what the writer or creator has chosen in order to show the audience that he or she has done homework on the subject and is knowledgeable about it. In addition, ask what the writer does to suggest or show that he or she is trustworthy and fair. What word choice or examples show that the writer is honest and credible?

Logical appeals. Even though recent research demonstrates that most people make decisions based on emotion more than anything

Critical Thinking & Argument: Constructing Arguments > LearningCurve (3)

else, logical appeals are still often thought to be the most persuasive for Western audiences. As some say, "The facts don't lie" (though facts can certainly be manipulated). In addition to checking the facts of any text, then, look for firsthand evidence drawn from observations, interviews, surveys or questionnaires, experiments, and personal experience, as well as secondhand evidence from authorities, precedents, the testimony of others, statistics, and other research sources. As you evaluate these sources, ask how trustworthy they are and whether all terms are clearly defined.

8b Analyzing the elements of an argument

According to philosopher Stephen Toulmin's framework for analyzing arguments, most arguments contain common features: a **claim** (or claims); reasons for the claim; stated or unstated assumptions that underlie the argument (Toulmin calls these **warrants**); **evidence** such as facts, authoritative opinion, examples, and statistics; and **qualifiers** that limit the claim in some way.

Suppose you read a brief argument about abolishing the Electoral College. The diagram below shows how you can use the elements of argument for analysis.

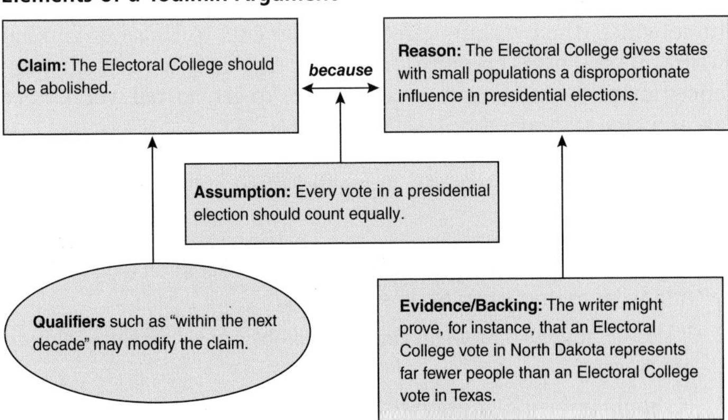

Critical Thinking & Argument: Constructing Arguments > Video Prompt

8c Arguing for a purpose

Since all language is in some sense argumentative, the purposes of argument vary widely.

Arguing to win. In the most traditional purpose of academic argument, arguing to win, you aim to present a position that prevails over or defeats the positions of others.

Arguing to convince. A frequent goal of argument is to convince others to change their minds about an issue. To convince, you must provide reasons so compelling that the audience willingly agrees with your conclusion.

Arguing to understand. Rogerian argument (named for psychologist Carl Rogers) and invitational argument (named by researchers Sonja Foss and Cindy Griffin) both call for understanding as a major goal of arguing. Your purpose in many situations will be to share information and perspectives in order to make informed political, professional, and personal choices.

8d Making an argument

Chances are you've been making convincing arguments since early childhood. But if family members and friends are not always easy to convince, then making effective arguments to those unfamiliar with you presents even more challenges, especially when such audiences are anonymous and in cyberspace. To get started, you'll need an arguable statement.

Arguable statements. An arguable statement must meet three criteria:

1. It should seek to convince readers of something, to change their minds, or to urge them to do something.
2. It should address a problem that has no obvious or absolute solution or answer.
3. It should present a position that readers can have varying perspectives on.

ARGUABLE STATEMENT	Violent video games lead to violent behavior.
UNARGUABLE STATEMENT	Video games earn millions of dollars every year.

Argumentative thesis or claim. To make the move from an arguable statement to an argumentative thesis, begin with an arguable statement:

ARGUABLE STATEMENT	Pesticides should be banned.

Attach at least one good reason.

REASON	Pesticides endanger the lives of farmworkers.

You now have a working argumentative thesis.

ARGUMENTATIVE THESIS	Because they endanger the lives of farmworkers, pesticides should be banned.

Develop the underlying assumption that supports your argument.

ASSUMPTION	Farmworkers have a right to a safe working environment.

Identifying this assumption will help you gather evidence in support of your argument. Finally, consider whether you need to qualify your claim in any way.

Ethical appeals. To make any argument effective, you need to establish your credibility. Here are some good ways to do so:

- Demonstrate that you are knowledgeable about the issues and topic.
- Show that you respect the views of your audience and have their best interests at heart.
- Demonstrate that you are fair and evenhanded by showing that you understand opposing viewpoints and can make a reasonable counterargument.

Visuals can also make ethical appeals. Just as you consider the impression your Facebook profile photo makes on your audience, you should think about what kind of case you're making when you choose images and design elements for your argument.

Logical appeals. Audiences almost always want proof—logical reasons that back up your argument. You can create good logical appeals in the following ways:

- Provide strong examples that are representative and that clearly support your point.
- Introduce precedents—particular examples from the past—that support your point.
- Use narratives or stories in support of your point.
- Cite authorities and their testimony, as long as each authority is timely and is genuinely qualified to speak on the topic.
- Establish that one event is the cause—or the effect—of another.

A Visual That Makes a Logical Appeal

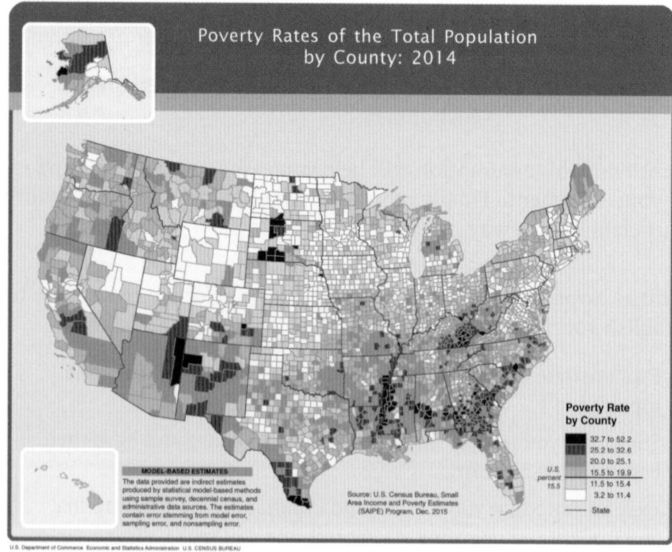

U.S. CENSUS BUREAU

Visuals that make logical appeals can be useful in arguments, since they present factual information that can be taken in at a glance. Consider how long it would take to explain all the information in the chart on p. 52 by using words alone.

Emotional appeals. Audiences can feel manipulated when an argument tries too hard to appeal to emotions like pity, anger, or fear. Nevertheless, you can appeal to the hearts as well as to the minds of your audience with the ethical use of strong emotional appeals:

- Introduce a powerful text that supports your point.
- Use concrete language and details to make your points more vivid.
- Use figurative language—metaphors, similes, analogies, and so on—to make your point both lively and memorable.

Visuals that make emotional appeals can add substance to your argument as long as you test them with potential readers to check whether they interpret the visual the same way you do.

8e Organizing an argument

Although there is no universally "ideal" organizational framework for an argument, the following pattern (often referred to as the classical system) has been used throughout the history of the Western world:

INTRODUCTION

- Gets readers' attention and interest
- Establishes your qualifications to write about your topic
- Establishes common ground with readers
- Demonstrates fairness
- States or implies your argumentative thesis

BACKGROUND

- Presents any necessary background data or information, including pertinent personal narratives or stories

LINES OF ARGUMENT

- Present good reasons and evidence (including logical and emotional appeals) in support of your thesis, usually in order of importance
- Demonstrate ways your argument is in readers' best interest

CONSIDERATION OF ALTERNATIVE ARGUMENTS

- Examines alternative or opposing points of view fairly
- Notes advantages and disadvantages of alternative views
- Explains why one view is better than other(s)

CONCLUSION

- May summarize the argument briefly
- Elaborates on the implication of your thesis
- Makes clear what you want readers to think and do
- Makes a strong ethical or emotional appeal in a memorable way

8f A student's argument essay

The digital resources for this book include an essay by Benjy Mercer-Golden, which argues that sustainability and capitalism can and must work together for an effective response to environmental degradation. (See the inside back cover for more details.)

9 Creating Portfolios

One especially good way to put your writing to work is by developing a portfolio that showcases your abilities and experiences. Your instructor may require you to assemble a portfolio of work in your course, but you may also want to keep a portfolio throughout your college career, adding outstanding examples of your work from year to year.

Critical Thinking & Argument: Constructing Arguments > Student Writing

9a Creating a portfolio for your course

Most instructors who assign portfolios as a culmination of the course will give you advice about what to include: a cover letter introducing the portfolio and pointing out its contents; a personal reflection on what you have learned about writing and improving your writing, with examples from your work; several polished pieces of your writing; an early draft accompanied by the final draft; examples of your work as a peer responder or as a participant in class forums or online discussion groups; and so on.

9b Assembling your portfolio

As you assemble your portfolio, keep these tips in mind:

- If the portfolio is assigned by your instructor, make sure you understand exactly what is to go into the portfolio and how it is to be organized.
- Decide, with your instructor's guidance, whether your portfolio will be print or digital.
- Consider audience and purpose: Who besides your instructor will see your portfolio? How can you most appropriately appeal to these readers?
- Choose pieces that show your strengths as a writer, and decide how many to include.
- Consider organization: what arrangement will make most sense to readers?
- Think about what layout and design will present your work most effectively.
- Be sure to get responses to your portfolio from classmates, friends, and your instructor. Ask if they find the portfolio easy to read and easy to follow.
- Edit and proofread very carefully, remembering that typos are often particularly hard to catch in digital texts.

9c A student's portfolio cover letter

The digital resources for this book include a reflective statement written by student James Kung to accompany his portfolio for his first-year college composition course. (See the inside back cover for more details.)

10 Writing in Academic Genres

Writing is important in every discipline or field, but putting your writing to work for you means different things in different fields. One of your jobs as a student is to learn to enter the conversations going on in different academic disciplines—learning to "talk the talk" and "walk the walk" in each one. You will begin to get a sense of such differences as you prepare assignments for courses in the humanities, social sciences, and natural sciences.

10a Recognizing expectations of disciplines and genres

It's frustrating to know that there is no one single "correct" style of communication in any country, including the United States. In addition, effective written styles differ from effective oral styles (Chapter 11), and what is considered good writing in one field of study may not be viewed as appropriate in another. Even the variety of English often referred to as "standard" covers a wide range of styles (19a). In each discipline you study, you will learn how to use different sets of conventions, strategies, and resources.

Early in your writing in any field, consider the **genre** or kind of text the instructor expects you to write: a lab report for biology, for example, or a review of the literature for psychology. If you are not sure what kind of text you are supposed to write, ask your instructor for clarification. (Examples may also be available at your school's writing center.) You may want to find multiple examples so that you can develop a sense of how different writers approach the same writing task.

 **Academic, Professional, and Public Writing: Academic Work in Any Discipline > Video Prompt**
Academic, Professional, and Public Writing: Writing for the Humanities > Student Writing (2)

10b Understanding vocabularies, styles, and evidence in academic genres

As you become familiar with the vocabularies, styles, and methods of proof used in the fields you study, you will slowly come to use them with ease—that is, to be an "insider" in a particular discipline.

Vocabulary. A good way to enter into the conversation of a field or discipline is to study its vocabulary. Highlight key terms in your reading or notes to help you distinguish any specialized terms. If you find only a little specialized vocabulary, try to master the new terms quickly by reading your textbook carefully, asking your instructor questions, and looking up key words or phrases.

Style. Study writing in the field to identify its stylistic features.

- How would you describe the overall tone of the writing? Do writers in the field usually strive for an objective stance? (See 1g.)
- Do they use the first person (*I*) or prefer such terms as *one* or *the investigator*? What is the effect of this choice?
- In general, how long are the sentences and paragraphs?
- Are verbs generally active or passive—and why? (See 21e.)
- How does the writing integrate visual elements—graphs, tables, charts, photographs, or maps—or include video or sound?
- How is the writing organized? Does it typically include certain features, such as an abstract, a discussion of methods, headings, or other formatting elements?

Evidence. As you grow familiar with any area of study, you will develop a sense of what it takes to prove a point in that field. As you read assigned materials, consider the following questions about evidence:

- How do writers in the field use precedent and authority?
- What kinds of quantitative data (items that can be counted and measured) and qualitative data (items that can be systematically observed) are used—and why?

Academic, Professional, and Public Writing: Writing for the Social Sciences > Student Writing

- How is logical reasoning used? How are definition, cause and effect, analogy, and example used in this discipline?
- What are the primary materials—the firsthand sources of information—in this field? What are the secondary materials—the sources of information derived from others? (See 13b.)
- How is research used and integrated into the text?
- What documentation style is typically used in this field? (See Chapters 45–48.)

EVIDENCE IN THE HUMANITIES. Evidence for assignments in the humanities may come from a primary source you are examining, such as a poem, a philosophical treatise, an artifact, or a painting. For certain assignments, secondary sources such as journal articles or reference works will also provide useful evidence. Ground your analysis of each source in key questions about the work you are examining that will lead you to a thesis.

EVIDENCE IN THE SOCIAL SCIENCES. You will need to understand both the quantitative and qualitative evidence used in your sources as well as other evidence you may create from research you conduct on your own. Summarizing and synthesizing information drawn from sources will be key to your success.

EVIDENCE IN THE NATURAL AND APPLIED SCIENCES. You will probably draw on two major sources of evidence: research—including studies, experiments, and analyses—conducted by credible scientists, and research you conduct by yourself or with others. Each source should provide a strong piece of evidence for your project.

10c Using conventional patterns and formats

To produce effective writing in a discipline, you need to know the field's generally accepted formats for organizing and presenting evidence. A typical laboratory report, for instance, follows a fairly standard organizational framework (often the "introduction, methods, results, and discussion" format known as IMRAD) and has a certain look.

Academic, Professional, and Public Writing: Writing for the Natural and Applied Sciences > Student Writing (2)

Ask your instructor to recommend some excellent examples of the kind of writing you will do in the course, or consult major scholarly journals to consider these questions about format:

- What types of documents are common in this field? What is the purpose of each?
- Do articles or other documents typically begin with an abstract? (See Chapter 13.)
- How is each type of text organized? What are its main parts? How are they labeled?
- What assumptions does the text take for granted? What points does it emphasize?

Remember that there is a close connection between the writing patterns and formats a particular area of study uses and the work that scholars in that field undertake.

10d Adapting genre structures

Learning to borrow and adapt transitional devices and pieces of sentence structure from other writing in the genre you are working in is one way to help you learn the conventions of that discipline. Don't copy the whole structure, however, or your borrowed sentences may seem plagiarized (Chapter 15). Find sample sentence structures from similar genres but on different topics so that you borrow a typical structure (which does not belong to anyone) rather than the idea or the particular phrasing. Write your own sentences first, and look at other people's sentences just to guide your revision.

ABSTRACT FROM A SOCIAL SCIENCE PAPER

Using the interpersonal communications research of J. K. Brilhart and G. J. Galanes, along with T. Hartman's personality assessment, I observed and analyzed the group dynamics of my project collaborators in a communications course. Based on results of the Hartman personality assessment, I predicted that a single leader would emerge. However, complementary individual

Academic, Professional, and Public Writing: Writing for Business > Student Writing (4)
Academic, Professional, and Public Writing: Writing for Business > Tutorial

strengths and gender differences encouraged a distributed leadership style.

EFFECTIVE BORROWING OF STRUCTURES

Drawing on the research of Deborah Tannen on conversational styles, I analyzed the conversational styles of six first-year students at DePaul University. Based on Tannen's research, I expected that the three men I observed would use features typical of male conversational style and the three women would use features typical of female conversational style. In general, these predictions were accurate; however, some exceptions were also apparent.

11 Creating Presentations

No doubt you will be assigned to create presentations throughout your college career. Yet many students say that they aren't completely comfortable with the "stand and deliver" format. This chapter will help you put your best foot forward in presentations.

11a Considering task, purpose, and audience

Think about how much time you have to prepare; where the presentation will take place; how long the presentation is to be; whether you will use written-out text or note cards; whether visual aids, handouts, or other accompanying materials are called for; and what equipment you will need. If you are making a group presentation, you will need time to divide duties and to practice with your classmates.

Consider the purpose of your presentation. Are you to lead a discussion? teach a lesson? give a report? make a proposal? present research findings? engage a group in an activity?

Consider your audience. What do they know about your topic, what opinions do they already hold about it, and what do they need to know to follow your presentation and perhaps accept your point of view?

Academic, Professional, and Public Writing: Writing for Business > Video Prompt

11b Writing a memorable introduction and conclusion

Listeners tend to remember beginnings and endings most readily. Consider making yours memorable by using a startling statement, opinion, or question; a vivid anecdote; or a powerful quotation or image. Make sure at the end that the audience gets the main takeaway!

11c Using explicit structure and signpost language

Organize your presentation clearly and carefully, and give an overview of your main points at the outset. (You may wish to recall these points toward the end of the talk.) Then pause between major points, and use signpost language as you move from one idea to the next. Such signposts should be clear and concrete: *The second crisis point in the breakup of the Soviet Union occurred hard on the heels of the first* instead of *Another thing about the Soviet Union's problems. . . .* You can also offer signposts by repeating key words and ideas; avoiding long, complicated sentences; and using as many concrete verbs and nouns as possible. If you are talking about abstract ideas, try to provide concrete examples for each.

11d Preparing a text for ease of presentation

If you decide to speak from a full text of your presentation, use fairly large double- or triple-spaced print that will be easy to read. End each page with the end of a sentence so that you won't have to pause while you turn a page. Whether you speak from a full text, a detailed outline, note cards, or points on flip charts or slides, mark the places where you want to pause, and highlight the words you want to emphasize. (If you are using presentation software, print out a paper version and mark it up.)

Designing and Performing Writing: Presentations > Video Prompts (4)

11e Planning visuals

Visuals carry a lot of the message the speaker wants to convey, so think of your visuals not as add-ons but as a major means of getting your points across. Many speakers use presentation software (such as PowerPoint or Prezi) to help keep themselves on track and to guide the audience. In addition, posters, flip charts, chalkboards, or interactive whiteboards can also help you make strong visual statements.

When you work with visuals for your own presentation, remember that they must be large enough to be easily seen and read. Be sure the information is simple, clear, and easy to understand. And remember *not* to read from your visuals or turn your back on your audience as you refer to them. Most important, make sure your visuals engage and help your listeners rather than distract them from your message. Try out each visual on your classmates, friends, or roommates: if they do not clearly grasp the meaning and purpose of the visual, scrap it and try again.

You may also want to prepare handouts for your audience: pertinent bibliographies, for example, or text too extensive to be presented otherwise. Unless the handouts include material you want your audience to use while you speak, distribute them at the end of the presentation.

Slides. Here are some guidelines for preparing effective slides:

- Don't put too much information on one slide; one simple word or picture may make your point most effectively. Avoid using more than three to five bullet points (or more than fifty words) on any slide, and never read them to your audience. Instead, say something to enhance, explain, or emphasize what's on the slide.
- Use light backgrounds in a darkened room, dark backgrounds in a lighted one.
- Make sure that audio or video clips with sound are clearly audible.
- Use only images that are large and sharp enough to be clearly visible to your audience.

Designing and Performing Writing: Presentations > Tutorial

Checklist

Reviewing Your Presentation

Before your instructor or another audience evaluates your presentation, do a review for yourself:

- Does your presentation have a clear thesis, a compelling introduction and conclusion, and a simple, clear structure?
- Do you use sources to support your points and demonstrate your knowledge? Do you include a works-cited slide at the end of the presentation?
- Is your use of media (posters, slides, video clips, and so on) appropriate for your topic and thesis? If you are using slides, will they appeal to your audience and make your points effectively?
- Do you use clear signpost language and effective repetition?
- Are you satisfied with your delivery—your tone and projection of voice, pacing, and stance?

11f Practicing

Set aside enough time to practice your presentation—including the use of all visuals—at least twice. You might also record your rehearsals, or practice in front of a mirror or with friends who can comment on content and style.

Timing your run-throughs will tell you whether you need to cut (or expand) material to make the presentation an appropriate length.

11g Delivering the presentation

To calm your nerves and get off to a good start, know your material thoroughly and use the following strategies to good advantage before, during, and after your presentation:

- Visualize your presentation with the aim of feeling comfortable during it.

- Consider doing some deep-breathing exercises before the presentation, and concentrate on relaxing; avoid too much caffeine.
- If possible, stand up. Most speakers make a stronger impression standing rather than sitting.
- Face your audience, and make eye contact as much as possible.
- Allow time for questions.
- Thank the audience at the end of your presentation.

11h A student's presentation

For her presentation "Words, Images, and the Mystical Way They Work Together in Alison Bechdel's *Fun Home*," Shuqiao Song developed a series of very simple slides aimed at underscoring her points and keeping her audience focused on them. The digital resources for this book include her full presentation. (See the inside back cover for more details.)

12 Writing to Make Something Happen in the World

A large group of college students participating in a research study were asked, "What is good writing?" The students kept coming back to one central idea: good writing "makes something happen in the world." They felt particular pride in the writing they did for family, friends, and community groups—and for many extracurricular activities that were meaningful to them. At some point during your college years or soon after, you are highly likely to create writing that is not just something that you turn in for a grade but writing that you do because you want to make a difference. The writing that matters most to many students and citizens, then, is writing that gets up off the page or screen, puts on its working boots, and marches out to get something done!

Designing and Performing Writing: Presentations > Student Writing

 Checklist

Characteristics of Writing That Makes Something Happen

- Public writing has a very clear *purpose*.
- It is intended for a specific *audience* and addresses those people directly.
- It uses the *genre* most suited to its purpose and audience (a poster, a newsletter, a brochure, a letter to the editor), and it appears in a *medium* (print, online, or both) where the intended audience will see it.
- It generally uses straightforward, everyday *language*.

12a Deciding what should happen

When you decide to write to make something happen, you'll generally have some idea of what effect you want that writing to have on your readers. Clarify what actions you want them to take in response to your writing, and then think about what people you most want to reach. Who will be interested in the topic you are writing about?

12b Connecting with your audience

Once you have a target audience in mind, you'll need to think carefully about where and how you are likely to find them, how you can get their attention so they will read what you write, and what you can say to get them to achieve your purpose.

If you want to convince your neighbors to pool time, effort, and resources to build a local playground, then you have a head start: you already know something about what they value and about what appeals would get their attention and convince them to join in this project. If you want to create a flash mob to publicize ineffective security at chemical plants near your city, on the other hand, you will need to reach as many people as possible, most of whom you will not know.

Genre and media. Even if you know the members of your audience, you still need to think about the genre and medium that will be most likely to reach them. To get neighbors involved in the playground project previously mentioned, you might decide that a print flyer delivered door-to-door and posted at neighborhood gathering places would work best. For a flash mob, however, an easily forwarded message—text, tweet, or email—will probably work best.

Appropriate language. For all public writing, think carefully about the audience you want to reach—as well as *unintended* audiences your message might reach. Doing so can help you craft writing that will be persuasive without being offensive.

Timing. Making sure your text will appear in a timely manner is crucial to the success of your project. If you want people to plan to attend an event, present your text to them at least two weeks ahead of time. If you are issuing a newsletter or blog, make sure that you create posts or issues often enough to keep people interested (but not so often that readers can't or won't keep up). If you are reporting information based on something that has already happened, make it available as soon as possible so that your audience won't consider your report "old news."

12c Sample writing that makes something happen in the world

Look on the following pages for some examples of the forms public writing can take.

Academic, Professional, and Public Writing: Writing to Make Something Happen in the World > Sample Writing (5)

Fundraising web page

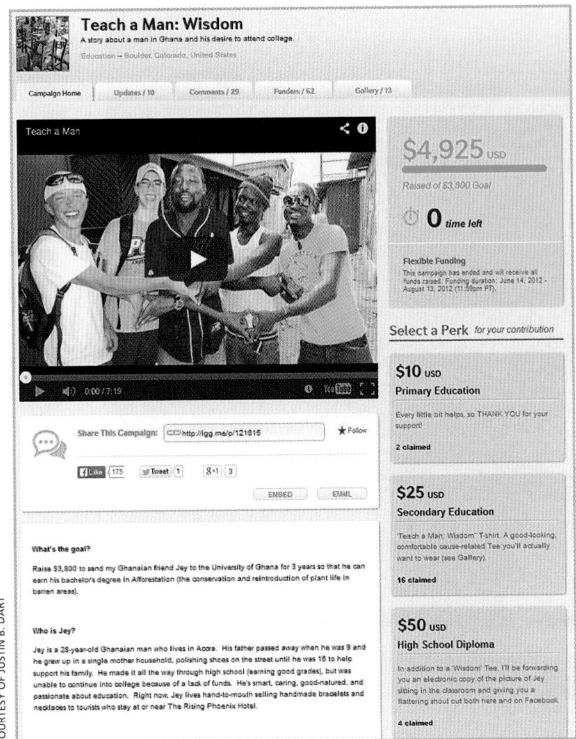

Student Justin Dart created this fundraising web page with a very clear purpose: to crowd-source the funding to help Jey, a young street vendor in Accra, Ghana, get a college education. Using the Indiegogo template, Justin posted a video spelling out the background and purpose of his fundraiser, a short written description of the project, and a list of perks for donors at various levels. Other tabs offered updates from Justin on his progress, comments from donors, photos, and more. To reach as many people as possible, Justin shared this page with his friends and acquaintances and urged them to share it on social media outlets. Justin ended up raising enough to pay for Jey's university tuition for his college career, as well as housing and incidentals.

Web comic

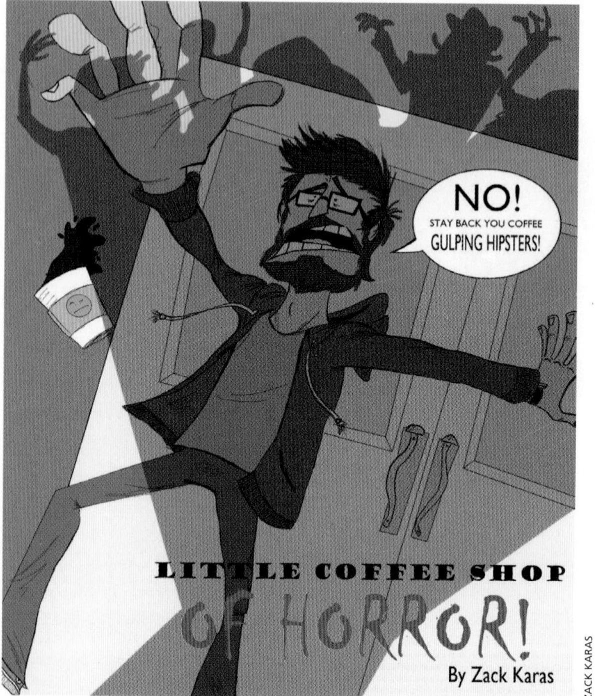

ZACK KARAS

Student Zack Karas worked with a team of classmates on an assignment to do field research in a public space. His group chose a local coffee shop, and after conducting observations of the environment and the interactions among people there, they presented a critical analysis of the coffee-drinking scene to the rest of the class.

Zack then used his team's coffee shop experience as the basis for a comic, which he posted on a blog created to host his artwork. The final panels include a twist: Zack's comic avatar fails to recognize that he, like many of the customers, is also a "post-ironic hipster . . . with facial hair, a hoodie, and an iPhone." Turning the report into a comic allowed Zack to reach an audience beyond his classmates—readers who share his interest in humor, online comics, and the critique of the coffee-culture demographic.

Newsletter

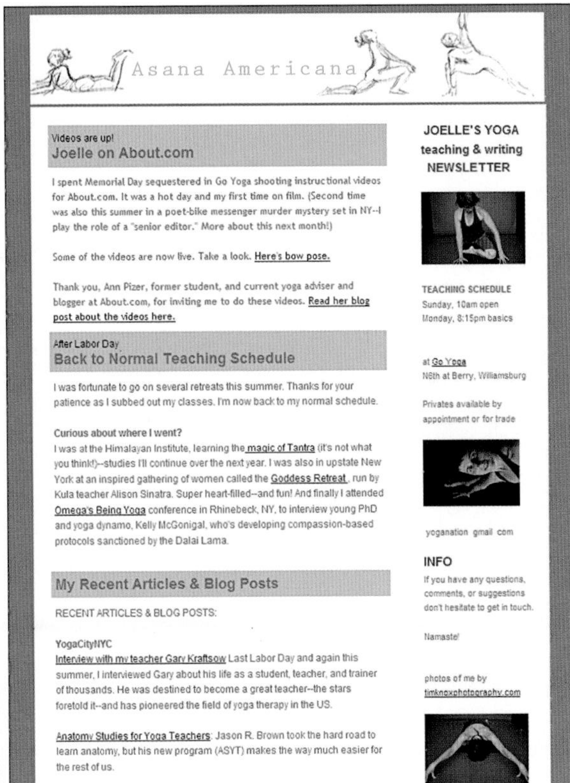

Asana Americana

JOELLE'S YOGA teaching & writing NEWSLETTER

Videos are up!
Joelle on About.com

I spent Memorial Day sequestered in Go Yoga shooting instructional videos for About.com. It was a hot day and my first time on film. (Second time was also this summer in a poet-bike messenger murder mystery set in NY--I play the role of a "senior editor." More about this next month!)

Some of the videos are now live. Take a look. Here's bow pose.

Thank you, Ann Pizer, former student, and current yoga adviser and blogger at About.com, for inviting me to do these videos. Read her blog post about the videos here.

After Labor Day
Back to Normal Teaching Schedule

I was fortunate to go on several retreats this summer. Thanks for your patience as I subbed out my classes. I'm now back to my normal schedule.

Curious about where I went?
I was at the Himalayan Institute, learning the magic of Tantra (it's not what you think!)--studies I'll continue over the next year. I was also in upstate New York at an inspired gathering of women called the Goddess Retreat, run by Kula teacher Alison Sinatra. Super heart-filled--and fun! And finally I attended Omega's Being Yoga conference in Rhinebeck, NY, to interview young PhD and yoga dynamo, Kelly McGonigal, who's developing compassion-based protocols sanctioned by the Dalai Lama.

My Recent Articles & Blog Posts

RECENT ARTICLES & BLOG POSTS:

YogaCityNYC
Interview with my teacher Gary Kraftsow Last Labor Day and again this summer, I interviewed Gary about his life as a student, teacher, and trainer of thousands. He was destined to become a great teacher--the stars foretold it--and has pioneered the field of yoga therapy in the US.

Anatomy Studies for Yoga Teachers: Jason R. Brown took the hard road to learn anatomy, but his new program (ASYT) makes the way much easier for the rest of us.

TEACHING SCHEDULE
Sunday, 10am open
Monday, 8:15pm basics

at Go Yoga
N6th at Berry, Williamsburg

Privates available by appointment or for trade

yoganation gmail com

INFO
If you have any questions, comments, or suggestions don't hesitate to get in touch.

Namaste!

photos of me by timknoxphotography.com

COURTESY OF JOELLE HANN

As with the creators of the fundraising web page and web comic, yoga teacher Joelle Hann has a clear purpose in mind for her e-newsletter: to provide information to her audience—students and others interested in her yoga classes and developments in the yoga community. Emailing the newsletter to her subscribers allows Joelle to reach an interested audience quickly and to provide links to more of the content she's discussing, and it also means that she can include photos, illustrations, and color to enhance her document's design impact.

Research

Writing Processes

Writing That Works

Research

Language

Grammar

Style

Punctuation/ Mechanics

Documentation

13 Conducting Research

Your employer asks you to recommend the best software for a project. You need to plan a week's stay in Toronto. Your instructor assigns a term project about a groundbreaking musician. Each of these situations calls for research, for examining various kinds of sources—and each calls for you to assess the data you collect, synthesize your findings, and come up with an original recommendation or conclusion. Many tasks that call for research require that your work culminate in a written document—whether print or digital—that refers to and lists the sources you used.

13a Beginning the research process

For academic research assignments, once you have a topic you need to move as efficiently as possible to analyze the research assignment, articulate a research question to answer, and form a hypothesis. Then, after your preliminary research is complete, you can refine your hypothesis into a working thesis and begin your research in earnest.

Considering the context for a research project. Ask yourself what the *purpose* of the project is—perhaps to describe, survey, analyze, persuade, explain, classify, compare, or contrast. Then consider your *audience.* Who will be most interested, and what will they need to know? What assumptions might they hold? What response do you want from them?

You should also examine your own *stance* or *attitude* toward your topic. Do you feel curious, critical, confused, or some other way about it? What influences have shaped your stance?

For a research project, consider how many and what *kinds of sources* you need to find. What kinds of evidence will convince your audience? What visuals—charts, photographs, and so on—might you need? Would it help to do field research, such as interviews, surveys, or observations?

Finally, consider practical matters, such as how long your project will be, how much time it will take, and when it is due.

Research: Preparing for a Research Project > Video Prompt

Formulating a research question and hypothesis. After analyzing your project's context, work from your general topic to a research question and a hypothesis.

TOPIC	Farming
NARROWED TOPIC	Small family farms in the United States
ISSUE	Making a living from a small family farm
RESEARCH QUESTION	How can small family farms in the United States successfully compete with big agriculture?
HYPOTHESIS	Small family farmers can succeed by growing specialty products that consumers want and by participating in farmers' markets and community-supported agriculture programs that forge relationships with customers.

After you have explored sources to test your hypothesis and sharpened it by reading, writing, and talking with others, you can refine it into a working thesis (2b).

WORKING THESIS	Although recent data show that small family farms are more endangered than ever, some enterprising farmers have reversed the trend by growing specialized products and connecting with consumers through farmers' markets and community-supported agriculture programs.

Planning research. Once you have formulated your hypothesis, determine what you already know about your topic and try to remember where you got your information. Think hard about the kinds of sources you expect to consult—articles, print or digital books, specialized reference works, experts on your own campus, and so on—and the number you think you will need, how current they should be, and where you might find them.

13b Choosing among types of sources

Keep in mind some important differences among types of sources.

Primary and secondary sources. Primary sources provide you with firsthand knowledge, while secondary sources report on or analyze the research of others. Primary sources are basic sources of raw information, including your own field research; films, works of art, or other objects you examine; literary works you read; and eyewitness accounts, photographs, news reports, and historical documents. Secondary sources are descriptions or interpretations of primary sources, such as researchers' reports, reviews, biographies, and encyclopedia articles. What constitutes a primary or secondary source depends on the purpose of your research. A film review, for instance, serves as a secondary source if you are writing about the film but as a primary source if you are studying the critic's writing.

Scholarly and popular sources. Nonacademic sources like magazines can help you get started on a research project, but you will usually want to depend more on authorities in a field, whose work generally appears in scholarly journals in print or online. The following list will help you to distinguish between scholarly and popular sources:

SCHOLARLY	POPULAR
Title often contains the word *Journal*	*Journal* usually does not appear in title
Source is available mainly through libraries and library databases	Source is generally available outside of libraries (at newsstands or from a home Internet connection)
Few or no commercial advertisements	Many advertisements
Authors are identified with academic credentials	Authors are usually journalists or reporters hired by the publication, not academics or experts
Summary or abstract appears on first page of article; articles are fairly long	No summary or abstract; articles are fairly short
Articles cite sources and provide bibliographies	Articles may include quotations but do not cite sources or provide bibliographies

SCHOLARLY

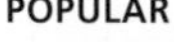

Older and more current sources. Most projects can benefit from both older, historical sources and more current ones. Some older sources are classics; others are simply dated.

13c Using library resources

Almost any research project should begin with resources in your school library, so you might begin by paying a visit.

Reference librarians. Your library's staff—especially reference librarians—can bc a valuable resource. You can talk with a librarian about your research project and get specific recommendations about databases and other helpful places to begin your research. Many libraries also have online tours and chat rooms where students can ask questions.

Catalogs. Library catalogs can tell you whether a book is housed in the library and, if so, offer a call number that enables you to find the book on the shelf. Browsing through other books near the

(TOP LEFT) *MICHIGAN QUARTERLY REVIEW*; (BOTTOM LEFT) COURTESY OF *ECOLOGY AND SOCIETY*

 Checklist

Effective Search Techniques

You can access many online catalogs, databases, and websites without actually going to the library. You can search the Internet by using carefully chosen keywords to limit the scope of your search, and refine your search depending on what you find.

- Advanced search tools let you focus your search more narrowly—by combining terms with AND or eliminating them with NOT, by specifying dates and media types, and so on—so they may give you more relevant results.
- If you don't see an advanced search option, start with keywords. (Simply entering terms in the search box may bring up an advanced search option.) Check the first page or two of results. If you get many irrelevant options, think about how to refine your keywords to get more targeted results.
- Databases and search engines don't all refine searches the same way—for instance, some use AND, while others use the + symbol. Look for tips on making the most of the search tool you're using.
- Most libraries classify material using the *Library of Congress Subject Headings*, or LCSH. When you find a library source that seems especially relevant, be sure to use the subject headings for that source as search terms to bring up all the entries under each heading.

one you've found in the catalog can help you locate other works related to your topic. Catalogs also indicate whether you can find a particular periodical, either in print or in an online database, at the library.

Indexes and databases. Remember that most college libraries subscribe to a large number of indexes and databases that students can access for free, and these sources contain much information that you will not have access to in a general Google search. Some databases include the full text of articles from newspapers, magazines, journals, and other works; some offer only short abstracts (summaries), which give an overview so you can decide whether to spend time finding and reading the whole text. Indexes of reviews provide information about a potential source's critical reception.

Check with a librarian for discipline-specific indexes and databases related to your topic.

Reference works. General reference works, such as encyclopedias, biographical resources, almanacs, digests, and atlases, can help you get an overview of a topic, identify subtopics, find more specialized sources, and identify keywords for searches.

Bibliographies. Bibliographies—lists of sources—in books or articles related to your topic can lead you to other valuable resources. Ask a librarian whether your library has more extensive bibliographies related to your research topic.

Other resources. Your library can help you borrow materials from other libraries (this can take time, so plan ahead). Check with reference librarians, too, about audio, video, multimedia, and art collections; government documents; and other special collections or archives that student researchers may be able to use.

13d Finding useful Internet sources

Many college students prefer to begin their research with general Internet searches, and much information—including authoritative sources identical to those your library provides—can be found online. But remember that library databases come from identifiable and professionally edited resources—often with materials that you can't access for free. Thus, you need to take special care to find out which information online is reliable and which is not (14a).

Internet searches. Research using a search tool such as Google usually begins with a keyword search (see the Checklist on the facing page). Many keyword searches bring up thousands of hits; you may find what you need on the first page or two of results, but if not, choose new keywords that lead to more specific sources.

Bookmarking tools. Today's powerful bookmarking tools can help you browse, sort, and track resources online. Social bookmarking sites allow users to tag information and share it with others. Users' tags are visible to all other users. If you find a helpful site, you can check how others have tagged it and browse similar tags for related information. You can also sort and group information with tags. Fellow users whose tags you trust can become part of your network so you can follow their sites of interest.

Web browsers can also help you bookmark online resources. However, unlike bookmarking tools in a browser, which are tied to one machine, you can use social bookmarking tools wherever you have an Internet connection.

Authoritative sources online. Many sources online are authoritative and reliable. You can browse collections in online virtual libraries, for example, or collections housed in government sites such as the Library of Congress, the National Institutes of Health, and the U.S. Census Bureau. For current national news, consult online versions of reputable newspapers such as the *Washington Post*, or electronic sites for news services such as C-SPAN. Google Scholar can help you limit searches to scholarly works.

Some journals (such as those from Berkeley Electronic Press) and general-interest magazines (such as *Salon*) are published only online; many other print publications make at least some of their content available free on the web.

13e Doing field research

For many research projects, you will need to collect field data. Consider *where* you can find relevant information, *how* to gather it, and *who* might be your best providers of information. You may also want to talk with your instructor about any field research you plan to do, to make sure your research will not violate your college's guidelines for doing research that involves people.

Interviews. Some information is best obtained by asking direct questions of other people. If you can talk with an expert—in person, on the telephone, or online—you may get information you cannot obtain through any other kind of research.

- Determine your exact purpose, and be sure it relates to your research question and your hypothesis.
- Set up the interview well in advance. Specify how long it will take, and if you wish to record the session, ask permission to do so.
- Prepare a written list of factual and open-ended questions. If the interview proceeds in a direction that seems fruitful, do not feel that you have to ask all of your prepared questions.
- Record the subject, date, time, and place of the interview.
- Thank those you interview, either in person or in a letter or email.

Observation. Trained observers report that making a faithful record of an observation requires intense concentration and mental agility.

- Determine the purpose of the observation, and be sure it relates to your research question and hypothesis.
- Brainstorm about what you are looking for, but don't be rigidly bound to your expectations.
- Develop an appropriate system for recording data. Consider using a split notebook or page: on one side, record your observations directly; on the other, record your thoughts or interpretations.
- Record the date, time, and place of observation.

Opinion surveys. Surveys usually depend on questionnaires. On any questionnaire, the questions should be clear and easy to understand and designed so that you can analyze the answers without difficulty. Questions that ask respondents to say *yes* or *no* or to rank items on a scale are easiest to tabulate.

- Write out your purpose, and determine the kinds of questions to ask.
- Figure out how to reach respondents—either online via email, apps, or social media; over the phone; or in person.
- Draft questions that call for short, specific answers.
- Test the questions on several people, and revise questions that seem unfair, ambiguous, or too hard or time-consuming.

- Draft a cover letter or invitation email. Be sure to state a deadline.
- If you are using a print questionnaire, leave adequate space for answers.
- Proofread the questionnaire carefully.

14 Evaluating Sources and Taking Notes

All research builds on the careful and sometimes inspired use of sources—that is, on research done by others. Since you want the information you glean from sources to be reliable and persuasive, evaluate each potential source carefully. Especially with online sources, practice what Howard Rheingold calls "crap detection," which means identifying information that is faulty or deceptive. Rheingold recommends finding three separate credible online sources that corroborate the point you want to make.

14a Evaluating the usefulness and credibility of potential sources

Use these guidelines to assess the value of a source, and add useful sources to your working bibliography with notes about why you need them.

- **Your purpose.** What will this source add to your research project? Does it help you support a major point, demonstrate that you have thoroughly researched your topic, or help establish your own credibility through its authority?
- **Relevance.** Is the source closely related to your research question? You may need to read beyond the title and opening paragraph to check for relevance.
- **Publisher's credentials.** What do you know about the publisher of the source you are using? For example, is it a major newspaper known for integrity in reporting, or is it a tabloid? Is the publisher

Research: Evaluating Sources > Student Writing (2)

a popular source, or is it sponsored by a professional or scholarly organization?

- **Author's credentials.** Is the author an expert on the topic? An author's credentials may be presented in the article, book, or website, or you can search the Internet for information on the author.
- **Date of publication.** Recent sources are often more useful than older ones, particularly in fields that change rapidly. However, the most authoritative works may be older ones. The publication dates of Internet sites can often be difficult to pin down. And even for sites that include the dates of posting, remember that the material posted may have been composed sometime earlier.
- **Accuracy of source.** How accurate and complete is the information in the source? How thorough is the bibliography or list of works cited that accompanies the source? Can you find other sources that corroborate what your source is saying?
- **Stance of source.** Identify the source's point of view or rhetorical stance, and scrutinize it carefully. Does the source present facts, or does it interpret or evaluate them? If it presents facts, what is included and what is omitted, and why? If it interprets or evaluates information that is not disputed, the source's stance may be obvious, but at other times you will need to think carefully about the source's goals. What does the author or sponsoring group want—to convince you of an idea? sell you something? call you to action in some way?
- **Cross-referencing.** Is the source cited in other works? If you see your source cited by others, looking at how they cite it and what they say about it can provide additional clues to its credibility.
- **Level of specialization.** General sources can be helpful as you begin your research, but you may then need the authority or currency of more specialized sources. On the other hand, extremely specialized works may be very hard to understand.
- **Audience of source.** Was the source written for the general public? specialists? advocates or opponents?

For more on evaluating web sources and articles, see the source maps on pp. 82–85.

SOURCE MAP: Evaluating Web Sources

Is the sponsor credible?

1. Who is the **sponsor or publisher** of the source? See what information you can get from the URL. The domain names for government sites may end in *.gov* or *.mil* and for educational sites in *.edu*. The ending *.org* may—but does not always—indicate a nonprofit organization. If you see a tilde (~) or percent sign (%) followed by a name, or if you see a word such as *users* or *members*, the page's creator may be an individual, not an institution. In addition, check the header and footer, where the sponsor may be identified. The web page shown on p. 83 comes from a site sponsored by the nonprofit Nieman Foundation for Journalism at Harvard University.

2. Look for an ***About* page** or a link to a home page for background information on the sponsor. Is a mission statement included? What are the sponsoring organization's purpose and point of view? Does the mission statement seem balanced? What is the purpose of the site (to inform, to persuade, to advocate for a cause, to advertise, or something else)? Does the information on the site come directly from the sponsor, or is the material reprinted from another source? If it is reprinted, check the original.

Is the author credible?

3. What are the **author's credentials**? Look for information accompanying the material on the page. You can also run a search on the author to find out more. Does the author seem qualified to write about this topic?

Is the information credible and current?

4. When was the information **posted or last updated**? Is it recent enough to be useful?

5. Does the page document sources with **footnotes or links**? If so, do the sources seem credible and current? Does the author include any additional resources for further information? Look for ways to corroborate the information the author provides.

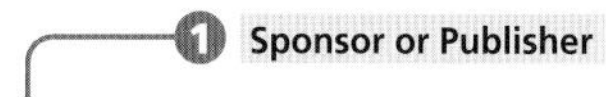

Nieman Foundation Fellowships Reports Lab Storyboard **Nieman**

NiemanReports

2 *About* Page

Exploring the Rise of Live Journalism: new projects are taking narrative from the page to the stage

Home Articles Watchdog Magazine Archives About Subscribe

COVER STORY: THE FUTURE OF FOREIGN NEWS

Date Posted 4 December 11, 2014

Nieman Reports Fall 2014

Embracing Encryption in an Age of Surveillance

Surveillance technologies make it more important for journalists abroad to protect sources

3 Author Information

ARTICLE BY

MICHAEL FITZGERALD

@riperian

Modern communications and the rise of the surveillance state make it harder than ever for journalists abroad to protect their sources. The consequences for sources can be dire, even fatal.

Journalists going abroad need to start by asking if encryption is legal where they will be. Does the government forbid certain kinds of apps? Do you need to show your ID to get a SIM card for your cell phone? "Find out the answers to these questions before you go," advises Susan E. McGregor, assistant director of Columbia's Tow Center for Digital Journalism. She adds that reporters also need to know if the telecommunications companies are state-owned. "If they are, you will need to be careful never to send specifics about people or locations via text message or e-mail especially."

Technology can also help journalists defend those who would talk to them. In countries that don't ban encryption, journalists can use encrypted e-mail tools, like Pretty Good Privacy, encrypted hard disks (FileVault2 for the Mac, PGP or

Tweet

Share

Email

Like

Comment

Print

TAGGED WITH

SOURCE MAP: Evaluating Articles

Determine the relevance of the source.

1. Look for an **abstract**, which provides a summary of the entire article. Is this source directly related to your research? Does it provide useful information and insights? Will your readers consider it persuasive support for your thesis?

Determine the credibility of the publication.

2. Consider the publication's **title**. Words in the title such as *Journal, Review*, and *Quarterly* may indicate that the periodical is a scholarly source. Most research projects rely on authorities in a particular field, whose work usually appears in scholarly journals. For more on distinguishing between scholarly and popular sources, see 13b.

3. Try to determine the **publisher or sponsor**. The journal on p. 85 is published by the University of Illinois. Academic presses such as this one generally review articles carefully before publishing them and bear the authority of their academic sponsors.

Determine the credibility of the author.

4. Evaluate the **author's credentials**. In this case, they are given in a note, which indicates that the author is a college professor.

Determine the currency of the article.

5. Look at the **publication date**, and think about whether your topic and your credibility depend on your use of very current sources.

Determine the accuracy of the article.

6. Look at the **sources cited** by the author of the article. Here, they are listed in a bibliography. Ask yourself whether the works the author has cited seem credible and current. Are any of these works cited in other articles you've considered?

In addition, consider the following questions:

- What is the article's stance or point of view? What are the author's goals? What does the author want you to know or believe?
- How does this source fit in with your other sources? Does any of the information it provides contradict or challenge other sources?

Elizabeth Tucker

Changing Concepts of Childhood: Children's Folklore Scholarship since the Late Nineteenth Century

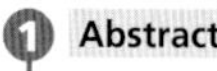

This essay examines children's folklore scholarship from the late nineteenth century to the present, tracing key concepts from the Gilded Age to the contemporary era. These concepts reflect significant social, cultural, political, and scientific changes. From the "savage child" to the "secret-keeping child," the "magic-making child," the "cerebral child," the "taboo-breaking child," the "monstrous child," and others, scholarly representations of young people have close connections to the eras in which they developed. Nineteenth-century children's folklore scholarship relied on evolutionism; now evolutionary biology provides a basis for children's folklore research, so we have re-entered familiar territory.

Since 1977, when the American Folklore Society decided to form a new section for scholars interested in young people's traditions, I have belonged to the Children's Folklore Section. It has been a joy to contribute to this dynamic organization, which has significantly influenced children's folklore scholarship and children's book authors' focus on folk tradition. This essay examines children's folklore scholarship from the late nineteenth century to the present, tracing key concepts from the Gilded Age to the contemporary era in the English language. These concepts reflect significant social, cultural, political, and scientific changes that have occurred since William Wells Newell, the first secretary of the American Folklore Society and the first editor of the *Journal of American Folklore*, published *Games and Songs of American Children* in 1883. They also reveal some very interesting commonalities. Those of us who pursue children's folklore scholarship today may consider ourselves to be light years away from nineteenth-century scholars' research but may find, when reading nineteenth-century works, that we have stayed fairly close to our scholarly "home base."

Before examining c[...] developed, I will offer a working definitio[...]eginning of childhood studies. I will also sum[...] work during the past thirty-four years. Acc[...]childhood con[...] "the state or stage of lif[...] a child; the tim[...]or birth to puberty" (2011[...]e between child[...]oo[...] and adolescence, which begins at puberty and follows pre-adolescence. The folklore

2 Title of Publication
Journal of American Folklore

4 Author's Credentials

Elizabeth Tucker is Professor of English at Binghamton University

Journal of American Folklore 125(498):389–410

3 Publisher
Board of Trustees of the University of Illinois

5 Publication Date
2012

6 Sources Cited

[...] and Humanities 3:145–60.
[...]. Why Children's Studies? *Centre for* [...] ca/pdf/papers/Carole.Carpenter.pdf.
[...]rancis. 1896. *The Child and Childhoo*[...]
[...] Fay. 1990. *Parenting with Love and* [...] Pinon Press.
Conrad, JoAnn. 2002. The War on Youth: A Modern Oedipal Tragedy. *Children's Folklore Review* 24(1–2):33–42.
Crandall, Bryan Ripley. 2009. *Cow Project*. bryanripleycrandall.files.wordpress.com/2009/05/slbscow-project.pdf.
Darwin, Charles. 1859. *On the Origin of Species by Means of Natural Selection, or the Preservation of Favoured Races in the Struggle for Life* (1st edition). London: John Murray.
Dégh, Linda. 2001. *Legend and Belief*. Bloomington: Indiana University Press.
Dorson, Richard M. 1968. *The British Folklorists: A History*. Chicago: University of Chicago Press.
Douglas, Norman. [1916] 1968. *London Street Games*. Detroit: Singing Tree Press.

14b Reading and interpreting sources

After you have determined that a source is potentially useful, read it carefully and critically, asking yourself the following questions about how this research fits your writing project:

- How relevant is this material to your research question and hypothesis?
- Does the source include counterarguments that you should address?
- How persuasive is the evidence? Does it represent opposing viewpoints fairly? Will the source be convincing to your audience?
- Will you need to change your thesis to account for this information?
- What quotations or paraphrases from this source might you want to use?

As you read and take notes on your sources, keep in mind that you will need to present data and sources to other readers so that they can understand your point.

14c Synthesizing sources

Analysis requires you to take apart something complex (such as an article in a scholarly journal) and look closely at each part to understand how the parts fit together into an effective (or ineffective) whole. Academic writing also calls for *synthesis*—grouping similar pieces of information together and looking for patterns—so you can put your sources and your own knowledge together in an original argument. Synthesis is the flip side of analysis: you assemble the parts into a new whole.

To synthesize sources for a research project, try the following tips:

- **Don't just grab a quotation and move on.** Rather, read the material carefully. (See Chapter 7.)
- **Understand the purpose of each source.** Make sure the source is relevant and necessary to your argument.
- **Determine the important ideas in each source.** Take notes on each source (14d). Identify and summarize the key ideas.

Research: Evaluating Sources > LearningCurve (2)
Research: Integrating Sources > Storyboards

- **Formulate a position.** Figure out how the pieces fit together. Look for patterns. After considering multiple perspectives, decide what you have to say.
- **Summon evidence to support your position.** You might use paraphrases, summaries, or direct quotations from your sources as evidence (15a), or your personal experience or prior knowledge. Keep your ideas central.
- **Consider counterarguments.** Acknowledge the existence of valid opinions that differ from yours, and try to understand them before explaining why they are incorrect or incomplete.
- **Combine your source materials effectively.** Be careful to avoid simply summarizing all of your research. Try to weave the various sources together rather than discussing each of your sources one by one.

Using sources effectively can pose challenges. A national study of first-year college writing found that student writers trying to incorporate research sometimes used sources that were not directly relevant to their point, too specific to support the larger claim being made, or otherwise ineffective. Another study showed that students tend to use sources *only* from the first one or two pages of a source, suggesting that they may not really know how relevant it is. Even after you have evaluated a source, take time to look at how well the source works in your specific situation. (If you change the focus of your work after you have begun doing research, be especially careful to check whether your sources still fit.)

14d Taking notes

While note-taking methods vary from one researcher to another, for each note you should (1) record enough information to help you recall the major points of the source; (2) put the information in the form in which you are most likely to incorporate it into your research project, whether a quotation, summary, or paraphrase; and (3) note all the information you will need to cite the source accurately. Keep a running list that includes citation information for each source in an electronic file or on note cards that you can

Research: Integrating Sources > Student Writing

rearrange and alter as your project takes shape. This working bibliography will simplify the process of documenting sources for your final project.

Quoting. Quoting involves bringing a source's exact words into your text. Use an author's exact words when the wording is so memorable or expresses a point so well that you cannot improve or shorten it without weakening it, when the author is a respected authority whose opinion supports your ideas, or when an author challenges or disagrees profoundly with others in the field.

- Copy quotations carefully, with punctuation, capitalization, and spelling exactly as in the original.
- Enclose the quotation in quotation marks (39a).
- Use brackets if you introduce words of your own into the quotation or make changes in it (40b). Use ellipses if you omit words from the quotation (40f). If you later incorporate the quotation into

Quotation-Style Note

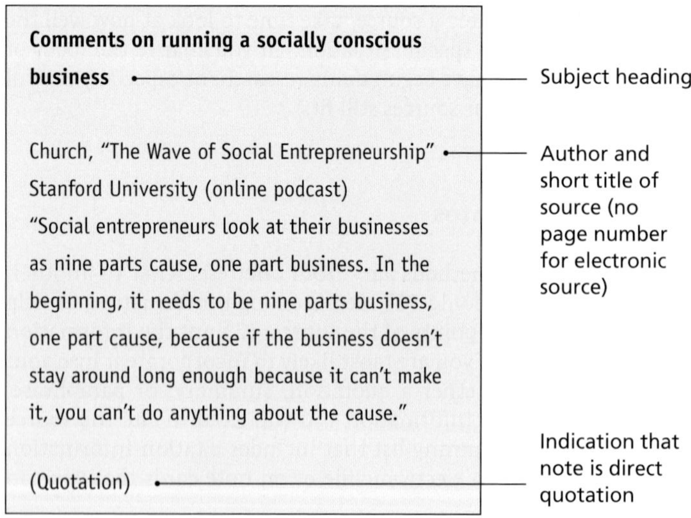

your research project, copy it from the note precisely, including brackets and ellipses.

- Record the author's name, shortened title of the source, and page number(s) on which the quotation appeared. Make sure you have a corresponding working-bibliography entry with complete source information.
- Label the note with a subject heading, and then identify it as a quotation.

Paraphrasing. When you paraphrase, you're putting brief material from an author (including major and minor points, usually in the order they are presented) into *your own words and sentence structures.* If you wish to cite some of the author's words within the paraphrase, enclose them in quotation marks.

- Include all main points and any important details from the original source in the same order in which the author presents them, but in your own words. Put the original source aside to avoid following the wording too closely.
- If you want to include any language from the original, enclose it in quotation marks.
- Save your comments, elaborations, or reactions for another note.
- Record the author, shortened title, and page number(s), if the source has them, on which the original material appeared.
- Make sure you have a corresponding working-bibliography entry.
- Label the note with a subject heading, and identify it as a paraphrase to avoid confusion with a summary.
- Recheck to be sure that the words and sentence structures are your own and that they express the author's meaning accurately.

The following examples of paraphrases resemble the original material either too little or too much.

ORIGINAL

Language play, the arguments suggest, will help the development of pronunciation ability through its focus on the properties of sounds and sound contrasts, such as rhyming. Playing with

> word endings and decoding the syntax of riddles will help the acquisition of grammar. Readiness to play with words and names, to exchange puns and to engage in nonsense talk, promotes links with semantic development. The kinds of dialogue interaction illustrated above are likely to have consequences for the development of conversational skills. And language play, by its nature, also contributes greatly to what in recent years has been called *metalinguistic awareness*, which is turning out to be of critical importance in the development of language skills in general and of literacy skills in particular.
>
> —David Crystal, *Language Play* (180)

UNACCEPTABLE PARAPHRASE: STRAYING FROM THE AUTHOR'S IDEAS

> Crystal argues that playing with language—creating rhymes, figuring out how riddles work, making puns, playing with names, using invented words, and so on—helps children figure out a great deal about language, from the basics of pronunciation and grammar to how to carry on a conversation. Increasing their understanding of how language works in turn helps them become more interested in learning new languages and in pursuing education (180).

This paraphrase starts off well enough, but it moves away from paraphrasing the original to inserting the writer's ideas; Crystal says nothing about learning new languages or pursuing education.

UNACCEPTABLE PARAPHRASE: USING THE AUTHOR'S WORDS

> Crystal suggests that language play, including rhyme, helps children improve pronunciation ability, that looking at word endings and decoding the syntax of riddles allows them to understand grammar, and that other kinds of dialogue interaction teach conversation. Overall, language play may be of critical importance in the development of language and literacy skills (180).

Because the highlighted phrases are either borrowed from the original without quotation marks or changed only superficially, this paraphrase plagiarizes.

UNACCEPTABLE PARAPHRASE: USING THE AUTHOR'S SENTENCE STRUCTURES

Language play, Crystal suggests, will improve pronunciation by zeroing in on sounds such as rhymes. Having fun with word endings and analyzing riddle structure will help a person acquire grammar. Being prepared to play with language, to use puns and talk nonsense, improves the ability to use semantics. These playful methods of communication are likely to influence a person's ability to talk to others. And language play inherently adds enormously to what has recently been known as *metalinguistic awareness*, a concept of great magnitude in developing speech abilities generally and literacy abilities particularly (180).

Here is a paraphrase of the same passage that expresses the author's ideas accurately and acceptably:

ACCEPTABLE PARAPHRASE: IN THE STUDENT WRITER'S OWN WORDS

Crystal argues that playing with language—creating rhymes, figuring out riddles, making puns, playing with names, using invented words, and so on—helps children figure out a great deal, from the basics of pronunciation and grammar to how to carry on a conversation. This kind of play allows children to understand the overall concept of how language works, a concept that is key to learning to use—and read—language effectively (180).

Summarizing. A summary is a significantly shortened version of a passage or even a whole chapter, article, film, or other work that captures main ideas *in your own words.* Unlike a paraphrase, a summary uses just enough information to record the points you wish to emphasize.

- Put the original aside to write your summary. If you later decide to include language from the original, enclose it in quotation marks.
- Record the author, shortened title, and page number(s) on which the original material appeared. For online or multimedia sources without page numbers, record any information that will help readers find the material.

- Make sure you have a corresponding working-bibliography entry.
- Label the note with a subject heading, and identify it as a summary to avoid confusion with a paraphrase.
- Recheck to be sure you have captured the author's meaning and that the words are entirely your own.

Annotating sources. You can annotate copies or printouts of sources you intend to use with your thoughts and questions as well as highlighting interesting quotations and key terms.

Try not to rely too heavily on copying or printing out whole pieces, however; you still need to read the material very carefully. And resist the temptation to treat copied material as notes, an action that could lead to inadvertent plagiarizing. Using a different color for text pasted from a source will help prevent this problem.

Summary Note

Note	
Language development	Subject heading
Crystal, *Language Play*, p. 180	Author, short title, page reference
Crystal argues that various kinds of language play contribute to awareness of how language works and to literacy.	
(Summary)	Label

For Multilingual Writers

Identifying Sources

While some language communities and cultures expect audiences to recognize the sources of important documents and texts, thereby eliminating the need to cite them directly, conventions for writing in North America call for careful attribution of any quoted, paraphrased, or summarized material. When in doubt, explicitly identify your sources.

15 Integrating Sources and Avoiding Plagiarism

In some ways, there is really nothing new under the sun, in writing and research as well as in life. Whatever writing you do has been influenced by what you have already read and experienced. As you work on your research project, you will need to know how to integrate and acknowledge the work of others. And all writers need to understand current definitions of plagiarism (which have changed over time and differ from culture to culture) as well as the concept of intellectual property—those works protected by copyright and other laws—so that they can give credit where credit is due.

15a Integrating quotations, paraphrases, and summaries

Integrate source materials into your writing with care to ensure that the integrated materials make grammatical and logical sense.

Quotations. Because your research project is primarily your own work, limit your use of quotations to those necessary to your thesis or memorable for your readers.

Short quotations should run in with your text, enclosed by quotation marks. Longer quotations should be set off from the text (39a). Integrate all quotations into your text so that they flow smoothly and clearly into the surrounding sentences. Be sure that the sentence containing the quotation is grammatically complete, especially if you incorporate a quotation into your own words.

SIGNAL PHRASES. Introduce the quotation with a signal phrase or signal **verb**, such as those highlighted in these examples.

- As Eudora Welty notes, "Learning stamps you with its moments. Childhood's learning," she continues, "is made up of moments. It isn't steady. It's a pulse" (9).
- In her essay, Haraway strongly opposes those who condemn technology outright, arguing that we must not indulge in a "demonology of technology" (181).

Research: Integrating Sources > LearningCurve (2)

Choose a signal verb that is appropriate to the idea you are expressing and that accurately characterizes the author's viewpoint. Other signal verbs include words such as *acknowledges, agrees, asserts, believes, claims, concludes, describes, disagrees, lists, objects, offers, remarks, reports, reveals, says, suggests*, and *writes*.

When you follow the Modern Language Association (MLA) style, used in the examples in this chapter, put verbs in signal phrases in the **present tense**. For *Chicago* style, use the present tense (or use the **past tense** to emphasize a point made in the past).

If you are using American Psychological Association (APA) style to describe research results, use the past tense or the **present perfect tense** (*the study showed, the study has shown*) in your signal phrase. Use the present tense to explain implications of research (*for future research, these findings suggest*).

When using the Council of Science Editors (CSE) style, in general use the present tense for research reports and the past tense to describe specific methods or observations, or to cite published research.

BRACKETS AND ELLIPSES. In direct quotations, enclose in brackets any words you change or add, and indicate any deletions with ellipsis points.

- **"There is something wrong in the [Three Mile Island] area," one farmer told the Nuclear Regulatory Commission after the plant accident ("Legacy" 33).**
- **Economist John Kenneth Galbraith pointed out that "large corporations cannot afford to compete with one another. . . . In a truly competitive market someone loses" (Key 17).**

Be careful that any changes you make in a quotation do not alter its meaning. Use brackets and ellipses sparingly; too many make for difficult reading and might suggest that you have removed some of the context for the quotation.

Paraphrases and summaries. Introduce paraphrases and summaries clearly, usually with a signal phrase that includes the author of the source, as the highlighted words in this example indicate.

▸ **Professor of linguistics Deborah Tannen illustrates how communication between women and men breaks down and then suggests that a full awareness of "genderlects" can improve relationships (297).**

15b Integrating visuals and media

Choose visuals and media wisely, whether you use video, audio, photographs, illustrations, charts and graphs, or any other kinds of images. Integrate all visuals and media smoothly into your text.

- **Does each visual or media file make a strong contribution to the message?** Purely decorative visuals and media may weaken the power of your writing.
- **Is each fair to your subject?** An obviously biased perspective may seem unfair to your audience.
- **Is each appropriate for your audience?**

While it is considered "fair use" to use such materials in an essay or other project for a college class, once that project is published on the web, you might infringe on copyright protections if you do not ask the copyright holder for permission to use the visual or media file. If you have questions about whether your work might infringe on copyright, ask your instructor for help.

Like quotations, paraphrases, and summaries, visuals and media need to be introduced and commented on in some way.

- Refer to the visual or media element in the text *before* it appears: *As Fig. 3 demonstrates.*
- Explain or comment on the relevance of the visual or media file. This can appear *after* the visual.
- Check the documentation system you are using to make sure you label visual and media elements appropriately; MLA, for instance, asks that you number and title tables and figures (*Table 1: Average Amount of Rainfall by Region*).
- If you are posting your work publicly, make sure you have permission to use any copyrighted visuals.

15c Knowing which sources to acknowledge

As you carry out research, it is important to understand the distinction between materials that require acknowledgment (in in-text citations, footnotes, or endnotes; and in the list of works cited or bibliography) and those that do not.

While you need to prepare accurate and thorough citations in most formal academic assignments, it's also important to understand that much of the writing you do outside of college will not require formal citations. In writing on social media, for example, or even in highly respected newspapers and magazines like the *New York Times* or the *Atlantic*, providing a link is often the only "citation" the authors need. So learn to be flexible: use formal citations when called for in formal college work, and weave in and acknowledge your sources more informally in most out-of-college writing.

Materials that do not require acknowledgment. You do not usually need to cite a source for the following:

- Common knowledge—facts that most readers are already familiar with
- Facts available in a wide variety of sources, such as encyclopedias, almanacs, or textbooks
- Your own findings from field research. You should, however, acknowledge people you interview as individuals rather than as part of a survey.

Materials that require acknowledgment. You should cite all of your other sources to be certain to avoid plagiarism. Follow the documentation style required (see Chapters 45–48), and list the source in a bibliography or list of works cited. Be especially careful to cite the following:

- Sources for quotations, paraphrases, and summaries that you include
- Facts not widely known or arguable assertions
- All visuals from any source, including your own artwork, photographs you have taken, and graphs or tables you create from data found in a source
- Any help provided by a friend, an instructor, or another person

Research: Acknowledging Sources and Avoiding Plagiarism > LearningCurve (2)
Research: Acknowledging Sources and Avoiding Plagiarism > Tutorial

15d Avoiding plagiarism

Academic integrity enables us to trust those sources we use and to demonstrate that our own work is equally trustworthy. Plagiarism is especially damaging to one's academic integrity, whether it involves inaccurate or incomplete acknowledgment of one's sources in citations—sometimes called unintentional plagiarism—or deliberate plagiarism that is intended to pass off one writer's work as another's.

Whether it is intentional or not, plagiarism can have serious consequences. Students who plagiarize may fail the course or be expelled. Others who have plagiarized, even inadvertently, have had degrees revoked or have been stripped of positions or awards.

Unintentional plagiarism. If your paraphrase is too close to the wording or sentence structure of a source (even if you identify the source); if after a quotation you do not identify the source (even if you include the quotation marks); or if you fail to indicate clearly the source of an idea that you did not come up with on your own, you may be accused of plagiarism even if your intent was not to plagiarize. This inaccurate or incomplete acknowledgment of one's sources often results either from carelessness or from not learning how to borrow material properly.

 **For Multilingual Writers**

Thinking about Plagiarism as a Cultural Concept

Many cultures do not recognize Western notions of plagiarism, which rest on a belief that writers can own their language and ideas. Indeed, in many cultures and communities, using the words and ideas of others without attribution is considered a sign of deep respect as well as an indication of knowledge. In academic writing in the United States, however, you should credit all materials except those that are common knowledge, that are available in a wide variety of sources, or that are your own creations or your own findings from field research.

Take responsibility for your research and for acknowledging all sources accurately. To guard against unintentional plagiarism, photocopy or print out sources and identify the needed quotations right on the copy. You can also insert footnotes or endnotes into the text as you write.

Deliberate plagiarism. Deliberate plagiarism—such as handing in an essay written by a friend or purchased or downloaded from an essay-writing company; cutting and pasting passages directly from source materials without marking them with quotation marks and acknowledging their sources; failing to credit the source of an idea or concept in your text—is what most people think of when they hear the word *plagiarism*. This form of plagiarism is particularly troubling because it represents dishonesty and deception: those who intentionally plagiarize present someone else's hard work as their own and claim knowledge they really don't have, thus deceiving their readers.

Deliberate plagiarism is also fairly simple to spot: your instructor will be well acquainted with your writing and likely to notice any sudden shifts in the style or quality of your work. In addition, by typing a few words from a project into a search engine, your instructor can identify "matches" very easily.

16 Writing a Research Project

When you are working on a research project, there comes a time to draw the strands of your research together and articulate your conclusions in writing.

16a Drafting your text

Once you have all the information you think you'll need, try arranging your notes and visuals to identify connections, main ideas, and possible organization. You may also want to develop a working outline, a storyboard, or an idea map.

Research: Writing a Research Project > Video Prompt

For almost all research projects, drafting should begin well before the deadline in case you need to gather more information or do more drafting. Begin drafting wherever you feel most confident. If you have an idea for an introduction, begin there.

Working title and introduction. The title and introduction set the stage for what is to come. Ideally, the title announces the subject in an intriguing or memorable way. The introduction should draw readers in and provide any background they will need to understand your discussion.

Conclusion. A good conclusion helps readers know what they have learned. One effective strategy is to begin with a reference to your thesis and then expand to a more general conclusion that reminds readers why your discussion is significant. Try to conclude with something that will have an impact—but avoid sounding preachy.

16b Reviewing and revising a research project

Once you've completed your draft, reread it slowly and carefully. As you do so, reconsider the project's purpose and audience, your stance and thesis, and the evidence you have gathered. Then, ask others to read and respond to your draft. (For more on reviewing and revising, see Chapter 4.)

16c Preparing a list of sources

Once you have a final draft with your source materials in place, you are ready to prepare your list of sources. Create an entry for each source used in your final draft, consulting your notes and working

For Multilingual Writers

Asking Experienced Writers to Review a Thesis

You might find it helpful to ask one or two classmates who have more experience with the particular type of academic writing to look at your explicit thesis. Ask if the thesis is as direct and clear as it can be, and revise accordingly.

bibliography. Then double-check your draft to make sure that you have listed every source mentioned in the in-text citations or notes and that you have omitted any sources not cited in your project. (For guidelines on documentation styles, see Chapters 45–48.)

16d Editing and proofreading

When you have revised your draft, check grammar, usage, spelling, punctuation, and mechanics. Proofread the final version of your project, and carefully consider the advice of spell checkers and grammar checkers before accepting it. (For more information on editing, see 4c.)

Language

Writing Processes

Writing That Works

Research

Language

Grammar

Style

Punctuation/ Mechanics

Documentation

17 Writing across Cultures

People today often communicate instantaneously across vast distances and cultures. Businesspeople complete multinational transactions, students take online classes at distant universities, and conversations circle the globe via social media. You may also find yourself writing to (or with) people from other cultures, language groups, and countries. In this era of rapid global communication, you must know how to write effectively across cultures.

17a Thinking about what seems "normal"

More than likely, your judgments about what is "normal" are based on assumptions that you are not aware of. Most of us tend to see our own way as the "normal" or right way to do things. If your ways seem inherently right, then perhaps you assume that other ways are somehow less than right. To communicate effectively with people across cultures, recognize the norms that guide your own behavior and how those norms differ from those of other people.

- Know that most ways of communicating are influenced by cultural contexts and differ from one culture to the next.
- Notice the ways that people from cultures other than your own communicate, and be flexible.
- Respect the differences among individuals within a culture. Don't assume that all members of a community behave in the same way or value the same things.

17b Clarifying meaning

All writers face challenges in trying to communicate across space, languages, and cultures. You can address these challenges by working to be sure that you understand what others say—and that they understand you. In such situations, take care to be explicit about the meanings of the words you use. In addition, don't hesitate to ask people to explain a point if you're not absolutely sure you understand, and invite responses by asking whether you're making yourself clear or what you could do to be *more* clear.

17c Meeting audience expectations

When you do your best to meet an audience's expectations about how a text should work, your writing is more likely to have the desired effect. In practice, figuring out what audiences want, need, or expect can be difficult—especially when you are writing in public spaces online and your audiences can be composed of anyone, anywhere. If you know little about your potential audiences, carefully examine your assumptions about your readers.

Expectations about your authority as a writer. Writers communicating across cultures often encounter audiences who have differing attitudes about authority and about the relationship between the writer and the people being addressed. In the United States, students are frequently asked to establish authority in their writing—by drawing on personal experience, by reporting on research, or by taking a position for which they can offer strong evidence and support. But some cultures position student writers as novices, whose job is to learn from others who have greater authority. When you write, think carefully about your audience's expectations and attitudes toward authority.

- What is your relationship to those you are addressing?
- What knowledge are you expected to have? Is it appropriate for you to demonstrate that knowledge—and if so, how?
- What is your goal—to answer a question? to make a point? to agree? something else?
- What tone is appropriate? If in doubt, show respect: politeness is rarely if ever inappropriate.

Expectations about persuasive evidence. You should think carefully about how to use evidence in writing, and pay attention to what counts as evidence to members of groups you are trying to persuade. Are facts, concrete examples, or firsthand experience convincing to the intended audience? Does the testimony of experts count heavily as evidence? What people are considered trustworthy experts, and why? Will the audience value citations from religious or philosophical texts, proverbs, or everyday wisdom? Are there other sources that would be considered strong evidence? If analogies are used as support, which kinds are most powerful?

Once you determine what counts as evidence in your own thinking and writing, consider where you learned to use and value this kind of evidence. You can ask these same questions about the use of evidence by members of other cultures.

Expectations about organization. The organizational patterns that you find pleasing are likely to be deeply embedded in your own culture. Many U.S. readers expect a well-organized piece of writing to use the following structure: introduction and thesis, necessary background, overview of the parts, systematic presentation of evidence, consideration of other viewpoints, and conclusion.

However, in cultures that value indirection, subtlety, or repetition, writers tend to prefer different organizational patterns. When writing for world audiences, think about how you can organize material to get your message across effectively. Consider where to state your thesis or main point (at the beginning, at the end, somewhere else, or not at all) and whether to use a straightforward organization or to employ digressions to good effect.

Expectations about style. Effective style varies broadly across cultures and depends on the rhetorical situation—purpose, audience, and so on. Even so, there is one important style question to consider when writing across cultures: what level of formality is most appropriate? In most writing to a general audience in the United States, a fairly informal style is often acceptable, even appreciated. Many cultures, however, tend to value a more formal approach. When in doubt, err on the side of formality in writing to people from other cultures, especially to your elders or to those in authority. Use appropriate titles (*Dr. Moss, Professor Mejía*); avoid slang and informal structures, such as **sentence fragments**; use complete words and sentences (even in email); and use first names only if invited to do so.

18 Language That Builds Common Ground

The supervisor who refers to her staff as "team members" (rather than as "my staff" or as "subordinates") has chosen language intended to establish common ground with people who are important to her. Your own language can work to build common ground if you carefully consider the sensitivities and preferences of others and if you watch for words that betray your assumptions, even though you have not directly stated them.

18a Examining assumptions and avoiding stereotypes

Unstated assumptions that enter into thinking and writing can destroy common ground by ignoring important differences. For example, a student in a religion seminar who uses *we* to refer to Christians and *they* to refer to members of other religions had better be sure that everyone in the class identifies as Christian, or some may feel left out of the discussion.

At the same time, don't overgeneralize about or stereotype a group of people. Because stereotypes are often based on half-truths, misunderstandings, and hand-me-down prejudices, they can lead to intolerance, bias, and bigotry.

Sometimes stereotypes and assumptions lead writers to call special attention to a group affiliation when it is not relevant to the point, as in *a woman plumber* or *a white basketball player*. Careful writers make sure that their language doesn't stereotype any group or individual.

18b Examining assumptions about gender

Powerful gender-related words can subtly affect our thinking and our behavior. For instance, at one time speakers commonly referred to hypothetical doctors or engineers as *he* (and then labeled a woman who worked as a doctor *a woman doctor*, as if to say, "She's an exception; doctors are normally men"). Similarly, a label like *male nurse* reflects stereotyped assumptions about proper roles for men. Equally problematic is the traditional use of *man* and *mankind* to refer to people of both sexes and the use of *he* and *him* to refer to generally to any human being. Because such usage ignores half of the people on earth, it hardly helps a writer build common ground.

Sexist language, those words and phrases that stereotype or ignore members of either sex or that unnecessarily call attention to gender, can usually be revised fairly easily. There are several alternatives to using masculine **pronouns** to refer to persons whose gender is unknown:

▶ **~~A lawyer~~ Lawyers must pass the bar exam before ~~he~~ they can practice.**

▶ **A lawyer must pass the bar exam before he or she can practice.**

▶ **A lawyer must pass the bar exam before ~~he can practice.~~ practicing.**

Try to eliminate common sexist **nouns** from your writing.

INSTEAD OF	TRY USING
anchorman, anchorwoman	anchor
businessman	businessperson, business executive
congressman	member of Congress, representative
fireman	firefighter
male nurse	nurse
man, mankind	humans, human beings, humanity, the human race, humankind
policeman, policewoman	police officer
woman engineer	engineer

18c Examining assumptions about race and ethnicity

In building common ground, watch for any words that ignore differences not only among individual members of a race or ethnic group but also among subgroups. Be aware, for instance, of the many nations to which American Indians belong and of the diverse places from which Americans of Spanish-speaking ancestry come.

Preferred terms. Identifying preferred terms is sometimes not an easy task, for they can change often and vary widely.

- The word *colored* was once widely used in the United States to refer to Americans of African ancestry. By the 1950s, the preferred term had become *Negro*; in the 1960s, *black* came to be preferred by most, though certainly not all, members of that community. Then, in the late 1980s, some leaders of the community urged that *black* be replaced by *African American*. Today, *African American* and *black* (or *Black*) are both widely used.
- The word *Oriental*, once used to refer to people of East Asian descent, is now considered offensive.
- Once widely preferred, the term *Native American* is challenged by those who argue that the most appropriate way to refer to indigenous peoples is by the specific name such as *Chippewa*, *Tlingit*, or *Hopi*. It has also become common for tribal groups to refer to themselves as *Indians* or *Indian tribes*.
- Among Americans of Spanish-speaking descent, the preferred terms of reference are many: *Chicano/Chicana*, *Hispanic*, *Latin American*, *Latino/Latina*, *Mexican American*, *Dominican*, and *Puerto Rican*, to name but a few.

Clearly, then, ethnic terminology changes often enough to challenge even the most careful writers—including writers who belong to the groups they are writing about. The best advice may be to consider your words carefully, to listen for the way members of a group refer to themselves (or ask about preferences), and to check in a current dictionary for any term you're unsure of.

18d Considering other kinds of difference

Remember that your audiences may include people from many areas of the United States as well as from other countries, of many different ages and socioeconomic backgrounds, of many different abilities, of differing religious views, and of different sexual orientations. In the latter case, it's important to recognize that people inhabit a very wide range of sexualities, including gay, lesbian, bisexual, transgender, intersexual, and asexual as well as heterosexual orientations. In short, you can almost never assume that audiences are just like you or that they share your background and experiences. Keeping this range of differences in mind can help you avoid overgeneralizing or stereotyping audiences—and thus help you build common ground.

19 Varieties of Language

Comedian Dave Chappelle has said, "Every black American is bilingual. We speak street vernacular, and we speak job interview." As Chappelle understands, English comes in many varieties that differ from one another in pronunciation, vocabulary, usage, and grammar. You probably already adjust the variety of language you use depending on how well—and how formally—you know the audience you are addressing. Language variety can improve your communication with your audience if you think carefully about the effect you want to achieve.

19a Using "standard" varieties of English appropriately

The key to shifting among varieties of English and among languages is appropriateness: you need to consider when such shifts will help your audience appreciate your message and when shifts may do just the opposite. Used appropriately and wisely, *any* variety of English can serve a good purpose.

One variety of English, usually referred to as the "standard" or "standard academic," is that taught prescriptively in schools, represented

Language: Language Variety > Video Prompt

 For Multilingual Writers

Recognizing Global Varieties of English

Like other world languages, English is used in many countries, so it has many global varieties. For example, British English differs somewhat from U.S. English in certain vocabulary (*bonnet* for *hood* of a car), syntax (*to hospital* rather than *to the hospital*), spelling (*centre* rather than *center*), and pronunciation. If you have learned a non-American variety of English, you will want to recognize, and to appreciate, the ways in which it differs from the variety widely used in U.S. academic settings.

in this and most other textbooks, used in the national media, and written and spoken widely by those wielding social and economic power. As the language used in business and most public institutions, "standard" English is a variety you will want to be completely familiar with. "Standard" English, however, is only one of many effective varieties of English and itself varies according to purpose and audience, from the more formal style used in academic writing to the informal style characteristic of casual conversation.

19b Using varieties of English to evoke a place or community

Weaving together regionalisms and standard English can be effective in creating a sense of place. Here, an anthropologist writing about one Carolina community takes care to let the residents speak their minds—and in their own words:

> For Roadville, schooling is something most folks have not gotten enough of, but everybody believes will do something toward helping an individual "get on." In the words of one oldtime resident, "Folks that ain't got no schooling don't get to be nobody nowadays."
>
> —Shirley Brice Heath, *Ways with Words*

Varieties of language, including slang and colloquial expressions, can also help writers evoke other kinds of communities. (See also 20a.)

19c Using varieties of English to build credibility with a community

Whether you are American Indian or trace your ancestry to Europe, Asia, Latin America, Africa, or elsewhere, your heritage lives on in the diversity of the English language. See how one Hawaiian writer uses a local variety of English to paint a picture of young teens hearing a "chicken skin" story from their grandmother.

> "—So, rather dan being rid of da shark, da people were stuck with many little ones, for dere mistake."
>
> Then Grandma Wong wen' pause, for dramatic effect, I guess, and she wen' add, "Dis is one of dose times. . . . Da time of da sharks."
>
> Those words ended another of Grandma's chicken skin stories. The stories she told us had been passed on to her by her grandmother, who had heard them from her grandmother. Always skipping a generation.
>
> —Rodney Morales, "When the Shark Bites"

Notice how the narrator of the story uses different varieties of English—presenting information necessary to the story line mostly in standard English and using a local, ethnic variety to represent spoken language. One important reason for the shift from standard English is to demonstrate that the writer is a member of the community whose language he is representing and thus to build credibility with others in the community. Take care, however, in using the language of communities other than your own. When used inappropriately, such language can have an opposite effect, perhaps destroying credibility and alienating your audience.

20 Word Choice

Deciding which word is the right word can be a challenge. It's not unusual to find many words that have similar but subtly different meanings, and each makes a different impression on your audience. For instance, the "pasta with marinara sauce" presented in a restaurant may look and taste much like the "macaroni and gravy" served at an Italian family dinner, but the choice of one label rather than the other tells us not only about the food but also about the people serving it and the people they expect to serve it to.

20a Using appropriate formality

In an email or letter to a friend or close associate, informal language is often appropriate. For most academic and professional writing, however, more formal language is appropriate, since you are addressing people you do not know well.

EMAIL TO SOMEONE YOU KNOW WELL

▸ **Myisha is great—hire her if you can!**

LETTER OF RECOMMENDATION TO SOMEONE YOU DO NOT KNOW

▸ **I am pleased to recommend Myisha Fisher. She will bring good ideas and extraordinary energy to your organization.**

Slang and colloquial language. Slang, or extremely informal language, is often confined to a relatively small group and changes very quickly, though some slang gains wide use (*ripoff, zine*). Colloquial language, such as *a lot*, *in a bind*, or *snooze*, is less informal, more widely used, and longer lasting than most slang.

Writers who use slang and colloquial language run the risk of not being understood or of not being taken seriously. If you are writing for a general audience about gun-control legislation and you use the term *gat*, some readers may not know what you mean, and others may be irritated by what they see as a frivolous reference to a deadly serious subject.

Jargon. Jargon is the special vocabulary of a trade or profession, enabling members to speak and write concisely to one another. Reserve jargon for an audience that will understand your terms. The example that follows, from a blog about fonts and typefaces, uses jargon appropriately for an interested and knowledgeable audience.

> RISQUÉ
> *Filmfax* №18
> CLASSIC SHOWMANSHIP
> ***Mr. Ed Wood***
> ED WOOD JR. was an American film director, screenwriter, producer, actor, author, and editor, who often performed in many of these functions simultaneously. In the 1950s, he made a run of many cheap and poorly produced *genre films*, humorously celebrated for their technical errors, dialogue, poor special effects, and outlandish plot elements.
> **Béla Lugosi**
>
> FONTSHOP.COM
>
> The Modern typeface classification is usually associated with Didones and display faces that often have too much contrast for text use. The Ingeborg family was designed with the intent of producing a Modern face that was readable at any size. Its roots might well be historic, but its approach is very contemporary. The three text weights (Regular, Bold, and Heavy) are functional and discreet while the Display weights (Fat and Block) catch the reader's eye with a dynamic form and a whole lot of ink on the paper. The family includes a boatload of extras like unicase alternates, swash caps, and a lined fill. —fontshop.com blog

Jargon can be irritating and incomprehensible—or extremely helpful. Before you use technical jargon, remember your readers: if they will not understand the terms, or if you don't know them well enough to judge, then say whatever you need to say in everyday language.

Pompous language, euphemisms, and doublespeak. Stuffy or pompous language is unnecessarily formal for the purpose, audience, or topic. It often gives writing an insincere or unintentionally humorous tone, making a writer's ideas seem insignificant or even unbelievable.

POMPOUS

- **Pursuant to the August 9 memorandum regarding the company carbon-footprint-reduction initiative, it is incumbent upon us to endeavor to make maximal utilization of telephonic and digital communication in lieu of personal visitation.**

REVISED

- **According to the August 9 memo, the company wants us to reduce our use of oil and gas, so we should telephone or email whenever possible rather than make personal visits.**

 For Multilingual Writers

Avoiding Fancy Language

In writing standard academic English, which is fairly formal, students are often tempted to use many "big words" instead of simple language. Although learning impressive words can be a good way to expand your vocabulary, it is usually best to avoid flowery or fancy language in college writing. Academic writing at U.S. universities tends to value clear, concise prose.

Euphemisms are words and **phrases** that make unpleasant ideas seem less harsh. *Your position is being eliminated* seeks to soften the blow of being fired or laid off. Although euphemisms can sometimes appeal to an audience by showing that you are considerate of people's feelings, they can also sound insincere or evasive.

Doublespeak is language used to hide or distort the truth. During massive layoffs in the business world, companies may describe a job-cutting policy as *employee repositioning*, *deverticalization*, or *rightsizing*. The public—and particularly those who lose their jobs—recognize such terms as doublespeak.

20b Considering denotation and connotation

The words *enthusiasm*, *passion*, and *obsession* all carry roughly the same denotation, or dictionary meaning. But the connotations, or associations, are quite different: an *enthusiasm* is a pleasurable and absorbing interest; a *passion* has a strong emotional component and may affect someone positively or negatively; an *obsession* is an unhealthy attachment that excludes other interests.

Note the differences in connotation among the following three statements:

- **Students Against Racism (SAR) erected a temporary barrier on the campus oval, saying the structure symbolized "the many barriers to those discriminated against by university policies."**
- **Left-wing agitators threw up an eyesore right on the oval to try to stampede the university into giving in to their demands.**

- **Supporters of human rights for all students challenged the university's investment in racism by erecting a protest barrier on campus.**

The first statement is the most neutral, merely stating facts (and quoting the assertion about university policy to represent it as someone's opinion); the second, by using words with negative connotations (*agitators*, *eyesore*, *stampede*), is strongly critical; the third, by using words with positive connotations (*supporters of human rights*) and presenting assertions as facts (*the university's investment in racism*), gives a favorable slant to the protest.

20c Using general and specific language effectively

Effective writers balance general words (those that name groups or classes) with specific words (those that identify individual and particular things). Abstractions, which are types of general words, refer to things we cannot perceive through our five senses. Specific words are often concrete, naming things we can see, hear, touch, taste, or smell.

GENERAL	LESS GENERAL	SPECIFIC	MORE SPECIFIC
book	dictionary	abridged dictionary	the fourth edition of the *American Heritage College Dictionary*

ABSTRACT	LESS ABSTRACT	CONCRETE	MORE CONCRETE
culture	visual art	painting	van Gogh's *Starry Night*

20d Using figurative language effectively

Figurative language, or figures of speech, paints pictures in readers' minds, allowing readers to "see" a point readily and clearly. Far from being a frill, such language is crucial to understanding.

Similes, metaphors, and analogies. Similes use *like*, *as*, *as if*, or *as though* to make explicit the comparison between two seemingly different things.

▸ **The comb felt as if it was raking my skin off.**

—Malcolm X, "My First Conk"

Metaphors are implicit comparisons, omitting the *like*, *as*, *as if*, or *as though* of similes.

▸ **The Internet is the new town square.** —Jeb Hensarling

Analogies compare similar features of two dissimilar things; they explain something unfamiliar by relating it to something more familiar.

▸ **The mouse genome . . . [is] the Rosetta Stone for understanding the language of life.** —Tom Friend

Clichés and mixed metaphors. A cliché is an overused figure of speech, such as *busy as a bee*. By definition, we use clichés all the time, especially in speech, and many serve usefully as shorthand for familiar ideas. But if you use clichés to excess in your writing, readers may conclude that what you are saying is not very new or is even insincere.

Mixed metaphors make comparisons that are inconsistent.

▸ **The lectures were like brilliant comets streaking through the night sky, ~~showering~~ ^dazzling^ listeners with ~~a torrential rain~~ ^flashes^ of insight.**

The images of streaking light and heavy precipitation are inconsistent; in the revised sentence, all of the images relate to light.

20e Making spell checkers work for you

Research conducted for this book shows that spelling errors have changed dramatically in the past twenty years, thanks to spell checkers. Although these programs have weeded out many once-common misspellings, they are not foolproof. Look out for these typical errors allowed by spell checkers:

- **Homonyms.** Spell checkers cannot distinguish between words such as *affect* and *effect* that sound alike but are spelled differently.
- **Proper nouns.** A spell checker cannot tell you when you misspell a name.
- **Compound words written as two words.** Spell checkers will not see a problem if you write *nowhere* incorrectly as *no where.*
- **Typos.** The spell checker will not flag *heat* even if you meant to write *heart.*

Spell checkers and wrong words. Wrong-word errors are the most common surface error in college writing today (see pp. 2–3), and spell checkers are partly to blame. Spell checkers may suggest bizarre substitutions for proper names and specialized terms, and if you accept the suggestions automatically, you may introduce wrong-word errors. A student who typed *fantic* instead of *frantic* found that the spell checker had substituted *fanatic,* a replacement that made no sense. Be careful not to take a spell checker's recommendation without paying careful attention to the replacement word.

Adapting spell checkers to your needs. Always proofread carefully, even after running the spell checker. The following tips can help:

- Check a dictionary if a spell checker highlights or suggests a word you are not sure of.
- If you can enter new words in your spell checker's dictionary, include names, non-English terms, or other specialized words that you use regularly. Be careful to enter the correct spelling!
- After you run the spell checker, look again for homonyms that you mix up regularly.
- Remember that spell checkers are not sensitive to capitalization.

Grammar

Writing Processes

Writing That Works

Research

Language

Grammar

Style

Punctuation/ Mechanics

Documentation

21 Verbs and Verb Phrases

One famous restaurant in New Orleans offers to bake, broil, pan-fry, deep-fry, poach, sauté, fricassee, blacken, or scallop any of the fish entrées on its menu. To someone ordering—or cooking—at this restaurant, the important distinctions lie entirely in the **verbs**.

21a Using regular and irregular verb forms

The past **tense** and past **participle** of a **regular verb** are formed by adding *-ed* or *-d* to the **base form**.

BASE FORM	PAST TENSE	PAST PARTICIPLE
love	loved	loved
honor	honored	honored
obey	obeyed	obeyed

An **irregular verb** does not follow the *-ed* or *-d* pattern. If you are unsure about whether a verb is regular or irregular, or what the correct form is, consult the following list or a dictionary. Dictionaries list any irregular forms under the entry for the base form.

Some common irregular verbs

BASE FORM	PAST TENSE	PAST PARTICIPLE
arise	arose	arisen
be	was/were	been
beat	beat	beaten
become	became	become
begin	began	begun
bite	bit	bitten, bit
blow	blew	blown
break	broke	broken

Grammar: Parts of Speech > LearningCurve (4)
Grammar: Parts of Sentences > LearningCurve (2)

BASE FORM	PAST TENSE	PAST PARTICIPLE
bring	brought	brought
build	built	built
burn	burned, burnt	burned, burnt
burst	burst	burst
buy	bought	bought
catch	caught	caught
choose	chose	chosen
come	came	come
cost	cost	cost
cut	cut	cut
dig	dug	dug
dive	dived, dove	dived
do	did	done
draw	drew	drawn
dream	dreamed, dreamt	dreamed, dreamt
drink	drank	drunk
drive	drove	driven
eat	ate	eaten
fall	fell	fallen
feel	felt	felt
fight	fought	fought
find	found	found
fly	flew	flown
forget	forgot	forgotten, forgot
freeze	froze	frozen
get	got	gotten, got
give	gave	given
go	went	gone

BASE FORM	PAST TENSE	PAST PARTICIPLE
grow	grew	grown
hang (suspend)[1]	hung	hung
have	had	had
hear	heard	heard
hide	hid	hidden
hit	hit	hit
keep	kept	kept
know	knew	known
lay	laid	laid
lead	led	led
leave	left	left
lend	lent	lent
let	let	let
lie (recline)[2]	lay	lain
lose	lost	lost
make	made	made
mean	meant	meant
meet	met	met
pay	paid	paid
prove	proved	proved, proven
put	put	put
read	read	read
ride	rode	ridden
ring	rang	rung
rise	rose	risen
run	ran	run

[1]*Hang* meaning "execute by hanging" is regular: *hang, hanged, hanged.*
[2]*Lie* meaning "tell a falsehood" is regular: *lie, lied, lied.*

BASE FORM	PAST TENSE	PAST PARTICIPLE
say	said	said
see	saw	seen
send	sent	sent
set	set	set
shake	shook	shaken
shoot	shot	shot
show	showed	showed, shown
shrink	shrank	shrunk
sing	sang	sung
sink	sank	sunk
sit	sat	sat
sleep	slept	slept
speak	spoke	spoken
spend	spent	spent
spread	spread	spread
spring	sprang, sprung	sprung
stand	stood	stood
steal	stole	stolen
strike	struck	struck, stricken
swim	swam	swum
swing	swung	swung
take	took	taken
teach	taught	taught
tear	tore	torn
tell	told	told
think	thought	thought
throw	threw	thrown
wake	woke, waked	waked, woken

BASE FORM	PAST TENSE	PAST PARTICIPLE
wear	wore	worn
win	won	won
write	wrote	written

21b Building verb phrases

Verb phrases can be built up out of a main **verb** and one or more **helping** (auxiliary) **verbs**.

- Immigration figures are rising every year.
- Immigration figures have risen every year.

Verb phrases have strict rules of order. If you try to rearrange the words in either of these sentences, you will find that most alternatives are impossible. You cannot say *Immigration figures rising are every year.*

Putting auxiliary verbs in order. In the sentence *Immigration figures may have been rising*, the main verb *rising* follows three auxiliaries: *may*, *have*, and *been*. Together these auxiliaries and the main verb make up a verb phrase.

Checklist

Editing the Verbs in Your Writing

- Check verb endings that cause you trouble. (21a)
- Double-check forms of *lie* and *lay*, *sit* and *set*, *rise* and *raise*. (21d)
- Refer to action in a literary work in the present tense. (21e)
- Check that verb tenses in your writing express meaning accurately. (21e and 21f)
- Use passive voice appropriately. (21g)

- *May* is a modal that indicates possibility; it is followed by the base form of a verb.
- *Have* is an auxiliary verb that in this case indicates the perfect tense; it must be followed by a past participle (*been*).
- Any form of *be*, when it is followed by a present participle ending in *-ing* (such as *rising*), indicates the progressive tense.
- *Be* followed by a past participle, as in *New immigration policies have <u>been passed</u> in recent years*, indicates the passive voice (21g).

As shown in the following chart, when two or more auxiliaries appear in a verb phrase, they must follow a particular order based on the type of auxiliary: (1) modal, (2) a form of *have* used to indicate a perfect tense, (3) a form of *be* used to indicate a progressive tense, and (4) a form of *be* used to indicate the passive voice. (Very few sentences include all four kinds of auxiliaries.)

	Modal	**Perfect *Have***	**Progressive *Be***	**Passive *Be***	**Main Verb**	
Sonia	—	has	—	been	invited	to visit a family in Prague.
She	should	—	—	be	finished	with school soon.
The invitation	must	have	—	been	sent	in the spring.
She	—	has	been	—	studying	Czech.
She	may	—	be	—	feeling	nervous.
She	might	have	been	—	expecting	to travel elsewhere.
The trip	will	have	been	being	planned	for a month by the time she leaves.

Only one modal is permitted in a verb phrase.

▸ **She will ~~can~~ ^be able to^ speak Czech much better soon.**

Forming auxiliary verbs. Whenever you use an auxiliary, check the form of the word that follows.

MODAL + BASE FORM. Use the base form of a verb after *can*, *could*, *will*, *would*, *shall*, *should*, *may*, *might*, and *must*: *Alice can read Latin.* In many other languages, modals like *can* or *must* are followed by the **infinitive** (*to* + base form). Do not substitute an infinitive for the base form in English.

▸ **Alice can ~~to~~ read Latin.**

PERFECT *HAVE, HAS,* OR *HAD* + PAST PARTICIPLE. To form the perfect tenses, use *have*, *has*, or *had* with a past participle: *Everyone has gone home. They have been working all day.*

PROGRESSIVE *BE* + PRESENT PARTICIPLE. A progressive form of the verb is signaled by two elements, a form of the auxiliary *be* (*am*, *is*, *are*, *was*, *were*, *be*, or *been*) and the *-ing* form of the next word: *The children are studying.* Be sure to include both elements.

▸ **The children ^are^ studying science.**

▸ **The children are ~~study~~ ^studying^ science.**

Some verbs are rarely used in progressive forms. These are verbs that express unchanging conditions or mental states rather than deliberate actions: *believe, belong, hate, know, like, love, need, own, resemble, understand.*

PASSIVE *BE* + PAST PARTICIPLE. Use *am*, *is*, *are*, *was*, *were*, *being*, *be*, or *been* with a past participle to form the passive voice.

▸ **Tagalog is spoken in the Philippines.**

Notice that the word following the progressive *be* (the present participle) ends in *-ing*, but the word following the passive *be* (the past participle) never ends in *-ing*.

PROGRESSIVE	Meredith is studying music.
PASSIVE	Natasha was taught by a famous violinist.

If the first auxiliary in a verb phrase is a form of *be* or *have*, it must show either present or past tense and must agree with the subject: *Meredith has played in an orchestra.*

21c Using infinitives and gerunds

Knowing whether to use an **infinitive** (*to read*) or a **gerund** (*reading*) in a sentence may be a challenge.

INFINITIVE

- **My adviser urged me to apply to several colleges.**

GERUND

- **Applying took a great deal of time.**

In general, infinitives tend to represent intentions, desires, or expectations, while gerunds tend to represent facts. The infinitive in the first sentence conveys the message that the act of applying was desired but not yet accomplished, while the gerund in the second sentence calls attention to the fact that the application process was actually carried out.

The association of intention with infinitives and facts with gerunds can often help you decide whether to use an infinitive or a gerund when another verb immediately precedes it.

INFINITIVES

- **Kumar expected to get a good job after graduation.**
- **Last year, Jorge decided to become a math major.**
- **The strikers have agreed to go back to work.**

GERUNDS

- **Jerzy enjoys going to the theater.**
- **We resumed working after our coffee break.**
- **Alycia appreciated getting candy from Sean.**

A few verbs can be followed by either an infinitive or a gerund. With some, such as *begin* and *continue*, the choice makes little difference in meaning. With others, however, the difference in meaning is striking.

▸ **Carlos was working as a medical technician, but he stopped to study English.**

The infinitive indicates that Carlos left his job because he intended to study English.

▸ **Carlos stopped studying English when he left the United States.**

The gerund indicates that Carlos actually studied English but then stopped.

The distinction between fact and intention is a tendency, not a rule, and other rules may override it. Always use a gerund—not an infinitive—directly following a **preposition**.

▸ **This fruit is safe for ~~to eat.~~ eating.**

You can also remove the preposition and keep the infinitive.

▸ **This fruit is safe ~~for~~ to eat.**

 For Multilingual Writers

Checking Usage with Search Engines

Search engines such as Google can provide a useful way of checking sentence structure and word usage. For example, if you are not sure whether you should use an **infinitive** form (*to* verb) or a **gerund** (*-ing*) for the verb *confirm* after the main verb *expect*, you can search for both *"expected confirming"* and *"expected to confirm"* to see which search term yields more results. A search for *"expected to confirm"* yields many more hits than a search for *"expected confirming."* These results indicate that *expected to confirm* is the more commonly used expression. Be sure to click through a few pages of the search engine's results to make sure that most results come from ordinary sentences rather than from headlines or phrases that may be constructed differently from standard English.

21d Using *lie* and *lay*, *sit* and *set*, *rise* and *raise*

These pairs of verbs cause confusion because both verbs in each pair have similar-sounding forms and somewhat related meanings. In each pair, one verb is transitive, meaning that it is followed by a direct **object** (*I lay the package on the counter*). The other is intransitive, meaning that it does not have an object (*He lies on the floor, unable to move*). The best way to avoid confusing these verbs is to memorize their forms and meanings.

BASE FORM	PAST TENSE	PAST PARTICIPLE	PRESENT PARTICIPLE	*-S* FORM
lie (recline)	lay	lain	lying	lies
lay (put)	laid	laid	laying	lays
sit (be seated)	sat	sat	sitting	sits
set (put)	set	set	setting	sets
rise (get up)	rose	risen	rising	rises
raise (lift)	raised	raised	raising	raises

- The doctor asked the patient to ~~lay~~ ^lie^ on his side.
- Tamika ~~sat~~ ^set^ the vase on the table.
- Jaime ~~rose~~ ^raised^ himself to a sitting position.

21e Using verb tenses

Tenses show when the verb's action takes place. The three **simple tenses** are the **present tense**, the **past tense**, and the **future tense**.

PRESENT TENSE	I ask, write
PAST TENSE	I asked, wrote
FUTURE TENSE	I will ask, will write

More complex aspects of time are expressed through **progressive**, **perfect**, and **perfect progressive** forms of the simple tenses.

PRESENT PROGRESSIVE	she is asking, is writing
PAST PROGRESSIVE	she was asking, was writing
FUTURE PROGRESSIVE	she will be asking, will be writing
PRESENT PERFECT	she has asked, has written
PAST PERFECT	she had asked, had written
FUTURE PERFECT	she will have asked, will have written
PRESENT PERFECT PROGRESSIVE	she has been asking, has been writing
PAST PERFECT PROGRESSIVE	she had been asking, had been writing
FUTURE PERFECT PROGRESSIVE	she will have been asking, will have been writing

The simple tenses locate an action only within the three basic time frames of present, past, and future. Progressive forms express continuing actions; perfect forms express completed actions; perfect progressive forms express actions that continue up to some point in the present, past, or future.

Special purposes of the present tense. When writing about action in literary works, use the present tense.

- ▸ **Ishmael slowly ~~realized~~ realizes all that ~~was~~ is at stake in the search for the white whale.**

General truths or scientific facts should be in the present tense, even when the **predicate** in the main **clause** is in the past tense.

- ▸ **Pasteur demonstrated that his boiling process ~~made~~ makes milk safe to drink.**

In general, when you are quoting, summarizing, or paraphrasing a work, use the present tense.

- ▸ **Adam Banks ~~wrote~~ writes that we should "fly on, reaching for the stars we cannot yet map, see, or scan."**

But when using APA (American Psychological Association) style, report the results of your experiments or another researcher's work in the past tense (*wrote*, *noted*) or the present perfect (*has discovered*). (For more on APA style, see Chapter 46.)

- **Comer (1995) ~~notes~~** *noted* **that protesters who deprive themselves of food are seen not as dysfunctional but rather as "caring, sacrificing, even heroic" (p. 5).**

21f Sequencing verb tenses

Careful and accurate use of tenses is important for clear writing. When you use the appropriate tense for each action, readers can follow time changes easily.

- **By the time he lent her the money, she** *had* **declared bankruptcy.**

  The revision makes clear that the bankruptcy occurred before the loan.

21g Using active and passive voice

Voice tells whether a **subject** is acting (*He questions us*) or being acted upon (*He is questioned*). When the subject is acting, the verb is in the **active voice**; when the subject is being acted upon, however, the verb is in the **passive voice**. Most contemporary writers use the active voice as much as possible because it makes their prose stronger and livelier. To shift a sentence from passive to active voice, make the performer of the action the subject of the sentence.

- *My sister took the* **~~The~~ prizewinning photograph. ~~was taken by my sister.~~**

Use the passive voice when you want to emphasize the recipient of an action rather than the performer of the action.

- **Colonel Muammar el-Qaddafi was killed during an uprising in his hometown of Surt.**

In scientific and technical writing, use the passive voice to focus attention on what is being studied.

- **The volunteers' food intake was closely monitored.**

21h Using mood appropriately

The **mood** of a verb indicates the writer's attitude toward what he or she is saying. The indicative mood states facts or opinions and asks questions: *I did the right thing.* The imperative mood gives commands and instructions: *Do the right thing.* The subjunctive mood (used primarily in **dependent clauses** beginning with *that* or *if*) expresses wishes and conditions that are contrary to fact: *If I were doing the right thing, I'd know it.*

The present subjunctive uses the base form of the verb with all subjects.

- **It is important that children be ready for a new sibling.**

The past subjunctive is the same as the simple past except for the verb *be*, which uses *were* for all subjects.

- **He spent money as if he had infinite credit.**
- **If the store were better located, it would attract more customers.**

Because the subjunctive creates a rather formal tone, many people today substitute the indicative mood in informal conversation.

INFORMAL

- **If the store was better located, it would attract more customers.**

For academic or professional writing, use the subjunctive in the following contexts:

CLAUSES EXPRESSING A WISH

- **He wished that his brother ~~was~~ were still living nearby.**

***THAT* CLAUSES EXPRESSING A REQUEST OR DEMAND**

▶ **The plant inspector insists that a supervisor ~~is~~** *be* **on site at all times.**

***IF* CLAUSES EXPRESSING A CONDITION THAT DOES NOT EXIST**

▶ **If public transportation ~~was~~** *were* **widely available, fewer Americans would commute by car.**

One common error is to use *would* in both clauses. Use the subjunctive in the *if* clause and *would* in the other clause.

▶ **If I ~~would have~~** had **played harder, I would have won.**

21i Using conditional sentences appropriately

English distinguishes among many different types of conditional sentences: sentences that focus on questions and that are introduced by *if* or its equivalent. Each of the following examples makes different assumptions about the likelihood that what is stated in the *if* **clause** is true.

▶ **If you *practice* (or *have practiced*) writing often, you *learn* (or *have learned*) what your main problems are.**

This sentence assumes that what is stated in the *if* clause may be true; any verb tense that is appropriate in a simple sentence may be used in both the *if* clause and the main clause.

▶ **If you *practice* writing for the rest of this term, you *will* (or *may*) *understand* the process better.**

This sentence makes a prediction and again assumes that what is stated may turn out to be true. Only the main clause uses the future tense (*will understand*) or a modal that can indicate future time (*may understand*). The *if* clause must use the present tense.

▶ **If you *practiced* (or *were to practice*) writing every day, it *would* eventually *seem* easier.**

This sentence indicates doubt that what is stated will happen. In the *if* clause, the verb is either past—actually, past subjunctive (21h)—or *were to* + the base form, though it refers to future time. The main clause contains *would* + the base form of the main verb.

- **If you *practiced* writing on Mars, *you would find* no one to read your work.**

  This sentence imagines an impossible situation. Again, the past subjunctive is used in the *if* clause, although here past time is not being referred to, and *would* + the base form is used in the main clause.

- **If you *had practiced* writing in ancient Egypt, you *would have used* hieroglyphics.**

  This sentence shifts the impossibility back to the past; obviously you won't find yourself in ancient Egypt. But a past impossibility demands a form that is "more past": the past perfect in the *if* clause and *would* + the present perfect form of the main verb in the main clause.

22 Nouns and Noun Phrases

Everyday life is filled with **nouns**: orange *juice, hip-hop,* the morning *news*, a *bus* to *work*, *meetings*, *pizza*, *email*, *Diet Coke*, *errands*, *dinner* with *friends*, a *chapter* in a good *book*. Every language includes nouns. In English, articles (*a* book, *an* email, *the* news) often accompany nouns.

22a Understanding count and noncount nouns

Nouns in English can be either **count nouns** or **noncount nouns**. Count nouns refer to distinct individuals or things that can be directly counted: *a doctor, an egg, a child; doctors, eggs, children*. Noncount nouns refer to masses, collections, or ideas without distinct parts: *milk, rice, courage*. You cannot count noncount nouns except with a preceding **phrase**: <u>*a glass of*</u> *milk*, <u>*three grains of*</u> *rice*, <u>*a little*</u> *courage*.

 Grammar: Parts of Speech > LearningCurve (4)
Grammar: Parts of Sentences > LearningCurve (2)

Count nouns usually have singular and plural forms: *tree*, *trees*. Noncount nouns usually have only a singular form: *grass*.

COUNT	NONCOUNT
people (plural of *person*)	humanity
tables, chairs, beds	furniture
letters	mail
pebbles	gravel
suggestions	advice

Some nouns can be either count or noncount, depending on their meaning.

COUNT	Before video games, children played with marbles.
NONCOUNT	The palace floor was made of marble.

When you learn a noun in English, you will therefore need to learn whether it is count, noncount, or both. Many dictionaries provide this information.

22b Using determiners

Determiners are words that identify or quantify a noun, such as <u>*this*</u> *study*, <u>*all*</u> *people*, <u>*his*</u> *suggestions*.

COMMON DETERMINERS

- the articles *a*, *an*, *the*
- *this*, *these*, *that*, *those*
- *my*, *our*, *your*, *his*, *her*, *its*, *their*
- possessive nouns and noun phrases (*Sheila's* <u>*paper*</u>, *my friend's* <u>*book*</u>)
- *whose*, *which*, *what*
- *all*, *both*, *each*, *every*, *some*, *any*, *either*, *no*, *neither*, *many*, *much*, (*a*) *few*, (*a*) *little*, *several*, *enough*
- the numerals *one*, *two*, etc.

These determiners . . .	. . . can precede these noun types	Examples
a, an, each, every	singular count nouns	a book an American each word every Buddhist
this, that	singular count nouns noncount nouns	this book that milk
(a) *little, much*	noncount nouns	a little milk much affection
some, enough	noncount nouns plural count nouns	some milk enough trouble some books enough problems
the	singular count nouns plural count nouns noncount nouns	the doctor the doctors the information
these, those, (a) *few, many,* *both, several*	plural count nouns	these books those plans a few ideas many students both hands several trees

Determiners with singular count nouns. Every singular count noun must be preceded by a determiner. Place any adjectives between the determiner and the noun.

my
▸ ^sister

the
▸ ^growing population

that
▸ ^old neighborhood

Determiners with plural nouns or noncount nouns. Noncount and plural nouns sometimes have determiners and sometimes do not. For example, *This research is important* and *Research is important* are both acceptable but have different meanings.

22c Using articles

Articles (*a*, *an*, and *the*) are a type of determiner. In English, choosing which article to use—or whether to use an article at all—can be challenging. Although there are exceptions, the following general guidelines can help.

Using *a* or *an*. Use indefinite articles *a* and *an* with singular count nouns. Use *a* before a consonant sound (*a car*) and *an* before a vowel sound (*an uncle*). Consider sound rather than spelling: *a house, an hour*.

A or *an* tells readers they do not have enough information to identify specifically what the noun refers to. Compare the following sentences:

- **I need a new coat for the winter.**
- **I saw a coat that I liked at Dayton's, but it wasn't heavy enough.**

The coat in the first sentence is hypothetical rather than actual. Since it is indefinite to the writer and the reader, it is used with *a*, not *the*. The second sentence refers to an actual coat, but since the writer cannot expect the reader to know which one, it is used with *a* rather than *the*.

If you want to speak of an indefinite quantity rather than just one indefinite thing, use *some* or *any* with a noncount noun or a plural count noun. Use *any* in either negative sentences or questions.

- **This stew needs some more salt.**
- **I saw some plates that I liked at Gump's.**
- **This stew doesn't need any more salt.**

Using *the*. Use the definite article *the* with both count and noncount nouns whose identity is known or is about to be made known to readers. The necessary information for identification can come from the noun phrase itself, from elsewhere in the text, from context, from general knowledge, or from a **superlative**.

- **Let's meet at ^the fountain in front of Dwinelle Hall.**

  The phrase *in front of Dwinelle Hall* identifies the specific fountain.

- **Last Saturday, a fire that started in a restaurant spread to a nearby clothing store. ~~Store~~ ^The store was saved, although it suffered water damage.**

  The word *store* is preceded by *the*, which directs our attention to the information in the previous sentence, where the store is first identified.

- **She asked him to shut ^the door when he left her office.**

  The context shows that she is referring to her office door.

- **~~Pope~~ ^The pope is expected to visit Mexico City in February.**

  There is only one living pope.

- **She is now one of ^the best hip-hop artists in the neighborhood.**

  The superlative *best* identifies the noun *hip-hop artists*.

No article. Noncount and plural count nouns can be used without an article to make generalizations:

- **In this world nothing is certain but death and taxes.**

  —Benjamin Franklin

Franklin refers not to a particular death or specific taxes but to death and taxes in general, so no article is used with *death* or with *taxes*.

English differs from many other languages that use the definite article to make generalizations. In English, a sentence like *The ants live in colonies* can refer only to particular, identifiable ants, not to ants in general.

23 Subject-Verb Agreement

In everyday terms, the word *agreement* refers to an accord of some sort: you reach an agreement with your boss about salary; friends agree to go to a movie; the members of a family agree to share household chores. This meaning covers grammatical **agreement** as well. Verbs must agree with their subjects in number (singular or plural) and in **person** (first, second, or third).

To make a verb in the **present tense** agree with a third-person singular subject, add *-s* or *-es* to the **base form**.

- **A vegetarian diet lowers the risk of heart disease.**

To make a verb in the present tense agree with any other subject, use the base form of the verb.

- **I miss my family.**
- **They live in another state.**

Have and *be* do not follow the *-s* or *-es* pattern with third-person singular subjects. *Have* changes to *has*; *be* has irregular forms in both the present tense and the past tense.

- **War is hell.**
- **The soldier was brave beyond the call of duty.**

23a Checking for words between subject and verb

Make sure the verb agrees with the simple **subject** and not with another **noun** that falls in between.

- **Many books on the best-seller list ~~has~~ have little literary value.**

  The simple subject is *books*, not *list*.

Be careful when you use *as well as*, *along with*, *in addition to*, *together with*, and similar phrases. They do not make a singular subject plural

---

Grammar: Parts of Speech > LearningCurve (4)

▸ **A passenger, as well as the driver, ~~were~~ was injured in the accident.**

Though this sentence has a grammatically singular subject, it would be clearer with a compound subject: *The driver and a passenger were injured in the accident.*

23b Checking agreement with compound subjects

Compound subjects joined by *and* are generally plural.

▸ **A backpack, a canteen, and a rifle ~~was~~ were issued to each recruit.**

When subjects joined by *and* are considered a single unit or refer to the same person or thing, they take a singular verb form.

▸ **The lead singer and chief songwriter *wants* to make the new songs available online.**

The singer and songwriter are the same person.

▸ **Drinking and driving ~~remain~~ remains a major cause of highway accidents and fatalities.**

In this sentence, *drinking and driving* is considered a single activity, and a singular verb is used.

With subjects joined by *or* or *nor*, the verb agrees with the part closer to the verb.

▸ **Neither my roommate nor my neighbors *like* my loud music.**

▸ **Either the witnesses or the defendant *is* lying.**

If you find this sentence awkward, put the plural noun closer to the verb: *Either the defendant or the witnesses* <u>*are*</u> *lying.*

Checklist

Editing for Subject-Verb Agreement

- Identify the subject that goes with each verb to check for agreement problems. (23a)
- Check compound subjects joined by *and*, *or*, and *nor.* (23b)
- Check any collective-noun subjects to determine whether they refer to a group as a single unit or as multiple members. (23c)
- Check indefinite-pronoun subjects. Most take a plural verb. (23d)

23c Making verbs agree with collective nouns

Collective nouns—such as *family*, *team*, *audience*, *group*, *jury*, *crowd*, *band*, *class*, and *committee*—and fractions can take either singular or plural verbs, depending on whether they refer to the group as a single unit or to the multiple members of the group. The meaning of a sentence as a whole is your guide.

- **After deliberating, the jury *reports* its verdict.**

  The jury acts as a single unit.

- **The jury still *disagree* on a number of counts.**

  The members of the jury act as multiple individuals.

- **Two-thirds of the park ~~have~~ has burned.**

  Two-thirds refers to the single portion of the park that burned.

- **One-third of the student body ~~was~~ were commuters.**

  One-third here refers to the students who commuted as individuals.

Treat phrases starting with *the number of* as singular and with *a number of* as plural.

SINGULAR	The number of applicants for the internship *was* unbelievable.
PLURAL	A number of applicants *were* put on the waiting list.

23d Making verbs agree with indefinite pronouns

Indefinite pronouns do not refer to specific persons or things. Most take singular verb forms.

SOME COMMON INDEFINITE PRONOUNS

another	each	much	one
any	either	neither	other
anybody	everybody	nobody	somebody
anyone	everyone	no one	someone
anything	everything	nothing	something

- **Of the two jobs, neither holds much appeal.**
- **Each of the plays ~~depict~~ depicts a hero undone by a tragic flaw.**

Both, *few*, *many*, *others*, and *several* are plural.

- **Though many apply, few are chosen.**

All, *any*, *enough*, *more*, *most*, *none*, and *some* can be singular or plural, depending on the noun they refer to.

- **All of the cake *was* eaten.**
- **All of the candidates *promise* to improve the schools.**

23e Making verbs agree with *who, which,* and *that*

When the relative **pronouns** *who*, *which*, and *that* are used as subjects, the verb agrees with the **antecedent** of the pronoun (26b).

▶ **Fear is an ingredient that goes into creating stereotypes.**

▶ **Guilt and fear are ingredients that go into creating stereotypes.**

Problems often occur with the words *one of the*. In general, *one of the* takes a plural verb, while *the only one of the* takes a singular verb.

▶ **Carla is one of the employees who always ~~works~~ work overtime.**

Some employees always work overtime. Carla is among them. Thus *who* refers to *employees*, and the verb is plural.

▶ **Ming is the only one of the employees who always ~~work~~ works overtime.**

Only one employee, Ming, always works overtime. Thus *one* is the antecedent of *who*, and the verb form must be singular.

23f Making linking verbs agree with subjects

A **linking verb** should agree with its subject, which usually precedes the verb, not with the subject complement, which follows it.

▶ **These three key treaties ~~is~~ are the topic of my talk.**

The subject is *treaties*, not *topic*.

▶ **Nero Wolfe's passion ~~were~~ was orchids.**

The subject is *passion*, not *orchids*.

23g Making verbs agree with subjects that end in *-s*

Some words that end in *-s* seem to be plural but are singular in meaning and thus take singular verb forms.

▸ **Measles still ~~strike~~ [strikes] many Americans.**

Some nouns of this kind (such as *statistics* and *politics*) may be either singular or plural, depending on context.

SINGULAR	Statistics *is* a course I really dread.
PLURAL	The statistics in that study *are* questionable.

23h Checking for subjects that follow the verb

In English, verbs usually follow subjects. When this order is reversed, make the verb agree with the subject, not with a noun that happens to precede it.

▸ **Beside the barn ~~stands~~ [stand] silos filled with grain.**

The subject, *silos*, is plural, so the verb must be *stand*.

In sentences beginning with *there is* or *there are* (or *there was* or *there were*), *there* is just an introductory word; the subject follows the verb.

▸ **There are five basic positions in classical ballet.**

23i Making verbs agree with titles and words used as words

Titles and words used as words always take singular verb forms, even if their own forms are plural.

▸ ***One Writer's Beginnings* ~~describe~~ [describes] Eudora Welty's childhood.**

▸ ***Steroids* ~~are~~ [is] a little word that packs a big punch in the world of sports.**

23j Considering spoken forms of *be*

Conventions for subject-verb agreement with *be* in spoken or vernacular varieties of English may differ from those of academic English. For instance, an Appalachian speaker might say "I been down" rather than "I have been down"; a speaker of African American vernacular might say "He be at work" rather than "He is at work," indicating that the person in question is habitually at work. You may want to quote such spoken phrases in your writing or to use them for special effect, but for much academic and professional writing, it's safest to follow the conventions of academic English. (For information on using varieties of English appropriately, see Chapter 19.)

24 Adjectives and Adverbs

Adjectives and **adverbs** can add indispensable differences in meaning to the words they describe or modify. In basketball, for example, there is an important difference between a *flagrant* foul and a *technical* foul, a layup and a *reverse* layup, and an *angry* coach and an *abusively angry* coach. In each instance, the **modifiers** are crucial to accurate communication.

Adjectives modify **nouns** and **pronouns**; they answer the questions *which? how many?* and *what kind?* Adverbs modify **verbs**, adjectives, and other adverbs; they answer the questions *how? when? where?* and *to what extent?* Many adverbs are formed by adding *-ly* to adjectives (*slight, slightly*), but some are formed in other ways (*outdoors*) or have forms of their own (*very*).

24a Using adjectives after linking verbs

When adjectives come after **linking verbs** (such as *is*), they usually describe the **subject**: *I am patient*. Note that in specific sentences, certain verbs may or may not be linking verbs—*appear, become, feel, grow, look, make, prove, seem, smell, sound,* and *taste,* for instance.

Grammar: Parts of Speech > LearningCurve (4)
Grammar: Parts of Sentences > LearningCurve (2)

For Multilingual Writers

Using Adjectives with Plural Nouns

In Spanish, Russian, and many other languages, adjectives agree in number with the nouns they modify. In English, adjectives do not change number in this way: *the kittens are cute* (not *cutes*).

When a word following one of these verbs modifies the subject, use an adjective; when it modifies the verb, use an adverb.

ADJECTIVE Fluffy looked angry.

ADVERB Fluffy looked angrily at the poodle.

Linking verbs suggest a state of being, not an action. In the preceding examples, *looked angry* suggests the state of being angry; *looked angrily* suggests an angry action.

In everyday conversation, you will often hear (and perhaps use) adjectives in place of adverbs. For example, people often say *go quick* instead of *go quickly*. When you write in academic and professional English, however, use adverbs to modify verbs, adjectives, and other adverbs.

▶ **You can feel the song's meter if you listen ~~careful.~~** carefully.

▶ **The audience was ~~real~~** really **disappointed by the show.**

***Good, well, bad,* and *badly*.** The modifiers *good*, *well*, *bad*, and *badly* cause problems for many writers because the distinctions between *good* and *well* and between *bad* and *badly* are often not observed in conversation. Problems also arise because *well* can function as either an adjective or an adverb.

▶ **I look ~~well~~** good **in blue.**

▶ **Now that the fever has broken, I feel ~~good~~** well **again.**

- He plays the trumpet ~~good.~~ well.
- I feel ~~badly~~ bad for the Toronto fans.
- Their team played ~~bad.~~ badly.

24b Using comparatives and superlatives

Most adjectives and adverbs have three forms: positive, **comparative**, and **superlative**. You usually form the comparative and superlative of one- or two-syllable adjectives by adding *-er* and *-est*: *short, shorter, shortest*. With some two-syllable adjectives, longer adjectives, and most adverbs, use *more* and *most* (or *less* and *least*): *scientific, more scientific, most scientific*; *elegantly, more elegantly, most elegantly*. Some short adjectives and adverbs have irregular comparative and superlative forms: *good, better, best*; *badly, worse, worst*.

Comparatives versus superlatives. In academic writing, use the comparative to compare two things; use the superlative to compare three or more things.

- Rome is a much *older* city than New York.
- Damascus is one of the ~~older~~ oldest cities in the world.

Double comparatives and superlatives. Double comparatives and superlatives are those that unnecessarily use both the *-er* or *-est* ending and *more* or *most*. Occasionally, these forms can add a special emphasis, as in the title of Spike Lee's movie *Mo' Better Blues*. In academic and professional writing, however, it's safest not to use *more* or *most* before adjectives or adverbs ending in *-er* or *-est*.

- Paris is the ~~most~~ loveliest city in the world.

Absolute concepts. Some readers consider modifiers such as *perfect* and *unique* to be absolute concepts; according to this view, a thing is either unique or it isn't, so modified forms of the concept don't make sense. However, many seemingly absolute words have multiple meanings, all of which are widely accepted as correct. For example, *unique* may mean *one of a kind* or *unequaled*, but it can also simply mean *distinctive* or *unusual*.

If you think your readers will object to a construction such as *more perfect* (which appears in the U.S. Constitution), then avoid such uses.

25 Modifier Placement

To be effective, **modifiers** should clearly refer to the words they modify and should be positioned close to those words. Consider this command:

DO NOT USE THE ELEVATORS IN CASE OF FIRE.

Should we avoid the elevators altogether, or only in case there is a fire? Repositioning the modifier *in case of fire* eliminates such confusion—and makes clear that we are to avoid the elevators only if there is a fire: IN CASE OF FIRE, DO NOT USE THE ELEVATORS.

25a Revising misplaced modifiers

Modifiers can cause confusion or ambiguity if they are not close enough to the words they modify or if they seem to modify more than one word in the sentence.

on voodoo
- **She teaches a seminar this term ~~on voodoo~~ at Skyline College.**

  The voodoo is not at the college; the seminar is.

He billowing from the window.
- **~~Billowing from the window, he~~ saw clouds of smoke.**

  People cannot billow from windows.

After he lost the 1962 race,
- **Nixon told reporters that he planned to get out of politics. ~~after he lost the 1962 race.~~**

  Nixon did not predict that he would lose the race.

Grammar: Parts of Speech > LearningCurve (4)

Limiting modifiers. Be especially careful with the placement of limiting modifiers such as *almost*, *even*, *just*, *merely*, and *only*. In general, these modifiers should be placed right before or after the words they modify. Putting them in other positions may produce not just ambiguity but a completely different meaning.

AMBIGUOUS	The court *only* hears civil cases on Tuesdays.
CLEAR	The court hears only civil cases on Tuesdays.
CLEAR	The court hears civil cases on Tuesdays only.

Squinting modifiers. If a modifier can refer either to the word before it or to the word after it, it is a squinting modifier. Put the modifier where it clearly relates to only a single word.

SQUINTING	Students who practice writing *often* will benefit.
REVISED	Students who often practice writing will benefit.
REVISED	Students who practice writing will often benefit.

25b Revising disruptive modifiers

Disruptive modifiers interrupt the connections between parts of a sentence, making it hard for readers to follow the progress of the thought.

If they are cooked too long, vegetables will
▶ **~~Vegetables will, if they are cooked too long,~~ lose most of their nutritional value.**

Split infinitives. In general, do not place a modifier between the *to* and the **verb** of an **infinitive** (*to often complain*). Doing so makes it hard for readers to recognize that the two go together.

surrender
▶ **Hitler expected the British to fairly quickly. ~~surrender.~~**

In certain sentences, however, a modifier sounds awkward if it does not split the infinitive. Most language experts consider split infinitives acceptable in such cases. Another option is to reword the sentence to eliminate the infinitive altogether.

SPLIT	I hope *to* almost *equal* my last year's income.
REVISED	I hope that I will earn almost as much as I did last year.

25c Revising dangling modifiers

Dangling modifiers are words or **phrases** that modify nothing in the rest of a sentence. They often *seem* to modify something that is implied but not actually present in the sentence. Dangling modifiers frequently appear at the beginnings or ends of sentences, as in the following example.

DANGLING	Exploding in rapid bursts of red, white, and blue, the picnickers cheered for the Fourth of July celebration.
REVISED	With fireworks exploding in rapid bursts of red, white, and blue, the picnickers cheered for the Fourth of July celebration.

To revise a dangling modifier, often you need to add a **subject** that the modifier clearly refers to; sometimes you have to turn the modifier into a phrase or a **clause**.

our family gave

▸ **Reluctantly, the hound ~~was given~~ to a neighbor.**

In the original sentence, was the dog reluctant, or was someone else who is not mentioned reluctant?

When he was

▸ **~~As~~ a young boy, his grandmother told stories of her years as a migrant worker.**

His grandmother was never a young boy.

My

▸ **~~Thumbing through the magazine, my~~ eyes automatically noticed the perfume ads~~.~~**

as I was thumbing through the magazine.

Eyes cannot thumb through a magazine.

26 Pronouns

As words that stand in for **nouns**, **pronouns** carry a lot of weight in our everyday discourse. The following directions show why it's important for a pronoun to refer clearly to a specific noun or pronoun **antecedent**:

- **When you see a dirt road on the left side of Winston Lane, follow it for two more miles.**

  The word *it* could mean either the dirt road or Winston Lane.

26a Considering a pronoun's role in the sentence

Most speakers of English usually know intuitively when to use *I*, *me*, and *my*. The choices reflect differences in **case**, the form a pronoun takes to indicate its function in a sentence. Pronouns functioning as **subjects** or subject complements are in the subjective case (*I*); those functioning as **objects** are in the objective case (*me*); those functioning as possessives are in the possessive case (*my*).

SUBJECTIVE	OBJECTIVE	POSSESSIVE
I	me	my/mine
we	us	our/ours
you	you	your/yours
he/she/it	him/her/it	his/her/hers/its
they	them	their/theirs
who/whoever	whom/whomever	whose

Problems tend to occur in the following situations.

In subject complements. Americans routinely use the objective case for subject complements in conversation: *Who's there? It's* <u>*me*</u>. If the subjective case for a subject complement sounds stilted or

Checklist

Editing Pronouns

- Make sure all pronouns in subject complements are in the subjective case. (26a)
- Check for correct use of *who, whom, whoever,* and *whomever.* (26a)
- In compound structures, check that pronouns are in the same case they would be in if used alone. (26a)
- When a pronoun follows *than* or *as,* complete the sentence mentally to determine whether the pronoun should be in the subjective or objective case. (26a)
- Check that pronouns agree with indefinite-pronoun antecedents, and revise sexist pronouns. (26b)
- Identify the antecedent that a pronoun refers to. Supply one if none appears in the sentence. If more than one possible antecedent is present, revise the sentence. (26c)

awkward (*It's I*), try rewriting the sentence using the pronoun as the subject (*I'm here*).

She was the
- ~~The~~ first person to see Kishore after the awards. ~~was she.~~

Before gerunds. Pronouns before a **gerund** should be in the possessive case.

his
- The doctor argued for ~~him~~ writing a living will.

With *who, whoever, whom,* and *whomever.* Today's speakers tend not to use *whom* and *whomever*, which can create a very formal tone. But for academic and professional writing in which formality is appropriate, remember that problems distinguishing between *who* and *whom* occur most often in two situations: when they begin a question, and when they introduce a **dependent clause** (29c). You can determine whether to use *who* or *whom* at the beginning of a question by answering the question using a personal pronoun. If

Grammar: Pronouns > LearningCurve

the answer is in the subjective case, use *who*; if it is in the objective case, use *whom*.

Whom
▸ **~~Who~~ did you visit?**

I visited *them*. *Them* is objective, so *whom* is correct.

Who
▸ **~~Whom~~ do you think wrote the story?**

I think *she* wrote the story. *She* is subjective, so *who* is correct.

If the pronoun acts as a subject or subject complement in the clause, use *who* or *whoever*. If the pronoun acts as an object in the clause, use *whom* or *whomever*.

who
▸ **Anyone can hypnotize a person ~~whom~~ wants to be hypnotized.**

The verb of the clause is *wants*, and its subject is *who*.

Whomever
▸ **~~Whoever~~ the party suspected of disloyalty was executed.**

Whomever is the object of *suspected* in the clause *whomever the party suspected of disloyalty*.

In compound structures. When a pronoun is part of a compound subject, complement, or object, put it in the same case you would use if the pronoun were alone.

he
▸ **When ~~him~~ and Zelda were first married, they lived in New York.**

her
▸ **The boss invited ~~she~~ and her family to dinner.**

me.
▸ **This morning saw yet another conflict between my sister and ~~I.~~**

In elliptical constructions. Elliptical constructions are sentences in which some words are understood but left out. When an elliptical construction ends in a pronoun, put the pronoun in the case it would be in if the construction were complete.

▸ **His sister has always been more athletic than *he* [is].**

In some elliptical constructions, the case of the pronoun depends on the meaning intended.

▶ **Willie likes Lily more than *she* [likes Lily].**

She is the subject of the omitted verb *likes.*

▶ **Willie likes Lily more than [he likes] *her*.**

Her is the object of the omitted verb *likes.*

With *we* and *us* before a noun. If you are unsure about whether to use *we* or *us* before a noun, use whichever pronoun would be correct if the noun were omitted.

▶ **~~Us~~ We fans never give up hope.**

Without *fans, we* would be the subject.

▶ **The Broncos depend on ~~we~~ us fans.**

Without *fans, us* would be the object of the preposition *on.*

26b Making pronouns agree with antecedents

The **antecedent** of a pronoun is the word the pronoun refers to. Pronouns and antecedents are said to agree when they match up in **person**, number, and gender.

SINGULAR	The choirmaster raised his baton.
PLURAL	The boys picked up their music.

Compound antecedents. Whenever a compound antecedent is joined by *or* or *nor*, the pronoun agrees with the nearer or nearest antecedent. If the parts of the antecedent are of different genders, however, this kind of sentence can be awkward and may need to be revised.

AWKWARD	Neither Annie nor Lu Ming got *his* work done.
REVISED	Annie didn't get *her* work done, and neither did Lu Ming.

When a compound antecedent contains both singular and plural parts, the sentence may sound awkward unless the plural part comes last.

▶ **Neither the blog nor the newspapers would reveal their sources.**

Collective-noun antecedents. A collective noun such as *herd*, *team*, or *audience* may refer to a group as a single unit. If so, use a singular pronoun.

▸ **The *committee* presented *its* findings to the board.**

When a collective noun refers to the members of the group as individuals, however, use a plural pronoun.

▸ **The *herd* stamped *their* hooves and snorted nervously.**

Indefinite-pronoun antecedents. **Indefinite pronouns** do not refer to specific persons or things. Most indefinite pronouns are always singular; a few are always plural. Some can be singular or plural depending on the context.

▸ **One of the ballerinas lost her balance.**

▸ **Many in the audience jumped to their feet.**

SINGULAR *Some* of the furniture was showing *its* age.

PLURAL *Some* of the farmers abandoned *their* land.

Sexist pronouns. Pronouns often refer to antecedents that may be either male or female. Writers used to use a masculine pronoun, known as the "generic *he*," to refer to such antecedents: *Everyone should know his legal rights.* However, such wording ignores or even excludes females—and thus should be revised: *Everyone should know his or her legal rights*, for example, or *People should know their legal rights.*

26c Making pronouns refer to clear antecedents

If a pronoun does not refer clearly to a specific antecedent, readers will have trouble making the connection between the two.

Ambiguous antecedents. In cases where a pronoun could refer to more than one antecedent, revise the sentence to make the meaning clear.

▸ **The car went over the bridge just before ~~it~~ [the bridge] fell into the water.**

What fell into the water—the car or the bridge? The revision makes the meaning clear.

▸ **Kerry told Ellen, ~~that she~~ ["I] should be ready soon.["]**

Reporting Kerry's words directly, in quotation marks, eliminates the ambiguity.

Vague use of *it, this, that,* and *which*. The words *it, this, that,* and *which* often function as a shortcut for referring to something mentioned earlier. Like other pronouns, each must refer to a specific antecedent.

▸ **When the senators realized the bill would be defeated, they tried to postpone the vote but failed. ~~It~~ [The entire effort] was a fiasco.**

▸ **Jasmine just found out that she won the lottery, ~~which~~ [and her sudden wealth] explains her resignation.**

Indefinite use of *you, it,* and *they*. In conversation, we often use *you, it,* and *they* in an indefinite sense in such expressions as *you never know* and *on television, they said.* In academic and professional writing, however, use *you* only to mean "you, the reader," and *they* or *it* only to refer to a clear antecedent.

▸ **Commercials try to make ~~you~~ [people] buy without thinking.**

▸ **~~On the~~ [The] Weather Channel~~, it~~ reported a powerful earthquake in China.**

▸ **~~In France, they~~ [Many restaurants in France] allow dogs. ~~in many restaurants.~~**

Implied antecedents. A pronoun may suggest a noun antecedent that is implied but not present in the sentence.

▸ **Detention centers routinely blocked efforts by ~~detainees'~~ families and lawyers to locate ~~them.~~ [detainees.]**

 27 Prepositions and Prepositional Phrases

Words such as *to* and *from*, which show the relations between other words, are **prepositions**. They are one of the more challenging elements of English writing.

27a Choosing the right preposition 

Even if you usually know where to use prepositions, you may have difficulty knowing which preposition to use. Each of the most common prepositions has a wide range of different applications, and this range never coincides exactly from one language to another. See, for example, how *in* and *on* are used in English.

- **The peaches are in the refrigerator.**
- **The peaches are on the table.**
- **Is that a diamond ring on your finger?**

The Spanish translations of these sentences all use the same preposition (*en*), a fact that might lead you astray in English.

There is no easy solution to the challenge of using English prepositions idiomatically, but a few strategies can make it less troublesome.

Know typical examples. The **object** of the preposition *in* is often a container that encloses something; the object of the preposition *on* is often a horizontal surface that supports something touching it.

IN	The peaches are *in* the refrigerator.
	There are still some pickles *in* the jar.
ON	The peaches are *on* the table.

Learn related examples. Prepositions that are not used in typical ways may still show some similarities to typical examples.

IN	You shouldn't drive *in* a snowstorm.

Like a container, the falling snow surrounds the driver. The preposition *in* is used for many weather-related expressions.

ON Is that a diamond ring *on* your finger?

The preposition *on* is used to describe things you wear.

Use your imagination. Mental images can help you remember figurative uses of prepositions.

IN Michael is *in* love.

Imagine a warm bath—or a raging torrent—in which Michael is immersed.

ON I've just read a book *on* social media.

Imagine the book sitting on a shelf labeled "Social Media."

Learn prepositions as part of a system. In identifying the location of a place or an event, the three prepositions *in*, *on*, and *at* can be used. *At* specifies the exact point in space or time; *in* is required for expanses of space or time within which a place is located or an event takes place; and *on* must be used with the names of streets (but not exact addresses) and with days of the week or month.

AT There will be a meeting tomorrow *at* 9:30 AM *at* 160 Main Street.

IN I arrived *in* the United States *in* January.

ON The airline's office is *on* Fifth Avenue.

I'll be moving to my new apartment *on* September 30.

27b Using two-word verbs idiomatically 

Some words that look like prepositions do not always function as prepositions. Consider the following sentences:

- **The balloon rose *off* the ground.**
- **The plane took *off* without difficulty.**

Grammar: Parts of Speech > LearningCurve (4)
Grammar: Prepositions and Prepositional Phrases > LearningCurve

In the first sentence, *off* is a preposition that introduces the prepositional phrase *off the ground*. In the second sentence, *off* neither functions as a preposition nor introduces a prepositional phrase. Instead, it combines with *took* to form a two-word **verb** with its own meaning. Such a verb is called a phrasal verb, and the word *off*, when used in this way, is called an adverbial particle. Many prepositions can function as particles to form phrasal verbs.

The verb + particle combination that makes up a phrasal verb is a single entity that cannot usually be torn apart.

- **The plane took off without difficulty. ~~off.~~**

Exceptions include some phrasal verbs that are transitive, meaning that they take a direct **object**. Some of these verbs have particles that may be separated from the verb by the object.

- **I *picked up my baggage* at the terminal.**
- **I *picked my baggage up* at the terminal.**

If a personal **pronoun** is used as the direct object, it *must* separate the verb from its particle.

- **I picked it up ~~it~~ at the terminal.**

In idiomatic two-word verbs where the second word is a preposition, the preposition can never be separated from the verb.

- **We *ran into* our neighbor on the train. [not *ran our neighbor into*]**

  The combination *run* + *into* has a special meaning (find by chance). Therefore, *run into* is a two-word verb.

28 Comma Splices and Fused Sentences

A **comma splice** results from placing only a comma between **independent clauses**—groups of words that can stand alone as a sentence. We often see comma splices used effectively to give slogans a catchy rhythm.

- **Dogs have owners, cats have staff.** —Bumper Sticker

A related construction is a **fused sentence**, or run-on, which results from joining two independent clauses with no punctuation or connecting word between them. The bumper sticker as a fused sentence would be "Dogs have owners cats have staff."

In academic and professional English, using comma splices or fused sentences will almost always be identified as an error, so be careful if you are using them for special effect.

28a Separating the clauses into two sentences

The simplest way to revise comma splices or fused sentences is to separate them into two sentences.

COMMA SPLICE My mother spends long hours every spring tilling the soil and moving manure~~,~~. ~~t~~This part of gardening is nauseating.

If the two clauses are very short, making them two sentences may sound abrupt and terse, so some other method of revision is probably preferable.

28b Linking the clauses with a comma and a coordinating conjunction

If the two clauses are closely related and equally important, join them with a comma and a **coordinating conjunction** (*and*, *but*, *or*, *nor*, *for*, *so*, or *yet*).

FUSED SENTENCE Interest rates fell, so people began borrowing more money.

28c Linking the clauses with a semicolon

If the ideas in the two clauses are closely related and you want to give them equal emphasis, link them with a semicolon.

Clarity: Comma Splices and Fused Sentences > LearningCurve

COMMA SPLICE This photograph is not at all realistic, ; it uses dreamlike images to convey its message.

Be careful when you link clauses with a **conjunctive adverb** like *however* or *therefore* or with a **transition** like *in fact.* In such sentences, the two clauses must be separated by a semicolon or by a comma and a coordinating conjunction.

COMMA SPLICE Many developing countries have high birthrates, ; therefore, most of their citizens are young.

28d Rewriting the two clauses as one independent clause

Sometimes you can reduce two spliced or fused independent clauses to a single independent clause.

FUSED SENTENCE ~~A large part~~ Most of my mail is advertisements ~~most of the rest is~~ and bills.

 **For Multilingual Writers**

Judging Sentence Length

In U.S. academic contexts, readers sometimes find a series of short sentences "choppy" and undesirable. If you want to connect two independent clauses into one sentence, join them using one of the methods discussed in this chapter to avoid creating a comma splice or fused sentence. Another useful tip for writing in American English is to avoid writing several very long sentences in a row. If you find this pattern in your writing, try breaking it up by including a shorter sentence occasionally.

28e Rewriting one independent clause as a dependent clause

When one independent clause is more important than the other, try converting the less important one to a **dependent clause** by adding an appropriate **subordinating conjunction**.

COMMA SPLICE Although ^ Zora Neale Hurston is now regarded as one of America's major novelists, she died in obscurity.

In the revision, the writer emphasizes the second clause and makes the first one into a dependent clause by adding the subordinating conjunction *although*.

FUSED SENTENCE The arts and crafts movement called for ^, which reacted against mass production, handmade objects. ~~it reacted against mass production.~~

In the revision, the writer chooses to emphasize the first clause (the one describing what the movement advocated) and make the second clause into a dependent clause.

28f Linking the two clauses with a dash

In informal writing, you can use a dash to join the two clauses, especially when the second clause elaborates on the first clause.

COMMA SPLICE Exercise trends come and go, ^— this year yoga is hot.

29 Sentence Fragments

Sentence fragments are often used to make writing sound conversational, as in this Facebook status update:

> Realizing that there are no edible bagels in this part of Oregon. Sigh.

Fragments—groups of words that are punctuated as sentences but are not sentences—are often seen in intentionally informal writing and in public writing, such as advertising, that aims to attract attention or give a phrase special emphasis. But think carefully before using fragments for special effect in academic or professional writing, where readers might regard them as errors.

29a Revising phrase fragments

A **phrase** is a group of words that lacks a **subject**, a **verb**, or both. When a phrase is punctuated like a sentence, it becomes a fragment. To revise a phrase fragment, attach it to an independent clause, or make it a separate sentence.

- **CNN is broadcasting the debates/ ~~With~~ with discussions afterward.**

  With discussions afterward is a prepositional phrase, not a sentence. The editing combines the phrase with an independent clause.

- **The town's growth is controlled by zoning laws/, ~~A~~ a strict set of regulations for builders and corporations.**

  A strict set of regulations for builders and corporations is a phrase renaming *zoning laws.* The editing attaches the fragment to the sentence containing that noun.

- **Kamika stayed out of school for three months after Linda was born. ~~To~~ She did so to recuperate and to take care of her baby.**

  The revision—adding a subject (*she*) and a verb (*did*)—turns the fragment into a separate sentence.

Fragments beginning with transitions. If you introduce an example or explanation with a transitional word or phrase like *also, for example, such as,* or *that,* be certain you write a sentence, not a fragment.

- **Joan Didion has written on many subjects/, ~~Such~~ such as the Hoover Dam and migraine headaches.**

  The second word group is a phrase, not a sentence. The editing combines it with an independent clause.

Clarity: Fragments > LearningCurve

29b Revising compound-predicate fragments

A fragment occurs when one part of a compound **predicate** lacks a subject but is punctuated as a separate sentence. Such a fragment usually begins with *and*, *but*, or *or*. You can revise it by attaching it to the independent clause that contains the rest of the predicate.

▸ **They sold their house~~.~~ ~~And~~ and moved into an apartment.**

29c Revising clause fragments

A **dependent clause** contains both a subject and a verb, but it cannot stand alone as a sentence; it depends on an independent clause to complete its meaning. A dependent clause usually begins with a **subordinating conjunction**, such as *after*, *because*, *before*, *if*, *since*, *that*, *though*, *unless*, *until*, *when*, *where*, *while*, *who*, or *which*. You can usually combine dependent-clause fragments with a nearby independent clause.

▸ **When I decided to switch to part-time work~~.~~, I gave up a lot of my earning potential.**

If you cannot smoothly attach a clause to a nearby independent clause, try deleting the opening subordinating word and turning the dependent clause into a sentence.

▸ **Most injuries in automobile accidents occur in two ways. ~~When an~~ An occupant either is hurt by something inside the car or is thrown from the car.**

Style

Writing Processes

Writing That Works

Research

Language

Grammar

Style

Punctuation/ Mechanics

Documentation

30 Consistency and Completeness

If you listen carefully to the conversations around you, you will hear speakers use different styles to get their points across. The words, tone, and structure they choose have a big impact on your impression of them—their personality and credibility, for example—and their ideas. Often, you will hear inconsistent and incomplete structures. For instance, during an NPR interview with journalist Shankar Vedantam, comedian Aziz Ansari discussed recent changes in modern romance:

> One of the big changes for people that are, like, dating now is you have more options than any generation of people ever. You know, when we talked to people that were living in retirement homes and stuff, it was really interesting. They talked about how, like—especially with the women it was really interesting. You know, they were saying, like, well, you know, I was 20 years old. I was living with my parents. I didn't have the opportunity to pursue education or my own career. . . . And there was some guy that lived in the neighborhood. He was pretty nice. And I wanted to get out of the house, and I was like, all right, I'll get married.

Because Ansari is talking casually, some of his sentences begin one way but then move in another direction. The mixed structures pose no problem for listeners, but sentences such as these can be confusing in writing.

30a Revising faulty sentence structure

Beginning a sentence with one grammatical pattern and then switching to another one confuses readers.

MIXED The fact that I get up at 5:00 AM, a wake-up time that explains why I'm always tired in the evening.

This sentence starts out with a **subject** (*The fact*) followed by a **dependent clause** (*that I get up at 5:00 AM*). The sentence needs a

predicate to complete the **independent clause**, but instead it moves to another **phrase** followed by a dependent clause (*a wake-up time that explains why I'm always tired in the evening*), and a **fragment** results.

REVISED The fact that I get up at 5:00 AM explains why I'm always tired in the evening.

Deleting *a wake-up time that* changes the rest of the sentence into a predicate.

REVISED I get up at 5:00 AM, a wake-up time that explains why I'm always tired in the evening.

Deleting *The fact that* turns the beginning of the sentence into an independent clause.

30b Matching subjects and predicates

Another kind of mixed structure, called faulty predication, occurs when a subject and predicate do not fit together grammatically or simply do not make sense together.

generosity.
▸ **A characteristic that I admire is ~~a person who is generous.~~**

A person is not a characteristic.

require that
▸ **The rules of the corporation ~~expect~~ employees ~~to~~ be on time.**

Rules cannot expect anything.

Is when, is where, the reason . . . is because. Although you will often hear these expressions in everyday use, such constructions are inappropriate in academic or professional writing.

an unfair characterization of
▸ **A stereotype is ~~when someone characterizes~~ a group. ~~unfairly.~~**

the practice of sending
▸ **Spamming is ~~where companies send~~ electronic junk mail.**

▸ **~~The reason~~ I like to play soccer ~~is~~ because it provides aerobic exercise.**

30c Using consistent compound structures

Sometimes writers omit certain words in compound structures. If the omitted word does not fit grammatically with other parts of the compound, the omission can be inappropriate.

► **His skills are weak, and his performance ^is^ only average.**

The omitted verb *is* does not match the verb in the other part of the compound (*are*), so the writer needs to include it.

30d Making complete comparisons

When you compare two or more things, the comparison must be complete and clear.

► **I was often embarrassed because my parents were so different/ ^from my friends' parents.^**

Adding *from my friends' parents* completes the comparison.

UNCLEAR	Aneil always felt more affection for his brother than his sister.
CLEAR	Aneil always felt more affection for his brother than his sister did.
CLEAR	Aneil always felt more affection for his brother than he did for his sister.

31 Coordination and Subordination

You may notice a difference between your spoken and your written language. In speech, people tend to use *and* and *so* as all-purpose connectors.

He enjoys psychology, and he has to study hard.

The meaning of this sentence may be perfectly clear in speech, which provides clues with voice, facial expressions, and gestures.

In writing, however, the same sentence could have more than one meaning.

> Although he enjoys psychology, he has to study hard.
>
> He enjoys psychology although he has to study hard.

The first sentence links two ideas with a **coordinating conjunction**, *and*; the other two sentences link ideas with a **subordinating conjunction**, *although*. A coordinating conjunction gives the ideas equal emphasis, and a subordinating conjunction emphasizes one idea more than another.

31a Relating equal ideas

When you want to give equal emphasis to different ideas in a sentence, link them with a coordinating conjunction (*and*, *but*, *for*, *nor*, *or*, *so*, *yet*) or a semicolon.

- **They acquired horses, and their ancient nomadic spirit was suddenly free of the ground.**
- **There is perfect freedom in the mountains, but it belongs to the eagle and the elk, the badger and the bear.**

—N. Scott Momaday, *The Way to Rainy Mountain*

Coordination can help make explicit the relationship between two separate ideas.

- **My son watches *The Simpsons* religiously/; ~~Forced~~ forced to choose, he would probably take Homer Simpson over his sister.**

  Connecting these two sentences with a semicolon strengthens the connection between two closely related ideas.

When you connect ideas in a sentence, make sure that the relationship between the ideas is clear.

- **Surfing the Internet is a common way to spend leisure time, ~~and~~ but it should not replace human contact.**

  What does being a common form of leisure have to do with replacing human contact? Changing *and* to *but* better relates the two ideas.

Style: Coordination and Subordination > LearningCurve

31b Distinguishing main ideas

Subordination allows you to distinguish major points from minor points or to bring supporting details into a sentence. If, for instance, you put your main idea in an **independent clause**, you might then put any less significant ideas in **dependent clauses**, **phrases**, or even single words. The following sentence highlights the subordinated point:

▸ **Mrs. Viola Cullinan was a plump woman who lived in a three-bedroom house somewhere behind the post office.**

—Maya Angelou, "My Name Is Margaret"

The dependent clause adds some important information about Mrs. Cullinan, but it is subordinate to the independent clause.

Notice that the choice of what to subordinate rests with the writer and depends on the intended meaning. Angelou might have given the same basic information differently:

▸ **Mrs. Viola Cullinan, a plump woman, lived in a three-bedroom house somewhere behind the post office.**

Subordinating the information about Mrs. Cullinan's size to that about her house would suggest a slightly different meaning. As a writer, you must think carefully about what you want to emphasize and subordinate information accordingly.

Subordination also establishes logical relationships among different ideas. These relationships are often specified by subordinating conjunctions.

SOME COMMON SUBORDINATING CONJUNCTIONS

after	if	though
although	in order that	unless
as	once	until
as if	since	when
because	so that	where
before	than	while
even though	that	

The following sentence highlights the subordinate clause and italicizes the subordinating word:

▶ **She usually rested her smile until late afternoon *when* her women friends dropped in and Miss Glory, the cook, served them cold drinks on the closed-in porch.**

—Maya Angelou, "My Name Is Margaret"

Using too many coordinate structures can be monotonous and can make it hard for readers to recognize the most important ideas. Subordinating lesser ideas can help highlight the main ideas.

▶ **Many people check email in the evening, and so they turn on the computer. ~~They~~ [Though they] may intend to respond only to urgent messages, a friend sends a link to a blog post, ~~and~~ [which] they decide to read ~~it~~ for just a short while/. ~~and~~ [Eventually,] they get engrossed in Facebook, and they end up spending the whole evening in front of the screen.**

Determining what to subordinate

▶ **~~Our~~ [Although our] new boss can be difficult, ~~although~~ she has revived and maybe even saved the division.**

The editing puts the more important information—that the new boss has saved part of the company—in an independent clause and subordinates the rest.

Avoiding excessive subordination. When too many subordinate clauses are strung together, readers may have trouble keeping track of the main idea expressed in the independent clause.

TOO MUCH SUBORDINATION

▶ **Philip II sent the Spanish Armada to conquer England, which was ruled by Elizabeth, who had executed Mary because she was plotting to overthrow Elizabeth, who was a Protestant, whereas Mary and Philip were Roman Catholics.**

REVISED

- **Philip II sent the Spanish Armada to conquer England, which was ruled by Elizabeth, a Protestant. She had executed Mary, a Roman Catholic like Philip, because Mary was plotting to overthrow her.**

  Putting the facts about Elizabeth executing Mary into an independent clause makes key information easier to recognize.

32 Conciseness

If you have a Twitter account, you probably know a lot about being concise—that is, about getting messages across in no more than 140 characters. In 2011, *New York Times* editor Bill Keller tweeted, "Twitter makes you stupid. Discuss." That little comment drew a large number of responses, including one from his wife that read, "I don't know if Twitter makes you stupid, but it's making you late for dinner. Come home."

No matter how you feel about the effects of Twitter on the brain (or stomach!), you can make any writing more effective by choosing words that convey exactly what you mean to say.

32a Eliminating redundant words

Sometimes writers add words for emphasis, saying that something is large *in size* or red *in color* or that two ingredients should be combined *together*. The italicized words are redundant (unnecessary for meaning), as are the deleted words in the following examples.

- **~~Compulsory a~~ A ttendance at assemblies is required.**
- **The auction featured ~~contemporary~~ "antiques" made recently.**
- **Many different forms of hazing occur, such as physical ~~abuse~~ and mental abuse.**

Style: Concise Writing > LearningCurve

32b Eliminating empty words

Words that contribute little or no meaning to a sentence include vague **nouns** like *area*, *kind*, *situation*, and *thing* as well as vague **modifiers** like *definitely*, *major*, *really*, and *very*. Delete such words, or find a more specific way to say what you mean.

▸ ~~The h~~ousing ~~situation~~ can ~~have a really significant impact~~ ~~on the social aspect of~~ a student's life.
(Inserted: "H" before "housing"; "strongly influence" after "can"; "social" before "life".)

32c Replacing wordy phrases

Many common **phrases** can be reduced to a word or two with no loss in meaning.

WORDY	CONCISE
at all times	always
at that point in time	then
at the present time	now/today
due to the fact that	because
for the purpose of	for
in order to	to
in spite of the fact that	although
in the event that	if

32d Simplifying sentence structure

Using the simplest grammatical structures can tighten and strengthen your sentences considerably.

▸ Hurricane Katrina, ~~which was certainly~~ one of the most powerful storms ever to hit the Gulf Coast, caused damage ~~to a very wide area.~~
(Inserted: "widespread" before "damage"; "." after "damage".)

Strong verbs. *Be* **verbs** (*is, are, was, were, been*) often result in wordiness.

▸ A high-fat, high-cholesterol diet ~~is bad for~~ harms your heart.

Expletives. Sometimes expletive constructions such as *there is, there are,* and *it is* introduce a topic effectively; often, however, your writing will be better without them.

▸ ~~There are m~~Many people ~~who~~ fear success because they believe they do not deserve it.

▸ ~~It is necessary for p~~Presidential candidates need to perform well on television.

Active voice. Some writing situations call for the passive **voice**, but it is always wordier than the active—and often makes for dull or even difficult reading (see 21g).

▸ ~~In Gower's research, it was~~ Gower found that pythons often dwell in trees.

33 Parallelism

If you look and listen, you will see parallel grammatical structures in everyday use. Bumper stickers often use parallelism to make their messages memorable (*Minds are like parachutes; both work best when open*), as do song lyrics and jump-rope rhymes. In addition to creating pleasing rhythmic effects, parallelism can help clarify meaning.

33a Making items in a series or list parallel

All items in a series should be in parallel form—all **nouns**, all **verbs**, all prepositional **phrases**, and so on. Parallelism makes a series both graceful and easy to follow.

Clarity: Parallelism > LearningCurve

- In the eighteenth century, armed forces could fight in open fields and on the high seas. Today, they can clash on the ground anywhere, on the sea, under the sea, and in the air.

  —Donald Snow and Eugene Brown, *The Contours of Power*

  The parallel structure of the phrases (highlighted here), and of the sentences themselves, highlights the contrast between the eighteenth century and today.

- The quarter horse skipped, pranced, and ~~was sashaying~~ ^sashayed onto the track.

- The children ran down the hill, skipped over the lawn, and ^jumped into the swimming pool.

- The duties of the job include baby-sitting, housecleaning, and ~~preparation of~~ ^preparing meals.

Items that are in a list, in a formal outline, and in headings should be parallel.

- Kitchen rules: (1) Coffee to be made only by library staff.

  (2) Coffee service to be closed at 4:00 AM. (3) Doughnuts to be kept in cabinet. (4) ~~No faculty members should handle~~ ^Coffee materials not to be handled ~~coffee materials.~~ ^by faculty.

33b Making paired ideas parallel

Parallel structures can help you pair two ideas effectively. The more nearly parallel the two structures are, the stronger the connection between the ideas will be.

- I type in one place, but I write all over the house.

  —Toni Morrison

- Writers are often more interesting on the page than they are in ~~person.~~ ^the flesh.

  In these examples, the parallel structures help readers see an important contrast between two ideas or acts.

With conjunctions. When you link ideas with *and*, *but*, *or*, *nor*, *for*, *so*, or *yet*, try to make the ideas parallel in structure. Always use the same structure after both parts of a **correlative conjunction**: *either . . . or*, *both . . . and*, *neither . . . nor*, *not . . . but*, *not only . . . but also*, *just as . . . so*, and *whether . . . or*.

- **Consult a friend** who is **in your class or who is good at math.**
- **The wise politician promises the possible and** ~~should accept~~ accepts **the inevitable.**
- **I wanted not only to go away to school but also to** live in **New England.**

33c Using words necessary for clarity

In addition to making parallel elements grammatically similar, be sure to include any words—**prepositions**, articles, verb forms, and so on—that are necessary for clarity.

- **We'll move to a city in the Southwest or** in **Mexico.**

  To a city in Mexico or to Mexico in general? The editing clarifies this.

34 Shifts

A shift in writing is an abrupt change that results in inconsistency. Sometimes a writer or speaker will shift deliberately, as Geneva Smitherman does in this passage from *Word from the Mother*:

> There are days when I optimistically predict that Hip Hop will survive—and thrive. . . . In the larger realm of Hip Hop culture, there is cause for optimism as we witness Hip Hop younguns tryna git they political activist game togetha.

Smitherman's shift from formal academic language to vernacular speech calls out for and holds our attention. Although writers make shifts for good rhetorical reasons, unintentional shifts can be confusing to readers.

34a Revising shifts in tense

If **verbs** in a passage refer to actions occurring at different times, they may require different **tenses**. Be careful, however, not to change tenses without a good reason.

▸ **A few countries produce almost all of the world's illegal drugs, but addiction ~~affected~~ ^affects many countries.**

34b Revising shifts in voice

Do not shift between the **active voice** (she *sold* it) and the **passive voice** (it *was sold*) without a reason. Sometimes a shift in voice is justified, but often it only confuses readers.

▸ **Two youths approached ~~me,~~ and ~~I was~~ asked ^me for my wallet.**

The original sentence shifts from active to passive voice, so it is unclear who asked for the wallet.

34c Revising shifts in point of view

Unnecessary shifts in point of view between first person (*I* or *we*), second person (*you*), and third person (*he*, *she*, *it*, *one*, or *they*), or between singular and plural subjects, can be very confusing to readers.

▸ **~~One~~ ^You can do well on this job if you budget your time.**

Is the writer making a general statement or giving advice to someone? Revising the shift eliminates this confusion.

34d Revising shifts between direct and indirect discourse

When you quote someone's exact words, you are using direct discourse: *She said, "I'm an editor."* When you report what someone says without repeating the exact words, you are using indirect

Clarity: Shifts > LearningCurve

discourse: *She said she was an editor.* Shifting between direct and indirect discourse in the same sentence can cause problems, especially with questions.

▸ **Bob asked what he could ~~he~~ do to help.**

The editing eliminates an awkward shift by reporting Bob's question indirectly. It could also be edited to quote Bob directly: *Bob asked, "What can I do to help?"*

34e Revising shifts in tone and diction

Watch out for shifts in your tone (overall attitude toward a topic or audience) and word choice. These shifts can confuse readers and leave them wondering what your real attitude is.

INCONSISTENT TONE

The question of child care forces a society to make profound decisions about its values. If some conservatives had their way, June Cleaver would still be in the kitchen baking cookies for Wally and the Beaver and waiting for Ward to bring home the bacon, but with only one income, the Cleavers would be lucky to afford hot dogs.

REVISED

The question of child care forces a society to make profound decisions about its values. Some conservatives believe that women with young children should not work outside the home, but many mothers are forced to do so for financial reasons.

The shift in diction from formal to informal makes readers wonder whether the writer is presenting a serious analysis or a humorous satire. As revised, the passage makes more sense because the words are consistently formal.

Punctuation/ Mechanics

Writing Processes

Writing That Works

Research

Language

Grammar

Style

Punctuation/ Mechanics

Documentation

35 Commas

It's hard to go through a day without encountering directions of some kind, and commas often play a crucial role in how you interpret instructions. See how important the comma is in the following directions for making hot cereal:

> Add Cream of Wheat slowly, stirring constantly.

That sentence tells the cook to *add the cereal slowly*. If the comma came before the word *slowly*, however, the cook might add all of the cereal at once and *stir slowly*.

35a Setting off introductory elements

In general, use a comma after any word, **phrase**, or **clause** that precedes the **subject** of the sentence.

- ▸ However, health care costs keep rising.
- ▸ Wearing new tap shoes, Audrey prepared for the recital.
- ▸ To win the game, players need both skill and luck.
- ▸ Fingers on the keyboard, Maya waited for the test to begin.
- ▸ While her friends watched, Lila practiced her gymnastics routine.

Some writers omit the comma after a short introductory element that does not seem to require a pause after it. However, you will never be wrong if you use a comma.

35b Separating clauses in compound sentences

A comma usually precedes a **coordinating conjunction** (*and*, *but*, *or*, *nor*, *for*, *so*, or *yet*) that joins two **independent clauses** in a compound sentence.

▸ **The climbers must reach the summit today, or they will have to turn back.**

With very short clauses, you can sometimes omit the comma (*She saw her chance and she took it*). But always use the comma if there is a chance the sentence will be misread without it.

▸ **I opened the heavy junk drawer, and the cabinet door jammed.**

Checklist

Editing for Commas

Research for this book shows that five of the most common errors in college writing involve commas.

- Check that a comma separates an introductory word, phrase, or clause from the main part of the sentence. (35a)
- Look at every sentence that contains a coordinating conjunction (*and*, *but*, *for*, *nor*, *or*, *so*, or *yet*). If the groups of words before and after this conjunction both function as complete sentences, use a comma before the conjunction. (35b)
- Look at each adjective clause beginning with *which*, *who*, *whom*, *whose*, *when*, or *where* and at each phrase and appositive. If the rest of the sentence would have a different meaning without the clause, phrase, or appositive, do not set off the element with commas. (35c)
- Make sure that adjective clauses beginning with *that* are not set off with commas. Do not use commas between subjects and verbs, verbs and objects or complements, or prepositions and objects; to separate parts of compound constructions other than compound sentences; to set off restrictive clauses; or before the first or after the last item in a series. (35i)
- Do not use a comma alone to separate your sentences. (See Chapter 28.)

Use a semicolon rather than a comma when the clauses are long and complex or contain their own commas.

- **When these early migrations took place, the ice was still confined to the lands in the far north; but eight hundred thousand years ago, when man was already established in the temperate latitudes, the ice moved southward until it covered large parts of Europe and Asia.**

—Robert Jastrow, *Until the Sun Dies*

35c Setting off nonrestrictive elements

Nonrestrictive elements are word groups that do not limit, or restrict, the meaning of the noun or pronoun they modify. Setting nonrestrictive elements off with commas shows your readers that the information is not essential to the meaning of the sentence. **Restrictive elements**, on the other hand, *are* essential to meaning and should *not* be set off with commas. The same sentence may mean different things with and without the commas:

- **The bus drivers rejecting the management offer remained on strike.**
- **The bus drivers, rejecting the management offer, remained on strike.**

The first sentence says that only *some* bus drivers, the ones rejecting the offer, remained on strike. The second says that *all* the drivers did.

Since the decision to include or omit commas influences how readers will interpret your sentence, you should think especially carefully about what you mean and use commas (or omit them) accordingly.

RESTRICTIVE Drivers *who have been convicted of drunken driving* should lose their licenses.

In the preceding sentence, the clause *who have been convicted of drunken driving* is essential because it explains that only drivers who have been convicted of drunken driving should lose their licenses. Therefore, it is *not* set off with commas.

NONRESTRICTIVE The two drivers involved in the accident, *who have been convicted of drunken driving*, should lose their licenses.

In this sentence, however, the clause *who have been convicted of drunken driving* is not essential to the meaning because it does not limit what it modifies, *The two drivers involved in the accident*, but merely provides additional information about these drivers. Therefore, the clause *is* set off with commas.

To decide whether an element is restrictive or nonrestrictive, mentally delete the element, and see if the deletion changes the meaning of the rest of the sentence. If the deletion *does* change the meaning, you should probably not set the element off with commas. If it *does not* change the meaning, the element probably requires commas.

Adjective and adverb clauses. An adjective clause that begins with *that* is always restrictive; do not set it off with commas. An adjective clause beginning with *which* may be either restrictive or nonrestrictive; however, some writers prefer to use *which* only for nonrestrictive clauses, which they set off with commas.

RESTRICTIVE CLAUSES

▸ **The claim *that men like seriously to battle one another to some sort of finish* is a myth.**

—John McMurtry, "Kill 'Em! Crush 'Em! Eat 'Em Raw!"

The adjective clause is necessary to the meaning because it explains which claim is a myth; therefore, the clause is not set off with commas.

▸ **The man~~,~~ who rescued Jana's puppy~~,~~ won her eternal gratitude.**

The adjective clause is necessary to the meaning because it identifies the man, so it takes no commas.

NONRESTRICTIVE CLAUSES

▸ **I borrowed books from the rental library of Shakespeare and Company, *which was the library and bookstore of Sylvia Beach at 12 rue de l'Odeon.***

—Ernest Hemingway, *A Moveable Feast*

The adjective clause is not necessary to the meaning of the independent clause and therefore is set off with a comma.

An adverb clause that follows a main clause does *not* usually require a comma to set it off unless the adverb clause expresses contrast.

▸ **The park became a popular gathering place, although nearby residents complained about the noise.**

The adverb clause expresses contrast; therefore, it is set off with a comma.

Phrases. Participial **phrases** may be restrictive or nonrestrictive. Prepositional phrases are usually restrictive, but sometimes they are not essential to the meaning of a sentence and thus are set off with commas.

NONRESTRICTIVE PHRASES

▸ **The NBA star's little daughter, refusing to be ignored, interrupted the interview.**

Using commas around the participial phrase makes it nonrestrictive.

Appositives. An **appositive** is a **noun** or noun phrase that renames a nearby noun. When an appositive is not essential to identify what it renames, it is set off with commas.

NONRESTRICTIVE APPOSITIVES

▸ **Savion Glover, the award-winning dancer, taps like poetry in motion.**

Savion Glover's name identifies him; the appositive *the award-winning dancer* provides extra information.

RESTRICTIVE APPOSITIVES

▸ **Mozart's opera/ *The Marriage of Figaro*/ was considered revolutionary.**

The phrase is restrictive because Mozart wrote more than one opera. Therefore, it is *not* set off with commas.

35d Separating items in a series

▸ **He has plundered our seas, ravaged our coasts, burnt our towns, and destroyed the lives of our people.**

—Declaration of Independence

You may see a series with no comma after the next-to-last item, particularly in newspaper writing. Occasionally, however, omitting the comma can cause confusion.

▸ **All the cafeteria's vegetables—broccoli, green beans, peas, and carrots—were cooked to a gray mush.**

Without the comma after *peas,* you wouldn't know if there were three choices (the third being a *mixture* of peas and carrots) or four.

Coordinate adjectives—two or more adjectives that relate equally to the noun they modify—should be separated by commas.

▸ **The long, twisting, muddy road led to a shack in the woods.**

In a sentence like *The cracked bathroom mirror reflected his face,* however, *cracked* and *bathroom* are not coordinate because *bathroom mirror* is the equivalent of a single word, which is modified by *cracked.* Hence they are *not* separated by commas.

You can usually determine whether adjectives are coordinate by inserting *and* between them. If the sentence makes sense with the *and* added, the adjectives are coordinate and should be separated by commas.

▸ **They are sincere *and* talented *and* inquisitive researchers.**

The sentence makes sense with the *ands,* so the adjectives should be separated by commas: *They are sincere, talented, inquisitive researchers.*

▸ **Byron carried an elegant ~~and~~ pocket watch.**

The sentence does not make sense with *and,* so the adjectives *elegant* and *pocket* should not be separated by commas: *Byron carried an elegant pocket watch.*

35e Setting off parenthetical and transitional expressions

Parenthetical expressions add comments or information. Because they often interrupt the flow of a sentence, they are usually set off with commas.

- Some studies have shown that chocolate, of all things, helps prevent tooth decay.

Transitions (such as *as a result*), **conjunctive adverbs** (such as *however*), and other expressions used to connect parts of sentences are usually set off with commas.

- Ozone is a by-product of dry cleaning, for example.

35f Setting off contrasting elements, interjections, direct address, and tag questions

- I asked you, *not your brother*, to sweep the porch.
- *Holy cow*, did you see that?
- Remember, *sir*, that you are under oath.
- The governor did not veto the bill, *did she?*

35g Setting off parts of dates and addresses

Dates. Use a comma between the day of the week and the month, between the day of the month and the year, and between the year and the rest of the sentence, if any.

- On Wednesday, November 26, 2008, gunmen arrived in Mumbai by boat.

Do not use commas with dates in inverted order or with dates consisting of only the month and the year.

- She dated the letter 5 August 2016.
- Thousands of Germans swarmed over the wall in November 1989.

Addresses and place names. Use a comma after each part of an address or a place name, including the state if there is no ZIP code. Do not precede a ZIP code with a comma.

▸ **Forward my mail to the Department of English, The Ohio State University, Columbus, Ohio 43210.**

▸ **Portland, Oregon, is much larger than Portland, Maine.**

35h Setting off quotations

Commas set off a quotation from words used to introduce or identify the source of the quotation. A comma following a quotation goes *inside* the closing quotation mark.

▸ **A German proverb warns, "Go to law for a sheep, and lose your cow."**

▸ **"All I know about grammar," said Joan Didion, "is its infinite power."**

Do not use a comma following a question mark or an exclamation point.

▸ **"Out, damned spot!/" cries Lady Macbeth.**

Do not use a comma to introduce a quotation with *that* or when you do not quote a speaker's exact words.

▸ **The writer of Ecclesiastes concludes that/ "all is vanity."**

▸ **Patrick Henry declared/ that he wanted either liberty or death.**

35i Avoiding unnecessary commas

Excessive use of commas can spoil an otherwise fine sentence.

Around restrictive elements. Do not use commas to set off restrictive elements—elements that limit, or define, the meaning of the words they modify or refer to (35c).

▶ **I don't let my children watch movies/ that are violent.**

▶ **The actor/ Benicio Del Toro/ might win the award.**

Between subjects and verbs, verbs and objects or complements, and prepositions and objects. Do not use a comma between a subject and its **verb**, a verb and its **object** or complement, or a **preposition** and its object.

▶ **Watching movies late at night/ allows me to relax.**

▶ **Parents must decide/ what time their children should go to bed.**

▶ **The winner of/ the prize for community service stepped forward.**

In compound constructions. In compound constructions other than compound sentences, do not use a comma before or after a coordinating conjunction that joins the two parts (35b).

▶ **Improved health care/ and more free trade were two of the administration's goals.**

The *and* joins parts of a compound subject, which should not be separated by a comma.

▶ **Mark Twain trained as a printer/ and worked as a steamboat pilot.**

The *and* joins parts of a compound predicate, which should not be separated by a comma.

In a series. Do not use a comma before the first or after the last item in a series.

▶ **The auction included/ furniture, paintings, and china.**

▶ **The swimmer took slow, elegant, powerful/ strokes.**

36 Semicolons

The following public-service announcement, posted in New York City subway cars, reminded commuters what to do with a used newspaper at the end of the ride:

Please put it in a trash can; that's good news for everyone.

The semicolon in the subway announcement separates two clauses that could have been written as separate sentences. Semicolons, which create a pause stronger than that of a comma but not as strong as the full pause of a period, show close connections between related ideas.

36a Linking independent clauses

Although a comma and a **coordinating conjunction** often join **independent clauses** (35b), semicolons provide writers with subtler ways of signaling closely related clauses. The clause following a semicolon often restates an idea expressed in the first clause; it sometimes expands on or presents a contrast to the first.

▸ **Immigration acts were passed; newcomers had to prove, besides moral correctness and financial solvency, their ability to read.** —Mary Gordon, "More Than Just a Shrine"

The semicolon gives the sentence an abrupt rhythm that suits the topic: laws that imposed strict requirements.

If two independent clauses joined by a coordinating conjunction contain commas, you may use a semicolon instead of a comma before the conjunction to make the sentence easier to read.

▸ **Every year, whether the Republican or the Democratic party is in office, more and more power drains away from the individual to feed vast reservoirs in far-off places; and we have less and less say about the shape of events which shape our future.** —William F. Buckley Jr., "Why Don't We Complain?"

A semicolon should link independent clauses joined by a **conjunctive adverb** such as *however* or *therefore* or a **transition** such as *as a result* or *for example*.

▸ **The circus comes as close to being the world in microcosm as anything I know; in a way, it puts all the rest of show business in the shade.** —E. B. White, "The Ring of Time"

Punctuation: Semicolons > LearningCurve

36b Separating items in a series containing other punctuation

Ordinarily, commas separate items in a series (35d). But when the items themselves contain commas or other punctuation, semicolons make the sentence clearer.

- Anthropology encompasses archaeology, the study of ancient civilizations through artifacts; linguistics, the study of the structure and development of language; and cultural anthropology, the study of language, customs, and behavior.

36c Avoiding misused semicolons

Use a comma, not a semicolon, to separate an independent clause from a **dependent clause** or **phrase**.

- The police found fingerprints, which they used to identify the thief.

- The new system would encourage students to register for courses online, thus streamlining registration.

Use a colon, not a semicolon, to introduce a series or list.

- The reunion tour includes the following bands: Urban Waste, Murphy's Law, Rapid Deployment, and Ism.

37 End Punctuation

Periods, question marks, and exclamation points often appear in advertising to create special effects:

You have a choice to make.

Where can you turn for advice?

Ask our experts today!

End punctuation tells us how to read each sentence—as a matter-of-fact statement, a question for the reader, or an enthusiastic exclamation.

37a Using periods

Use a period to close sentences that make statements or give mild commands.

- **All books are either dreams or swords.** —Amy Lowell
- **Don't use a fancy word if a simpler word will do.** —George Orwell, "Politics and the English Language"

A period also closes indirect questions, which report rather than ask questions.

- **I asked how old the child was.**

In American English, periods are used with most abbreviations. However, more and more abbreviations are currently appearing without periods.

Mr.	MD	BCE *or* B.C.E.
Ms.	PhD	AD *or* A.D.
Sen.	Jr.	PM *or* p.m.

Some abbreviations rarely if ever appear with periods. These include the postal abbreviations of state names, such as *FL* and *TN*, and most groups of initials (*GE, CIA, AIDS, YMCA, UNICEF*). If you are not sure whether a particular abbreviation should include periods, check a dictionary or follow the particular style guidelines you are using for a research paper. (For more about abbreviations, see Chapter 42.)

Do not use an additional period when a sentence ends with an abbreviation that has its own period.

- **The social worker referred me to John Pintz Jr./**

37b Using question marks

Use question marks to close sentences that ask direct questions.

- **How is the human mind like a computer, and how is it different?** —Kathleen Stassen Berger and Ross A. Thompson, *The Developing Person through Childhood and Adolescence*

Question marks do not close indirect questions, which report rather than ask questions.

▶ **She asked whether I opposed his nomination?.**

37c Using exclamation points

Use an exclamation point to show surprise or strong emotion. Use these marks sparingly because they can distract your readers or suggest that you are exaggerating.

▶ **In those few moments of geologic time will be the story of all that has happened since we became a nation. And what a story it will be!**

—James Rettie, "But a Watch in the Night"

37d Using end punctuation in informal writing

In informal writing, especially on social media, writers today are more likely to omit end punctuation entirely. Research also shows that ellipses (. . .), or "dots," are on the rise; they can be used to signal a trailing off of a thought, to raise questions about what is being left out, to leave open the possibility of further communication, or simply to indicate that the writer doesn't want or need to finish the sentence. Exclamation marks can convey an excited or a chatty tone, so they are used more frequently in informal writing. And some writers have argued that using a period at the end of a text or tweet rather than no punctuation at all can suggest that the writer is irritated or angry. The meaning of end punctuation is changing in informal contexts, so pay attention to how others communicate, and use what you learn in your own social writing.

38 Apostrophes

The little apostrophe can make a big difference in meaning. The following sign at a neighborhood swimming pool, for instance, says something different from what the writer probably intended:

> Please deposit your garbage (and your guests) in the trash receptacles before leaving the pool area.

The sign indicates that the guests, not their garbage, should be deposited in trash receptacles. Adding a single apostrophe would offer a more neighborly statement: *Please deposit your garbage (and your guests') in the trash receptacles before leaving the pool area.*

38a Signaling possessive case

The possessive case denotes ownership or possession. Add an apostrophe and *-s* to form the possessive of most singular **nouns**, including those that end in *-s*, and of **indefinite pronouns** (23d). The possessive forms of personal **pronouns** do not take apostrophes: *yours, his, hers, its, ours, theirs.*

- ▶ **The bus's fumes overpowered her.**
- ▶ **George Lucas's movies have been wildly popular.**
- ▶ **Anyone's guess is as good as mine.**

Plural nouns. To form the possessive case of plural nouns not ending in *-s*, add an apostrophe and *-s*. For plural nouns ending in *-s*, add only the apostrophe.

- ▶ **The men's department sells business attire.**
- ▶ **The clowns' costumes were bright green and orange.**

Compound nouns. For compound nouns, make the last word in the group possessive.

- ▶ **Both her daughters-in-law's birthdays fall in July.**

Two or more nouns. To signal individual possession by two or more owners, make each noun possessive.

- ▶ **Great differences exist between Jerry Bruckheimer's and Ridley Scott's films.**

  Bruckheimer and Scott produce different films.

Punctuation: Apostrophes > LearningCurve

To signal joint possession, make only the last noun possessive.

▸ **Wallace and Gromit's creator is Nick Park.**

Wallace and Gromit have the same creator.

38b Signaling contractions

Contractions are two-word combinations formed by leaving out certain letters, which are replaced by an apostrophe (*it is, it has/it's; will not/won't*).

Contractions are common in conversation and informal writing. Academic and professional work, however, often calls for greater formality.

Distinguishing *its* and *it's*. *Its* is a possessive **pronoun**—the possessive form of *it*. *It's* is a contraction for *it is* or *it has*.

▸ **This disease is unusual; its symptoms vary from person to person.**

▸ **It's a difficult disease to diagnose.**

38c Understanding apostrophes and plural forms

Many style guides now advise against using apostrophes for plurals.

▸ **The gymnasts need marks of 8s and 9s in order to qualify for the finals.**

Other guidelines call for an apostrophe and *-s* to form the plural of numbers, letters, and words referred to as terms.

▸ **The five Shakespeare's in the essay were spelled five different ways.**

Check your instructor's preference.

39 Quotation Marks

"Hilarious!" "A great family movie!" "A must see!" The quotation marks are a key component of statements like these from movie ads; they make the praise more believable by indicating that it comes from people other than the movie promoter. Quotation marks identify a speaker's exact words or the titles of short works.

39a Signaling direct quotation

- **The crowd chanted "Yes, we can" as they waited for the speech to begin.**
- **She smiled and said, "Son, this is one incident that I will never forget."**

Use quotation marks to enclose the words of each speaker within running dialogue. Mark each shift in speaker with a new paragraph.

> "I want no proof of their affection," said Elinor; "but of their engagement I do."
>
> "I am perfectly satisfied of both."
>
> "Yet not a syllable has been said to you on the subject, by either of them." —Jane Austen, *Sense and Sensibility*

Single quotation marks. Single quotation marks enclose a quotation within a quotation. Open and close the quoted passage with double quotation marks, and change any quotation marks that appear *within* the quotation to single quotation marks.

- **Baldwin says, "The title 'The Uses of the Blues' does not refer to music; I don't know anything about music."**

Long quotations. To quote a passage that is more than four typed lines, set the quotation off by starting it on a new line and indenting it one-half inch from the left margin. This format, known as block quotation, does not require quotation marks.

In "Suspended," Joy Harjo tells of her first awareness of jazz as a child:

> My rite of passage into the world of humanity occurred then, via jazz. The music made a startling bridge between the familiar and strange lands, an appropriate vehicle, for . . . we were there when jazz was born. I recognized it, that humid afternoon in my formative years, as a way to speak beyond the confines of ordinary language. I still hear it. (84)

Punctuation: Quotation Marks > LearningCurve

This block quotation, including the ellipsis dots and the page number in parentheses at the end, follows the style of the Modern Language Association, or MLA (see Chapter 45). The American Psychological Association, or APA, has different guidelines for setting off block quotations (see Chapter 46).

Poetry. When quoting poetry, if the quotation is brief (fewer than four lines), include it within your text. Separate the lines of the poem with slashes, each preceded and followed by a space, in order to tell the reader where one line of the poem ends and the next begins.

> In one of his best-known poems, Robert Frost remarks, "Two roads diverged in a yellow wood, and I—/ I took the one less traveled by / And that has made all the difference."

To quote more than three lines of poetry, indent the block one-half inch from the left margin. Do not use quotation marks. Take care to follow the spacing, capitalization, punctuation, and other features of the original poem.

> The duke in Robert Browning's poem "My Last Duchess" is clearly a jealous, vain person, whose arrogance is illustrated through this statement:
>
> > She thanked men—good! but thanked
> > Somehow—I know not how—as if she ranked
> > My gift of a nine-hundred-years-old name
> > With anybody's gift. (lines 31–34)

39b Identifying titles of short works and definitions

Use quotation marks to enclose the titles of short poems, short stories, articles, essays, songs, sections of books, and episodes of television and radio programs. Quotation marks also enclose definitions.

- **The essay "The Art of Stephen Curry" analyzes some reasons for the success of the Warriors' star.**

▸ In social science, the term *sample size* means "the number of individuals being studied in a research project."

—Kathleen Stassen Berger and Ross A. Thompson, *The Developing Person through Childhood and Adolescence*

39c Using quotation marks with other punctuation

Periods and commas go *inside* closing quotation marks.

▸ "Don't compromise yourself," said Janis Joplin. "You are all you've got."

Colons, semicolons, and footnote numbers go *outside* closing quotation marks.

▸ I felt one emotion after finishing "Eveline": sorrow.

▸ Tragedy is defined by Aristotle as "an imitation of an action that is serious and of a certain magnitude."[1]

Question marks, exclamation points, and dashes go *inside* if they are part of the quoted material, *outside* if they are not.

PART OF THE QUOTATION

▸ The cashier asked, "Would you like to super-size that?"

NOT PART OF THE QUOTATION

▸ What is the theme of "The Birth-Mark"?

39d Avoiding misused quotation marks

Do not use quotation marks for indirect quotations—those that do not use someone's exact words.

▸ Mother smiled and said that "she was sure she would never forget the incident."

 For Multilingual Writers

Quoting in American English

Remember that the way you mark quotations in American English (" ") may not be the same as in other languages. In French, for example, quotations are marked with *guillemets* (« »), while in German, quotations take split-level marks („ "). American English and British English offer opposite conventions for double and single quotation marks. If you are writing for an American audience, follow the U.S. conventions for quotation marks.

Do not use quotation marks merely to add emphasis to particular words or phrases.

▸ **The hikers were startled by the appearance of a "gigantic" grizzly bear.**

Do not use quotation marks around slang or colloquial language; they create the impression that you are apologizing for using those words. If you have a good reason to use slang or a colloquial term, use it without quotation marks.

▸ **After our twenty-mile hike, we were completely exhausted and ready to "turn in."**

40 Other Punctuation

Parentheses, brackets, dashes, colons, slashes, and ellipses are everywhere. Every URL includes colons and slashes, many sites use brackets or parentheses to identify updates and embedded media, and dashes and ellipses are increasingly common in writing that expresses conversational informality.

You can also use these punctuation marks for more formal purposes: to signal relationships among parts of sentences, to create particular rhythms, and to help readers follow your thoughts.

40a Using parentheses

Use parentheses to enclose material that is of minor or secondary importance in a sentence—material that supplements, clarifies, comments on, or illustrates what precedes or follows it.

▸ **Inventors and men of genius have almost always been regarded as fools at the beginning (and very often at the end) of their careers.**

—Fyodor Dostoyevsky

▸ **During my research, I found problems with the flat-rate income tax (a single-rate tax with no deductions).**

Parentheses are also used to enclose textual citations and numbers or letters in a list.

▸ **Freud and his followers have had a most significant impact on the ways abnormal functioning is understood and treated (Joseph, 1991).** —Ronald J. Comer, *Abnormal Psychology*

The in-text citation in this sentence shows the style of the American Psychological Association (APA).

▸ **Five distinct styles can be distinguished: (1) Old New England, (2) Deep South, (3) Middle American, (4) Wild West, and (5) Far West or Californian.** —Alison Lurie, *The Language of Clothes*

With other punctuation. A period may be placed either inside or outside a closing parenthesis, depending on whether the parenthetical text is part of a larger sentence. A comma, if needed, is always placed *outside* a closing parenthesis (and never before an opening one).

▸ **Gene Tunney's single defeat in an eleven-year career was to a flamboyant and dangerous fighter named Harry Greb ("The Human Windmill"), who seems to have been, judging from boxing literature, the dirtiest fighter in history.**

—Joyce Carol Oates, "On Boxing"

40b Using brackets

Use brackets to enclose any parenthetical elements in material that is itself within parentheses. Brackets should also be used to enclose any explanatory words or comments that you are inserting into a quotation.

▸ **Eventually, the investigation had to examine the major agencies (including the National Security Agency [NSA]) that were conducting covert operations.**

Punctuation: Other Punctuation Marks > LearningCurve

▶ **Massing notes that "on average, it [Fox News] attracts more than eight million people daily—more than double the number who watch CNN."**

The bracketed words *Fox News* clarify the meaning of *it* in the original quotation.

In the quotation in the following sentence, the artist Gauguin's name is misspelled. The bracketed word *sic*, which means "so," tells readers that the person being quoted—not the writer who has picked up the quotation—made the mistake.

▶ **One admirer wrote, "She was the most striking woman I'd ever seen—a sort of wonderful combination of Mia Farrow and one of Gaugin's [*sic*] Polynesian nymphs."**

40c Using dashes

Use dashes to insert a comment or to highlight material in a sentence.

▶ **The pleasures of reading itself—who doesn't remember?—were like those of Christmas cake, a sweet devouring.**

—Eudora Welty, "A Sweet Devouring"

A single dash can be used to emphasize material at the end of a sentence, to mark a sudden change in tone, to indicate hesitation in speech, or to introduce a summary or an explanation.

▶ **In the twentieth century it has become almost impossible to moralize about epidemics—except those which are transmitted sexually.**

—Susan Sontag, *AIDS and Its Metaphors*

▶ **In walking, the average adult person employs a motor mechanism that weighs about eighty pounds—sixty pounds of muscle and twenty pounds of bone.** —Edwin Way Teale

Dashes give more emphasis than parentheses to the material they enclose or set off. Many word-processing programs automatically convert two typed hyphens with no spaces before or after into a solid dash.

40d Using colons

Use a colon to introduce an explanation, an example, an appositive, a series, a list, or a quotation.

- At the baby's one-month birthday party, Ah Po gave him the Four Valuable Things: ink, inkslab, paper, and brush.

  —Maxine Hong Kingston, *China Men*

Use a colon rather than a comma to introduce a quotation when the lead-in is a complete sentence on its own.

- The 2013 State of the Union address ended with a bold challenge: "Well into our third century as a nation, it remains the task of us all . . . to be the authors of the next great chapter in our American story."

Colons are also used after salutations in letters; with numbers indicating hours, minutes, and seconds; with ratios; with biblical chapters and verses; with titles and subtitles; and in bibliographic entries.

- Dear Dr. Chapman:
- 4:59 PM
- a ratio of 5:1
- Ecclesiastes 3:1
- *The Joy of Insight: Passions of a Physicist*
- Boston: Bedford/St. Martin's, 2016

Misused colons. Do not put a colon between a **verb** and its **object** or complement (unless the object is a quotation), between a **preposition** and its object, or after such expressions as *such as*, *especially*, and *including*.

- Some natural fibers are: cotton, wool, silk, and linen.
- In poetry, additional power may come from devices such as: simile, metaphor, and alliteration.

40e Using slashes

Use a slash to separate alternatives.

- ▸ **Then there was Daryl, the cabdriver/bartender.**

—John L'Heureux, *The Handmaid of Desire*

Use a slash, preceded and followed by a space, to divide lines of poetry quoted within running text.

- ▸ **The speaker of Sonnet 130 says of his mistress, "I love to hear her speak, yet well I know / That music hath a far more pleasing sound."**

Slashes also separate parts of fractions and Internet addresses.

40f Using ellipses

An ellipsis is three equally spaced dots that indicate that something has been omitted from a quoted passage. Just as you should carefully use quotation marks around any material that you are quoting directly from a source, so you should carefully use an ellipsis to indicate that you have left out part of a quotation that otherwise appears to be a complete sentence. Ellipses have been used in the following example to indicate two omissions—one in the middle of the first sentence and one at the end of the second sentence.

ORIGINAL TEXT

- ▸ **The quasi-official division of the population into three economic classes called high-, middle-, and low-income groups rather misses the point, because as a class indicator the amount of money is not as important as the source.**

—Paul Fussell, "Notes on Class"

WITH ELLIPSES

- ▸ **As Paul Fussell argues, "The quasi-official division of the population into three economic classes . . . rather misses the point. . . ."**

When you omit the last part of a quoted sentence, add a period before the ellipsis—for a total of four dots. Be sure a complete sentence comes before the four dots. If your shortened quotation ends with a source citation (such as a page number, a name, or a title), place the documentation source in parentheses after the three ellipsis points and the closing quotation mark but before the period.

▸ **Packer argues, "The Administration is right to reconsider its strategy . . ." (34).**

You can also use an ellipsis to indicate a pause or a hesitation in speech in the same way that you can use a dash for that purpose. (For more uses of ellipses in informal writing, see 37d.)

▸ **Then the voice, husky and familiar, came to wash over us—"The winnah, and still heavyweight champeen of the world . . . Joe Louis."**

—Maya Angelou, *I Know Why the Caged Bird Sings*

41 Capital Letters

Capital letters are a key signal in everyday life. Look around any store to see their importance: you can shop for Levi's or *any* blue jeans, for Pepsi or *any* cola, for Kleenex or *any* tissue. In each of these instances, the capital letter indicates the name of a particular brand.

41a Capitalizing the first word of a sentence

With very few exceptions, capitalize the first word of a sentence. If you are quoting a full sentence, capitalize its first word.

▸ **Kennedy said, "Let us never negotiate out of fear."**

Capitalization of a nonquoted sentence following a colon is optional.

▸ **Gould cites the work of Darwin: The [*or* the] theory of natural selection incorporates the principle of evolutionary ties among all animals.**

Mechanics: Capital Letters > LearningCurve

Capitalize a sentence within parentheses unless the parenthetical sentence is inserted into another sentence.

- **Gould cites the work of Darwin. (Other researchers cite more recent evolutionary theorists.)**
- **Gould cites the work of Darwin (see p. 150).**

When citing poetry, follow the capitalization of the original poem. Though most poets capitalize the first word of each line in a poem, some do not.

- **Morning sun heats up the young beech tree**
  leaves and almost lights them into fireflies

—June Jordan, "Aftermath"

41b Capitalizing proper nouns and proper adjectives

Capitalize proper **nouns** (those naming specific persons, places, and things) and most **adjectives** formed from proper nouns. All other nouns are common nouns and are not capitalized unless they are used as part of a proper noun: *a street*, but *Elm Street*.

Capitalized nouns and adjectives include personal names; nations, nationalities, and languages; months, days of the week, and holidays (but not seasons of the year); geographical names; structures and monuments; ships, trains, aircraft, and spacecraft; organizations, businesses, and government institutions; academic institutions and courses; historical events and eras; and religions, with their deities, followers, and sacred writings. For trade names, follow the capitalization you see in company advertising or on the product itself.

PROPER	COMMON
Alfred Hitchcock, Hitchcockian	a director
Brazil, Brazilian	a nation, a language
Pacific Ocean	an ocean
Challenger	a spaceship
Library of Congress	a federal agency

Political Science 102	a political science course
the Qur'an	a holy book
Catholicism	a religion
Cheerios, iPhone	cereal, a smartphone
Halloween	a holiday in the fall

41c Capitalizing titles before proper names

When used alone or following a proper name, most titles are not capitalized. One common exception is the word *president*, which many writers capitalize whenever it refers to the President of the United States.

Professor Gordon Chang	my history professor
Dr. Teresa Ramirez	Teresa Ramirez, our doctor

41d Capitalizing titles of works

Capitalize most words in titles of books, articles, speeches, stories, essays, plays, poems, documents, films, paintings, and musical compositions. Do not capitalize articles (*a*, *an*, *the*), **prepositions**, **conjunctions**, and the *to* in an **infinitive** unless they are the first or last words in a title or subtitle.

Walt Whitman: A Life	Declaration of Independence
"As Time Goes By"	*Hamilton*
"Crazy in Love"	*The Living Dead*

41e Revising unnecessary capitalization

Capitalize compass directions only if the word designates a specific geographical region.

- ▸ **John Muir headed west, motivated by the desire to explore.**
- ▸ **Water rights are an increasingly contentious issue in the West.**

 For Multilingual Writers

Learning English Capitalization

Capitalization systems vary considerably. Arabic, Chinese, Hebrew, and Hindi, for example, do not use capital letters at all. English may be the only language to capitalize the first-person singular pronoun (*I*), but Dutch and German capitalize some forms of the second-person pronoun (*you*)—and German also capitalizes all nouns.

Capitalize family relationships only if the word is used as part of a name or as a substitute for the name.

- **When she was a child, my mother shared a room with my aunt.**
- **I could always tell when Mother was annoyed with Aunt Rose.**

42 Abbreviations and Numbers

Anytime you look up an address, you see an abundance of abbreviations and numbers, as in the following listing from a Google map:

Tarrytown Music Hall   13 Main St   Tarrytown, NY

Abbreviations and numbers allow writers to present detailed information in a small amount of space.

42a Using abbreviations

Certain titles are normally abbreviated.

Ms. Susanna Moller	Henry Louis Gates Jr.
Mr. Mark Otuteye	Karen Lancry, MD

Religious, academic, and government titles should be spelled out in academic writing but can be abbreviated in other writing when they appear before a full name.

Rev. Fleming Rutledge	Reverend Rutledge
Prof. Jaime Mejía	Professor Mejía
Sen. Christopher Dodd	Senator Dodd

Business, government, and science terms. As long as you can be sure your readers will understand them, use common abbreviations such as *PBS*, *NASA*, and *DNA*. If an abbreviation may be unfamiliar, spell out the full term the first time you use it, and give the abbreviation in parentheses; after that, you can use the abbreviation by itself. Use abbreviations such as *Co.*, *Inc.*, *Corp.*, and *&* only if they are part of a company's official name.

- ▶ **The Comprehensive Test Ban (CTB) Treaty was first proposed in the 1950s. For those nations signing it, the CTB would bring to a halt all nuclear weapons testing.**
- ▶ **Sears, Roebuck & Co. was the only large ~~corp.~~ corporation in town.**

With numbers. The following abbreviations are acceptable with specific years and times.

399 BCE ("before the common era") *or* 399 BC ("before Christ")

49 CE ("common era") *or* AD 49 (*anno Domini*, Latin for "year of our Lord")

11:15 AM (*or* a.m.)

9:00 PM (*or* p.m.)

Symbols such as % and $ are acceptable with figures (*$11*) but not with words (*eleven dollars*). Units of measurement can be abbreviated in charts and graphs (*4 in.*) but not in the body of a paper (*four inches*).

In notes and source citations. Some Latin abbreviations required in notes and in source citations are not appropriate in the body of a paper.

cf.	compare (*confer*)
e.g.	for example (*exempli gratia*)
et al.	and others (*et alia*)

etc.	and so forth (*et cetera*)
i.e.	that is (*id est*)
N.B.	note well (*nota bene*)

In addition, except in notes and source citations, do not abbreviate such terms as *chapter*, *page*, and *volume* or the names of months, states, cities, or countries. Two exceptions are *Washington, D.C.*, and *U.S.* The latter abbreviation is acceptable as an **adjective** but not as a **noun**: *U.S. borders* but *in the United States.*

42b Using numbers

If you can write out a number in one or two words, do so. Use figures for longer numbers.

thirty-eight
▶ **Her screams were ignored by ~~38~~ people.**

216
▶ **A baseball is held together by ~~two hundred sixteen~~ red stitches.**

If one of several numbers *of the same kind* in the same sentence requires a figure, you should use figures for all the numbers in that sentence.

$100
▶ **An audio system can range in cost from ~~one hundred dollars~~ to $2,599.**

When a sentence begins with a number, either spell out the number or rewrite the sentence.

Taxpayers spent sixteen million dollars for
▶ **119 years of CIA labor. ~~cost taxpayers sixteen million dollars.~~**

In general, use figures for the following:

ADDRESSES	23 Main Street; 175 Fifth Avenue
DATES	September 17, 1951; 6 June 1983; 4 BCE; the 1860s
DECIMALS AND FRACTIONS	65.34; 8½
EXACT AMOUNTS OF MONEY	$7,348; $1.46 trillion; $2.50; thirty-five (*or* 35) cents

PERCENTAGES	77 percent (*or* 77%)
SCORES AND STATISTICS	an 8–3 Red Sox victory; an average age of 22
TIME OF DAY	6:00 AM (*or* a.m.)

43 Italics

The slanted type known as *italics* is more than just a pretty typeface. Indeed, italics give words special meaning or emphasis. In the sentence "Many people read *People* on the subway every day," the italics (and the capital letter) tell us that *People* is a publication. You may use your computer to produce italic type; if not, underline words that you would otherwise italicize.

43a Italicizing titles

In general, use italics for titles and subtitles of long works; use quotation marks for shorter works (39b).

BOOKS	*Fun Home: A Family Tragicomic*
CHOREOGRAPHIC WORKS	Agnes de Mille's *Rodeo*
FILMS AND VIDEOS	*Star Wars*
LONG MUSICAL WORKS	*The Magic Flute*
LONG POEMS	*Bhagavad Gita*
MAGAZINES AND JOURNALS	*Ebony;* the *New England Journal of Medicine*
NEWSPAPERS	the Cleveland *Plain Dealer*
PAINTINGS AND SCULPTURE	Georgia O'Keeffe's *Black Iris*
PAMPHLETS	Thomas Paine's *Common Sense*
PLAYS	*Les Misérables*
RADIO SERIES	*All Things Considered*

ALBUM-LENGTH RECORDINGS	*The Ramones Leave Home*
SOFTWARE	*Quicken*
TELEVISION SERIES	*Breaking Bad*

Do not italicize titles of sacred books, such as the Bible and the Qur'an; public documents, such as the Constitution and the Magna Carta; or your own papers.

43b Italicizing words, letters, and numbers used as terms

- **On the back of his jersey was the famous *24*.**
- **One characteristic of some New York speech is the absence of postvocalic *r*—for example, pronouncing the word *four* as "fouh."**

43c Italicizing non-English words

Italicize words from other languages unless they have become part of English—like the French "bourgeois" or the Italian "pasta," for example. If a word is in an English dictionary, it does not need italics.

- **At last one of the phantom sleighs gliding along the street would come to a stop, and with gawky haste Mr. Burness in his fox-furred *shapka* would make for our door.**

—Vladimir Nabokov, *Speak, Memory*

43d Italicizing names of aircraft, ships, and trains

Spirit of St. Louis Amtrak's *Silver Star* U.S.S. *Iowa*

43e Using italics for emphasis

Italics can help create emphasis in writing, but use them sparingly for this purpose. It is usually better to create emphasis with sentence structure and word choice.

▸ **Great literature and a class of literate readers are nothing new in India. What is new is the emergence of a gifted generation of Indian writers *working in English.*** —Salman Rushdie

44 Hyphens

Hyphens are undoubtedly confusing to many people—hyphen problems are now one of the twenty most common surface errors in student writing (see p. 10). The confusion is understandable. Over time, the conventions for hyphen use in a given word can change (*tomorrow* was once spelled *to-morrow*). New words, even compounds such as *firewall*, generally don't use hyphens, but controversy continues to rage over whether to hyphenate *email* (or is it *e-mail?*). And some words are hyphenated when they serve one kind of purpose in a sentence and not when they serve another.

44a Using hyphens with compound words

Compound nouns. Some are one word (*rowboat*), some are separate words (*hard drive*), and some require hyphens (*sister-in-law*). You should consult a dictionary to be sure.

Compound adjectives. Hyphenate most compound **adjectives** that precede a noun, but not those that follow a noun.

a *well-liked* boss	My boss is *well liked.*
a *six-foot* plank	The plank is *six feet long.*

In general, the reason for hyphenating compound adjectives is to make meaning clear.

▶ **Designers often use potted plants as living-room dividers.**

Without the hyphen, *living* may seem to modify *room dividers.*

Never hyphenate an *-ly* adverb and an adjective.

▶ **They used a widely/distributed mailing list.**

Fractions and compound numbers. Use a hyphen to write out fractions and to spell out compound numbers from twenty-one to ninety-nine.

one-seventh   fifty-four thousand

44b Using hyphens with prefixes and suffixes

The majority of words containing prefixes or suffixes are written without hyphens, such as *antiwar* or *Romanesque*. Following are some exceptions:

BEFORE CAPITALIZED BASE WORDS	un-American, non-Catholic
WITH FIGURES	pre-1960, post-1945
WITH CERTAIN PREFIXES AND SUFFIXES	all-state, ex-partner, self-possessed, quasi-legislative, mayor-elect, fifty-odd
WITH COMPOUND BASE WORDS	pre-high school, post-cold war
FOR CLARITY OR EASE OF READING	re-cover, anti-inflation, troll-like

Re-cover means "cover again"; the hyphen distinguishes it from *recover*, meaning "get well." In *anti-inflation* and *troll-like*, the hyphens separate confusing clusters of vowels and consonants.

Checklist

Editing for Hyphens

- Double-check compound words to be sure they are properly closed up, separated, or hyphenated. If in doubt, consult a dictionary. (44a)
- Check all terms that have prefixes or suffixes to see whether you need hyphens. (44b)
- Do not hyphenate two-word verbs or word groups that serve as subject complements. (44c)

44c Avoiding unnecessary hyphens

Unnecessary hyphens are at least as common a problem as omitted ones. Do not hyphenate the parts of a two-word verb such as *depend on*, *turn off*, or *tune out* (27b).

- **Each player must pick/up a medical form before football tryouts.**

  The words *pick up* act as a verb and should not be hyphenated.

However, be careful to check that two words do indeed function as a verb in the sentence; if they function as an adjective, a hyphen may be needed.

- **Let's sign up for the early class.**

  The verb *sign up* should not have a hyphen.

- **Where is the sign-up sheet?**

  The adjective *sign-up*, which modifies the noun *sheet*, needs a hyphen.

Do not hyphenate a subject complement—a word group that follows a linking verb (such as a form of *be* or *seem*) and describes the subject.

- **Audrey is almost three/years/old.**

Documentation

Writing Processes

Writing That Works

Research

Language

Grammar

Style

Punctuation/ Mechanics

Documentation

45 MLA Style

Many fields in the humanities ask students to follow Modern Language Association (MLA) style to format manuscripts and to document various kinds of sources. This chapter introduces MLA guidelines. For further reference, consult the *MLA Handbook*, Eighth Edition (2016).

45a Understanding MLA citation style

Why does academic work call for very careful citation practices when writing for the general public may not? The answer is that readers of your academic work expect source citations for several reasons:

- Source citations demonstrate that you've done your homework on your topic and that you are a part of the conversation surrounding it. Careful citation shows your readers what you know, where you stand, and what you think is important.
- Source citations show your readers that you understand the need to give credit when you make use of someone else's intellectual property. Especially in academic writing, when it's better to be safe than sorry, include a citation for any source you think you might need to cite. (See 15c.)
- Source citations give explicit directions to guide readers who want to look for themselves at the works you're using.

The guidelines for MLA style help you with this last purpose, giving you instructions on exactly what information to include in your citation and how to format that information.

45b Considering the context of your sources

New kinds of sources crop up regularly. As the *MLA Handbook* confirms, there are often several "correct" ways to cite a source, so you will need to think carefully about *your own context* for using the source so you can identify the pieces of information that you should emphasize or include and any other information that might be helpful to your readers.

Elements of MLA citations. The first step is to identify elements that are commonly found in most works writers cite.

AUTHOR AND TITLE. The first two elements, both of which are needed for many sources, are the author's name and the title of the work. Each of these elements is followed by a period.

Author. Title.

Even in these elements, your context is important. The author of a novel may be obvious, but who is the "author" of a television episode? The director? The writer? The show's creator? The star? The answer may depend on the focus of your own work. If an actor's performance is central to your discussion, then MLA guidelines ask you to identify the actor as the author. If the plot is your focus, you might name the writer of the episode as the author.

CONTAINER. The next step is to identify elements of what the MLA calls the "container" for the work. The context in which you are discussing the source and the context in which you find the source will help you determine what counts as a container in each case. If you watch a movie in a theater, you won't identify a separate container after the film title. But if you watch the same movie as part of a DVD box set of the director's work, the container title is the name of the box set. If you read an article in a print journal, the first container will be the journal that the article appears in. If you read it online, the journal may also be part of a second, larger container, such as a database. Thinking about a source as nested in larger containers may help you to visualize how a citation works.

The elements you may include in the "container" part of your citation include the following, in this order: the title of the larger container, if it's different from the title of the work; the names of any contributors such as editors or translators; the version or edition; the volume and issue numbers; the publisher or sponsor; the date of publication; and a location such as the page numbers,

DOI, permalink, or URL. These elements are separated by commas, and the end of the container is marked with a period.

Author. Title. Container title, contributor names, version or edition, volume and issue numbers, publisher, date, location.

Most sources won't include all these pieces of information, so include only the elements that are available and relevant to create an acceptable citation. If you need a second container—for instance, if you are citing an article from a journal you found in a database—you simply add it after the first one, beginning with the container title and including as many of the same container elements as you can find. The rest of this chapter offers many examples of how elements and containers are combined to create citations.

Examples from student work

ARTICLE IN A DATABASE. David Craig, whose research writing appears in 45f, found a potentially useful article in Academic Search Premier, a database he accessed through his library website. Many databases are digital collections of articles that originally appeared in print periodicals, and the articles usually have the same written-word content as they did in print form, without changes or updates.

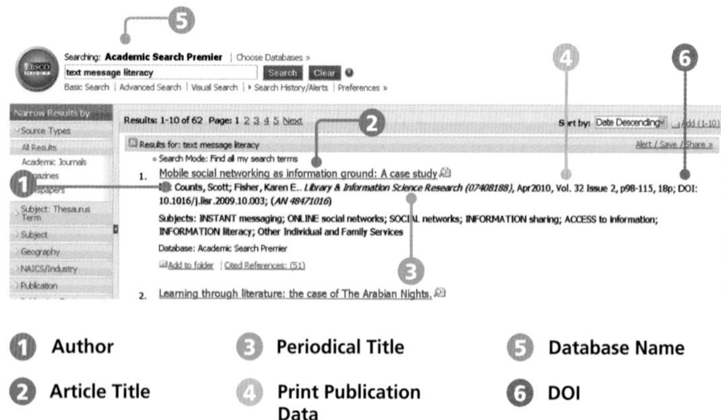

From the page shown on p. 216, David Craig was able to click through to read the full text of the article. He printed this computer screen in case he needed to cite the article: the image has all the information that he would need to create a complete MLA citation, including the original print publication information for the article, the name of the database, and the location (here, a "digital object identifier" or DOI, which provides the source's permanent location).

A complete citation for this article would look like this:

Counts, Scott, and Karen E. Fisher. "Mobile Social Networking as Information Ground: A Case Study." *Library and Information Science Research*, vol. 32, no. 2, Apr. 2010, pp. 98-115. *Academic Search Premier*, doi:10.1016/j.lisr.2009.10.003.

Note that the periodical, *Library and Information Science Research*, is the first container of the article, and the database, *Academic Search Premier*, is the second container. Notice, too, that the first container includes just four relevant elements—the journal title, number (here, that means the volume and issue numbers), date, and page numbers; and the second container includes just two—the database title and location. Publisher information is not readily available for journals and databases, so it is not required.

Types of sources. Look at the Directory to MLA Style on pp. 227–28 for guidelines on citing various types of sources, including print books, print periodicals (journals, magazines, and newspapers), digital written-word sources, and other sources (films, artwork) that consist mainly of material other than written words. A digital version of a source may include updates or corrections that the print version of the same work lacks, so MLA guidelines ask you to indicate where you found the source. If you can't find a model exactly like the source you've selected, see "Citing sources that don't match any model exactly" on p. 229.

Parts of citations. MLA citations appear in two parts—a brief in-text citation in parentheses in the body of your written text, and a full citation in the list of works cited, to which the in-text citation directs readers. A basic in-text citation includes the author's name and the page number (for a print source), but many variations on this format are discussed in 45d.

In the text of his research project (see 45f), David Craig quotes material from a print book and from an online report. He cites both parenthetically, pointing readers to entries on his list of works cited, as shown on p. 268. These examples show just two of the many ways to cite sources using in-text citations and a list of works cited. You'll need to make case-by-case decisions based on the types of sources you include.

for good reason. According to David Crystal, an internationally recognized scholar of linguistics at the University of Wales, as young children develop and learn how words string together to express ideas, they go through many phases of language play. The singsong rhymes and nonsensical chants of preschoolers are vital to learning language, and a healthy appetite for wordplay leads to a better command of language later in life (182).

Craig 10

...nd in SAT ...Is Yielding ...Concern. College Board, 2002.

Crystal, David. *Language Play*. U of Chicago P, 1998.

Ferguson, Niall. "Texting Makes U Stupid." *Newsweek,* vol. 158, no. 12, 19 Sept. 2011, p. 11. *EBSCOHost,* connection.ebscohost.com/c/articles/65454341/texting-makes-u-stupid.

Leibowitz, Wendy R. "Technology Transforms Writing and the Teaching of Writing." *Chronicle of Higher Education,* 26 Nov. 1999, pp. A67-A68.

Lenhart, Amanda. *Teens, Smartphones, & Texting*. Pew Research Center, 19 Mar. 2012, www.pewinternet.org/files/old-media//Files/Reports/2012/PIP_Teens_Smartphones_and_Texting.pdf.

Lenhart, Amanda, et al. *Writing, Technology & Teens*. Pew Research Center, 24 Apr. 2008, www.pewinternet.org/2008/04/24/writing-technology-and-teens/.

Lenhart, Amanda, and Oliver Lewis. *Teenage Life Online: The Rise of the Instant-Message Generation and the Internet's Impact on Friendships and Family Relationships*. Pew Research Center, 21 June 2001, www.pewinternet.org/2001/06/20/the-rise-of-the-instant-message-generation/.

...?" *Bedford Bits*, 9 Apr. 2015, .../the-english-community/bedford ...ma-queen.

...ext-Messaging Skills Can Score ...11 Mar. 2005, www ...sc.html.

"SAT Trends 2011." *Collegeboard.org,* 14 Sept. 2011, research.collegeboard.org/programs/sat/data/archived/cb-seniors-2011/tables.

is rising among the young. According to the Pew Internet & American Life Project, 85 percent of those aged twelve to seventeen at least occasionally write text messages, instant messages, or comments on social networking sites (Lenhart et al.) In 2001, the most conservative estimate based on

Explanatory notes. MLA citation style asks you to include explanatory notes for information that doesn't readily fit into your text but is needed for clarification or further explanation. In addition, MLA permits bibliographic notes for information about or evaluation of a source, or to list multiple sources that relate to a single point. Use superscript numbers in the text to refer readers to the notes, which may appear as endnotes (under the heading *Notes* on a separate page immediately before the list of works cited) or as footnotes at the bottom of each page where a superscript number appears.

EXAMPLE OF SUPERSCRIPT NUMBER IN TEXT

Although messaging relies on the written word, many messagers disregard standard writing conventions. For example, here is a snippet from an IM conversation between two teenage girls:[1]

EXAMPLE OF EXPLANATORY NOTE

1. This transcript of an IM conversation was collected on 20 Nov. 2016. The teenagers' names are concealed to protect their privacy.

45c Following MLA manuscript format

The MLA recommends the following format for the manuscript of a research paper. However, check with your instructor before preparing the final draft of a print work.

First page and title. The MLA does not require a title page. Type each of the following items on a separate line on the first page, beginning one inch from the top and flush with the left margin: your name, the instructor's name, the course name and number, and the date. Double-space between each item; then double-space again and center the title. Double-space between the title and the beginning of the text.

Margins and spacing. Leave one-inch margins at the top and bottom and on both sides of each page. Double-space the entire text, including set-off quotations, notes, and the list of works cited. Indent the first line of a paragraph one-half inch. Indent set-off quotations one-half inch.

Page numbers. Include your last name and the page number on each page, one-half inch below the top and flush with the right margin.

Long quotations. When quoting a long passage (more than four typed lines), set the quotation off by starting it on a new line and indenting each line one-half inch from the left margin. Do not enclose the passage in quotation marks (39a).

Headings. MLA style allows, but does not require, headings. However, many students and instructors find them helpful. (See 3b for guidelines on using headings and subheadings.)

Visuals. Visuals (such as photographs, drawings, charts, graphs, and tables) should be placed as near as possible to the relevant text. (See 15b for guidelines on incorporating visuals into your text.) Tables should have a label and number (*Table 1*) and a clear caption. The label and caption should be aligned on the left, on separate lines. Give the source information below the table. All other visuals should be labeled *Figure* (abbreviated *Fig.*), numbered, and captioned. The label and caption should appear on the same line, followed by source information. Remember to refer to each visual before it appears in your text, indicating how it contributes to the point(s) that you are making.

45d Creating MLA in-text citations

MLA style requires a citation in the text of a writing project for every quotation, paraphrase, summary, or other material requiring documentation (see 15c). In-text citations document material from other sources with both signal phrases and parenthetical references. Parenthetical references should include the information your readers need to locate the full reference in the list of works cited at the end of the text. An in-text citation in MLA style gives the reader two kinds of information: (1) it indicates which source on the works-cited page the writer is referring to, and (2) it explains where in the source the material quoted, paraphrased, or summarized can be found, if the source has page numbers or other numbered sections.

The basic MLA in-text citation includes the author's last name either in a signal phrase introducing the source material (see 15a) or in parentheses at the end of the sentence. For sources with stable page numbers, it also includes the page number in parentheses at the end of the sentence.

SAMPLE CITATION USING A SIGNAL PHRASE

In his discussion of Monty Python routines, Crystal notes that the group relished "breaking the normal rules" of language (107).

SAMPLE PARENTHETICAL CITATION

A noted linguist explains that Monty Python humor often relied on "bizarre linguistic interactions" (Crystal 108).

(For digital sources without stable page numbers, see model 3.)

Note in the examples on the following pages where punctuation is placed in relation to the parentheses.

DIRECTORY TO MLA STYLE

MLA style for in-text citations

1. AUTHOR NAMED IN A SIGNAL PHRASE. The MLA recommends using the author's name in a signal phrase to introduce the material and citing the page number(s) in parentheses.

> Lee claims that his comic-book creation, Thor, was "the first regularly published superhero to speak in a consistently archaic manner" (199).

2. AUTHOR NAMED IN A PARENTHETICAL REFERENCE. When you do not mention the author in a signal phrase, include the author's last name before the page number(s), if any, in the parentheses. Use no punctuation between the author's name and the page number(s).

> The word *Bollywood* is sometimes considered an insult because it implies that Indian movies are merely "a derivative of the American film industry" (Chopra 9).

3. DIGITAL OR NONPRINT SOURCE. Give enough information in a signal phrase or in parentheses for readers to locate the source in your list of works cited. Many works found online or in electronic databases lack stable page numbers; you can omit the page number in such cases. However, if you are citing a work with stable pagination, such as an article in PDF format, include the page number in parentheses.

DIGITAL SOURCE WITHOUT STABLE PAGE NUMBERS

> As a *Slate* analysis explains, "Prominent sports psychologists get praised for their successes and don't get grief for their failures" (Engber).

DIGITAL SOURCE WITH STABLE PAGE NUMBERS

> According to Whitmarsh, the British military had experimented with using balloons for observation as far back as 1879 (328).

If the source includes numbered sections, paragraphs, or screens, include the abbreviation (*sec.*), paragraph (*par.*), or screen (*scr.*) number in parentheses.

4. TWO AUTHORS. Use both authors' last names in a signal phrase or in parentheses.

> Gilbert and Gubar point out that in the Grimm version of "Snow White," the king "never actually appears in this story at all" (37).

5. THREE OR MORE AUTHORS. Use the first author's name and *et al.* ("and others"), unless your instructor asks you to list every name.

> Similarly, as Belenky et al. assert, examining the lives of women expands our understanding of human development (7).

6. ORGANIZATION AS AUTHOR. Give the group's full name in a signal phrase; in parentheses, abbreviate any common words in the name.

> Any study of social welfare involves a close analysis of "the impacts, the benefits, and the costs" of its policies (Social Research Corp. iii).

7. UNKNOWN AUTHOR. Use the full title, if it is brief, in your text—or the first word of the title in parentheses.

> One analysis defines *hype* as "an artificially engendered atmosphere of hysteria" (*Today's* 51).

8. AUTHOR OF TWO OR MORE WORKS CITED IN THE SAME PROJECT. If your list of works cited has more than one work by the same author, include the title of the work you are citing in a signal phrase or the first word of the title in parentheses to prevent reader confusion.

> Gardner shows readers their own silliness in his description of a "pointless, ridiculous monster, crouched in the shadows, stinking of dead men, murdered children, and martyred cows" (*Grendel* 2).

9. TWO OR MORE AUTHORS WITH THE SAME LAST NAME. Include the author's first *and* last names in a signal phrase or first initial and last name in a parenthetical reference.

> Children will learn to write if they are allowed to choose their own subjects, James Britton asserts, citing the Schools Council study of the 1960s (37-42).

10. MULTIVOLUME WORK. In a parenthetical reference, note the volume number first and then the page number(s), with a colon and one space between them.

> Modernist writers prized experimentation and gradually even sought to blur the line between poetry and prose, according to Forster (3: 150).

If you name only one volume of the work in your list of works cited, include only the page number in the parentheses.

11. LITERARY WORK. Because literary works are usually available in many different editions, cite the page number(s) from the edition you used followed by a semicolon, and then give other identifying information that will lead readers to the passage in any edition. Indicate the act and/or scene in a play (*37; sc. 1*). For a novel, indicate the part or chapter (*175; ch. 4*).

> In utter despair, Dostoyevsky's character Mitya wonders aloud about the "terrible tragedies realism inflicts on people" (376; bk. 8, ch. 2).

For a poem, cite the part (if there is one) and line(s), separated by a period. If you are citing only line numbers, use the word *line(s)* in the first reference (*lines 33-34*).

> Whitman speculates, "All goes onward and outward, nothing collapses, / And to die is different from what anyone supposed, and luckier" (6.129-30).

For a verse play, give only the act, scene, and line numbers, separated by periods.

> The witches greet Banquo as "lesser than Macbeth, and greater" (1.3.65).

12. WORK IN AN ANTHOLOGY OR COLLECTION. For an essay, short story, or other piece of prose reprinted in an anthology, use the name of the author of the work, not the editor of the anthology, but use the page number(s) from the anthology.

> Narratives of captivity play a major role in early writing by women in the United States, as demonstrated by Silko (219).

13. SACRED TEXT. To cite a sacred text such as the Qur'an or the Bible, give the title of the edition you used, the book, and the chapter and verse (or their equivalent) separated by a period. In your text, spell out the names of books. In parenthetical references, use abbreviations for books with names of five or more letters (*Gen.* for *Genesis*).

> He ignored the admonition "Pride goes before destruction, and a haughty spirit before a fall" (*New Oxford Annotated Bible,* Prov. 16.18).

14. ENCYCLOPEDIA OR DICTIONARY ENTRY. An entry from a reference work—such as an encyclopedia or a dictionary—without an author will appear on the works-cited list under the entry's title. Enclose the entry title in quotation marks, and place it in parentheses. Omit the page number for print reference works that arrange entries alphabetically.

> The term *prion* was coined by Stanley B. Prusiner from the words *proteinaceous* and *infectious* and a suffix meaning *particle* ("Prion").

15. GOVERNMENT SOURCE WITH NO AUTHOR NAMED. Because entries for sources authored by government agencies will appear on your list of works cited under the name of the country (see 45e, item 69), your in-text citation for such a source should include the name of the country as well as the name of the agency responsible for the source.

> To reduce the agricultural runoff into the Chesapeake Bay, the United States Environmental Protection Agency has argued that "[h]igh nutrient loading crops, such as corn and soybean, should be replaced with alternatives in environmentally sensitive areas" (2-26).

16. ENTIRE WORK. Include the reference in the text, without any page numbers.

> Krakauer's *Into the Wild* both criticizes and admires the solitary impulses of its young hero, which end up killing him.

17. INDIRECT SOURCE (AUTHOR QUOTING SOMEONE ELSE). Use the abbreviation *qtd. in* to indicate that you are quoting from someone else's report of a source.

> As Arthur Miller says, "When somebody is destroyed everybody finally contributes to it, but in Willy's case, the end product would be virtually the same" (qtd. in Martin and Meyer 375).

18. TWO OR MORE SOURCES IN ONE CITATION. Separate the information with semicolons.

> Economists recommend that *employment* be redefined to include unpaid domestic labor (Clark 148; Nevins 39).

19. VISUAL. When you include an image in your text, number it and include a parenthetical reference (*see Fig. 2*). Number figures (photos, drawings, cartoons, maps, graphs, and charts) and tables separately. Each visual should include a caption with the figure or table number and information about the source—either a complete citation or enough information to direct readers to the works-cited entry.

> This trend is illustrated in a chart distributed by the College Board as part of its 2011 analysis of aggregate SAT data (see Fig. 1).

Soon after the preceding sentence, readers find the following figure and a caption referring them to the entry in the list of works cited (see 45f):

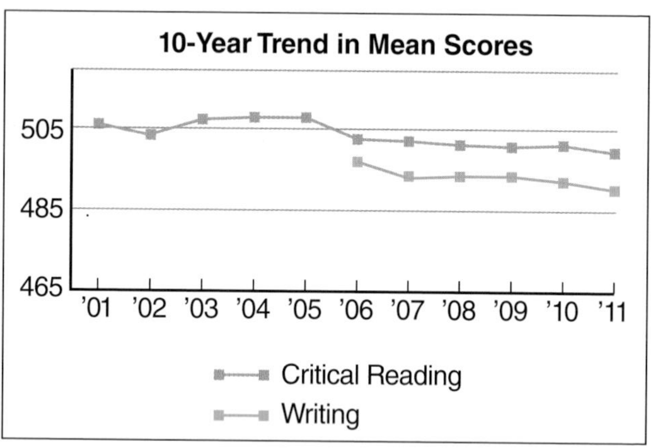

Fig. 1. Ten-year trend in mean SAT reading and writing scores (2001-2011). Data source: "SAT Trends 2011."

An image that you create might appear with a caption like this:

> Fig. 4. Young women reading magazines. Personal photograph by author.

Documentation: MLA Style > Tutorials (4)

45e Creating an MLA list of works cited

A list of works cited is an alphabetical list of the sources you have referred to in your essay. (If your instructor asks you to list everything you have read as background, call the list *Works Consulted*.)

DIRECTORY TO MLA STYLE

MLA style for a list of works cited

DIRECTORY TO MLA STYLE

MLA style for a list of works cited, *continued*

Checklist

Citing Sources That Don't Match Any Model Exactly

What should you do if your source doesn't match any of the models exactly? Suppose, for instance, that your source is a translated essay that appears in the fifth edition of an anthology.

- Identify a basic model to follow. For example, if you decide that your source looks most like an essay in an anthology, you would start with a citation that looks like model 10.
- After listing author and title information (if given), enter as many of the elements of the container as you can find (see 45b): title of the larger container, if any; other contributors, such as editor or translator; version or edition; volume; publisher; date; and page numbers or other location information such as a URL or DOI. End the container with a period. If the container is nested in a larger container, collect the information from the second container as well.
- If you aren't sure which model to follow or how to create a combination model with multiple containers, ask your instructor.

Formatting a list of works cited

- Start your list on a separate page after the text of your document and any notes.
- Center the heading *Works Cited* (not italicized or in quotation marks) one inch from the top of the page.
- Begin each entry flush with the left margin, but indent subsequent lines one-half inch. Double-space the entire list.
- List sources alphabetically by the first word. Start with the author's name, if available, or the editor's name. If no author or editor is given, start with the title.
- List the author's last name first, followed by a comma and the first name. If a source has two authors, the second author's name appears first name first (see model 2).
- Capitalize every important word in titles and subtitles. Italicize titles of books and long works, but put titles of shorter works in quotation marks.

Guidelines for author listings

The list of works cited is always arranged alphabetically. The in-text citations in your writing point readers toward particular sources on the list.

NAME CITED IN SIGNAL PHRASE IN TEXT

Crystal explains . . .

NAME IN PARENTHETICAL CITATION IN TEXT

. . . (Crystal 107).

BEGINNING OF ENTRY ON LIST OF WORKS CITED

Crystal, David.

Models 1–5 explain how to arrange author names. The information that follows the name depends on the type of work you are citing—a book (models 6–27); a print periodical (models 28–34); a written text from a digital source, such as an article from a website or database (models 35–51); sources from art, film, comics, or other media, including live performances (models 52–67); and academic, government, and legal sources (models 68–75). Consult the model that most closely resembles the source you are using.

1. ONE AUTHOR. Put the last name first, followed by a comma, the first name (and initial, if any), and a period.

Crystal, David.

2. MULTIPLE AUTHORS. For two authors, list the first author with the last name first (see model 1). Follow this with a comma, the word *and*, and the name of the second author with the first name first.

Gilbert, Sandra M., and Susan Gubar.

For three or more authors, list the first author followed by a comma and *et al.* ("and others").

> Lupton, Ellen, et al.

3. ORGANIZATION OR GROUP AUTHOR. Give the name of the group, government agency, corporation, or other organization listed as the author.

> Getty Trust.

> United States. Government Accountability Office.

4. UNKNOWN AUTHOR. When the author is not identified, begin the entry with the title, and alphabetize by the first important word. Italicize titles of books and long works, but put titles of articles and other short works in quotation marks.

> "California Sues EPA over Emissions."

> *New Concise World Atlas.*

5. TWO OR MORE WORKS BY THE SAME AUTHOR. Arrange the entries alphabetically by title. Include the author's name in the first entry, but in subsequent entries, use three hyphens followed by a period. (For the basic format for citing a book, see model 6. For the basic format for citing an article from an online newspaper, see model 38.)

> Chopra, Anupama. "Bollywood Princess, Hollywood Hopeful." *The New York Times*, 10 Feb. 2008, nyti.ms/1QEtNpF.

> ---. *King of Bollywood: Shah Rukh Khan and the Seductive World of Indian Cinema*. Warner Books, 2007.

Note: Use three hyphens only when the work is by *exactly* the same author(s) as the previous entry.

Print books

6. BASIC FORMAT FOR A BOOK. Begin with the author name(s). (See models 1–5.) Then include the title and subtitle, the publisher, and the publication year. The source map on pp. 234–35 shows where to find this information in a typical book.

Crystal, David. *Language Play*. U of Chicago P, 1998.

Note: Place a period and a space after the name and title, and end with a period. Place a comma after the publisher, and in the publisher's name, omit *Co.* or *Inc.*, and abbreviate *University Press* to *UP.*

7. AUTHOR AND EDITOR BOTH NAMED

Bangs, Lester. *Psychotic Reactions and Carburetor Dung*. Edited by Greil Marcus, Alfred A. Knopf, 1988.

Note: To cite the editor's contribution instead, begin the entry with the editor's name.

Marcus, Greil, editor. *Psychotic Reactions and Carburetor Dung*. By Lester Bangs, Alfred A. Knopf, 1988.

8. EDITOR, NO AUTHOR NAMED

Wall, Cheryl A., editor. *Changing Our Own Words: Essays on Criticism, Theory, and Writing by Black Women*. Rutgers UP, 1989.

9. ANTHOLOGY. Cite an entire anthology the same way you would cite a book with an editor and no named author (see model 8).

Walker, Dale L., editor. *Westward: A Fictional History of the American West.* Forge Books, 2003.

10. WORK IN AN ANTHOLOGY OR CHAPTER IN A BOOK WITH AN EDITOR. List the author(s) of the selection; the selection title, in quotation marks; the title of the book, italicized; the words *edited by* and the name(s) of the editor(s); the publisher; the year; and the abbreviation *pp.* with the selection's page numbers.

Komunyakaa, Yusef. "Facing It." *The Seagull Reader*, edited by Joseph Kelly, W. W. Norton, 2000, pp. 126-27.

Note: To provide original publication information for a reprinted selection, use the original publication information as a second container (see 45b):

Byatt, A. S. "The Thing in the Forest." *The O. Henry Prize Stories 2003*, edited by Laura Furman, Anchor Books, 2003, pp. 3-22. Originally published in *The New Yorker*, 3 June 2002, pp. 80-89.

11. TWO OR MORE ITEMS FROM THE SAME ANTHOLOGY. List the anthology as one entry (see model 9). Also list each selection separately with a cross-reference to the anthology.

Estleman, Loren D. "Big Tim Magoon and the Wild West." Walker, pp. 391-404.

Salzer, Susan K. "Miss Libbie Tells All." Walker, pp. 199-212.

12. TRANSLATION

Bolaño, Roberto. *2666*. Translated by Natasha Wimmer, Farrar, Straus and Giroux, 2008.

13. BOOK WITH BOTH TRANSLATOR AND EDITOR. List the editor's and translator's names after the title, in the order they appear on the title page.

Kant, Immanuel. *"Toward Perpetual Peace" and Other Writings on Politics, Peace, and History*. Edited by Pauline Kleingeld, translated by David L. Colclasure, Yale UP, 2006.

14. TRANSLATION OF A SECTION OF A BOOK. If different translators have worked on various parts of the book, identify the translator of the part you are citing.

García Lorca, Federico. *"The Little Mad Boy."* Translated by W. S. Merwin. *The Selected Poems of Federico García Lorca*, edited by Francisco García Lorca and Donald M. Allen, Penguin, 1969, pp. 51-53.

15. TRANSLATION OF A BOOK BY AN UNKNOWN AUTHOR

Grettir's Saga. Translated by Denton Fox and Hermann Palsson, U of Toronto P, 1974.

MLA SOURCE MAP: Books

Take information from the book's title page and copyright page (on the reverse side of the title page), not from the book's cover or a library catalog.

1. **Author.** List the last name first. End with a period. For variations, see models 2–5.
2. **Title.** Italicize the title and any subtitle; capitalize all major words. End with a period.
3. **Publisher.** Identify the publisher's name as given on the book's title page. If more than one publisher appears on the title page, separate the names with a slash, leaving a space before and after the slash. If no publisher is listed on the title page, check the copyright page. Abbreviate *University* and *Press* as *U* and *P* (*Oxford UP*). Omit terms such as *Company* and *Incorporated*. Follow the publisher's name with a comma.
4. **Year of publication.** If more than one copyright date is given, use the most recent one. End with a period.

A citation for the book on p. 235 would look like this:

Patel, Raj. *The Value of Nothing: How to Reshape Market Society and Redefine Democracy.* Picador, 2009.

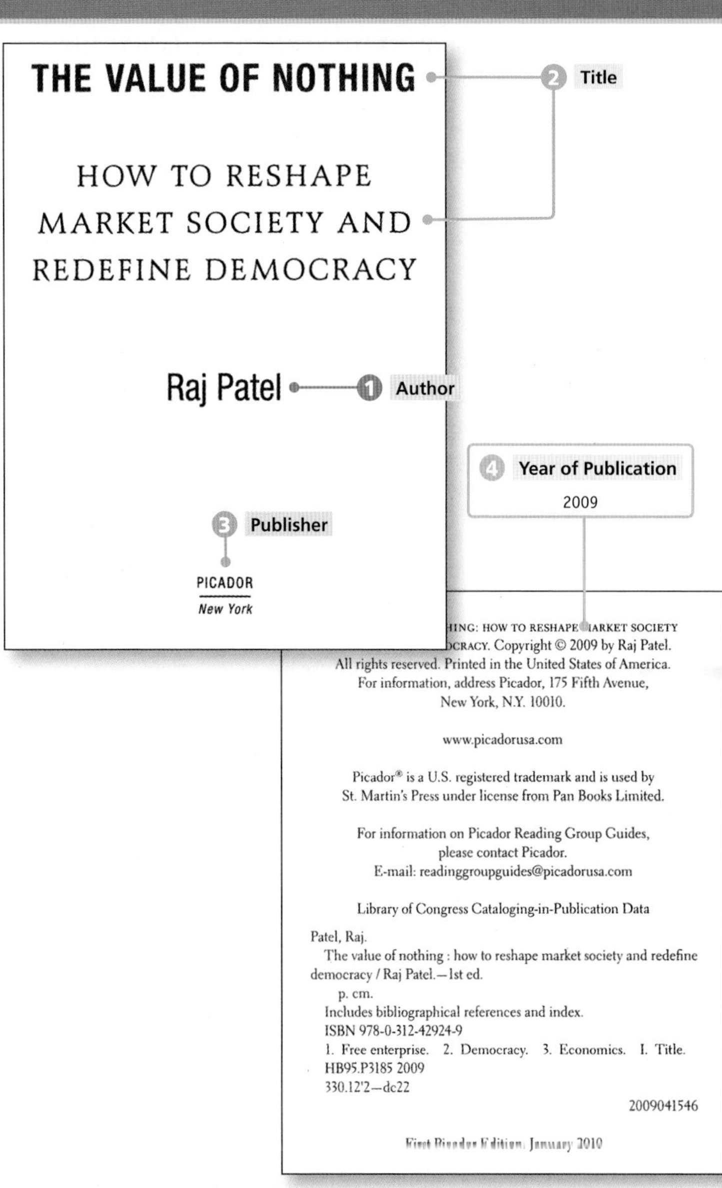

THE VALUE OF NOTHING

HOW TO RESHAPE MARKET SOCIETY AND REDEFINE DEMOCRACY

Raj Patel

PICADOR
New York

(2) **Title**

(1) **Author**

(3) **Publisher**

(4) **Year of Publication**
2009

HING: HOW TO RESHAPE MARKET SOCIETY
DCRACY. Copyright © 2009 by Raj Patel.
All rights reserved. Printed in the United States of America.
For information, address Picador, 175 Fifth Avenue,
New York, N.Y. 10010.

www.picadorusa.com

Picador® is a U.S. registered trademark and is used by
St. Martin's Press under license from Pan Books Limited.

For information on Picador Reading Group Guides,
please contact Picador.
E-mail: readinggroupguides@picadorusa.com

Library of Congress Cataloging-in-Publication Data

Patel, Raj.
The value of nothing : how to reshape market society and redefine democracy / Raj Patel.—1st ed.
p. cm.
Includes bibliographical references and index.
ISBN 978-0-312-42924-9
1. Free enterprise. 2. Democracy. 3. Economics. I. Title.
HB95.P3185 2009
330.12'2—dc22

2009041546

First Picador Edition: January 2010

16. BOOK IN A LANGUAGE OTHER THAN ENGLISH. Include a translation of the title in brackets, if necessary.

Benedetti, Mario. *La borra del café* [*The Coffee Grind*]. Editorial Sudamericana, 2000.

17. GRAPHIC NARRATIVE OR COMIC. If the words and images are created by the same person, cite a graphic narrative just as you would with a book (model 6).

Bechdel, Alison. *Are You My Mother? A Comic Drama*. Houghton Mifflin Harcourt, 2012.

If the work is a collaboration, indicate the author or illustrator who is most important to your research before the title of the work. List other contributors after the title, in the order of their appearance on the title page. Label each person's contribution to the work.

Stavans, Ilan, writer. *Latino USA: A Cartoon History*. Illustrated by Lalo Arcaraz, Basic Books, 2000.

18. EDITION OTHER THAN THE FIRST

Walker, John A. *Art in the Age of Mass Media*. 3rd ed., Pluto Press, 2001.

19. ONE VOLUME OF A MULTIVOLUME WORK. Give the number of the volume cited after the title. Including the total number of volumes after the publication date is optional.

Ch'oe, Yong-Ho, et al., editors. *Sources of Korean Tradition*. Vol. 2, Columbia UP, 2000. 2 vols.

20. TWO OR MORE VOLUMES OF A MULTIVOLUME WORK

Ch'oe, Yong-Ho, et al., editors. *Sources of Korean Tradition*. Columbia UP, 2000. 2 vols.

21. PREFACE, FOREWORD, INTRODUCTION, OR AFTERWORD. After the writer's name, describe the contribution. After the title, indicate the book's author (with *by*) or editor (with *edited by*).

Atwan, Robert. Foreword. *The Best American Essays 2002*, edited by Stephen Jay Gould, Houghton Mifflin, 2002, pp. viii-xii.

Moore, Thurston. Introduction. *Confusion Is Next: The Sonic Youth Story*, by Alec Foege, St. Martin's Press, 1994, p. xi.

22. ENTRY IN A REFERENCE BOOK. For a well-known encyclopedia, note the edition (if identified) and year of publication. If the entries are alphabetized, omit the page number.

Kettering, Alison McNeil. "Art Nouveau." *World Book Encyclopedia*, 2002 ed.

23. BOOK THAT IS PART OF A SERIES. Cite the series name (and number, if any) from the title page.

Nichanian, Marc, and Vartan Matiossian, editors. *Yeghishe Charents: Poet of the Revolution*. Mazda, 2003. Armenian Studies Ser. 5.

24. REPUBLICATION (MODERN EDITION OF AN OLDER BOOK). Indicate the original publication date after the title.

Austen, Jane. *Sense and Sensibility*. 1813. Dover Publications, 1996.

25. MORE THAN ONE PUBLISHER'S NAME. If the title page gives two publishers' names, separate them with a slash. Include spaces on both sides of the slash.

Hornby, Nick. *About a Boy*. Riverhead / Penguin Putnam, 1998.

26. BOOK WITH A TITLE WITHIN THE TITLE. Do not italicize the title of a book or other long work within a book title. For an article title within a title, italicize as usual and place the article title in quotation marks.

Mullaney, Julie. *Arundhati Roy's* The God of Small Things: *A Reader's Guide*. Continuum, 2002.

Rhynes, Martha. *"I, Too, Sing America": The Story of Langston Hughes*. Morgan Reynolds Publishing, 2002.

27. SACRED TEXT. To cite any individual published editions of sacred books, begin the entry with the title.

Qur'an: The Final Testament (Authorized English Version) with Arabic Text. Translated by Rashad Khalifa, Universal Unity, 2000.

Print periodicals

Begin with the author name(s). (See models 1–5.) Then include the article title, the title of the periodical, the date and volume information, and the page numbers. The source map on pp. 240–41 shows where to find this information in a sample periodical.

28. ARTICLE IN A PRINT JOURNAL. Follow the journal title with a comma; the abbreviation *vol.* and volume number; a comma; the abbreviation *no.* and issue number; a comma; the month (abbreviated except for May, June, and July), day (if given), and the year or the season and year of publication; a comma; and the abbreviation *p.* or *pp.* and page numbers.

Gigante, Denise. "The Monster in the Rainbow: Keats and the Science of Life." *PMLA*, vol. 117, no. 3, May 2002, pp. 433-48.

29. ARTICLE IN A PRINT MAGAZINE. Provide the date from the magazine cover instead of volume or issue numbers.

Surowiecki, James. "The Stimulus Strategy." *The New Yorker*, 25 Feb. 2008, p. 29.

Taubin, Amy. "All Talk?" *Film Comment*, Nov.-Dec. 2007, pp. 45-47.

30. ARTICLE IN A PRINT NEWSPAPER. Include the edition (if listed) and the section number or letter (if listed).

Fackler, Martin. "Japan's Foreign Minister Says Apologies to Wartime Victims Will Be Upheld." *The New York Times*, 9 Apr. 2014, late ed., p. A6.

Note: For locally published newspapers, add the city in brackets after the name if it is not part of the name: *Globe and Mail [Toronto]*.

31. ARTICLE THAT SKIPS PAGES. When an article skips pages, give only the first page number and a plus sign.

Tyrnauer, Matthew. "Empire by Martha." *Vanity Fair*, Sept. 2002, pp. 364+.

32. EDITORIAL OR LETTER TO THE EDITOR. Include the writer's name, if given, and the title, if any. Then end with the label *Editorial* or *Letter*.

"California Dreaming." *The Nation*, 25 Feb. 2008, p. 4. Editorial.

MacEwan, Valerie. *The Believer*, vol. 12, no. 1, Jan. 2014, p. 4. Letter.

33. REVIEW

Nussbaum, Emily. "Change Agents: Review of *The Americans* and *Silicon Valley*." *The New Yorker*, 31 Mar. 2014, p. 68.

Schwarz, Benjamin. Review of *The Second World War: A Short History*, by R. A. C. Parker, *The Atlantic Monthly*, May 2002, pp. 110-11.

34. UNSIGNED ARTICLE

"Performance of the Week." *Time*, 6 Oct. 2003, p. 18.

Digital written-word sources

Digital sources such as websites differ from print sources in the ease with which they can be changed, updated, or eliminated. The most commonly cited electronic sources are documents from websites and databases.

35. WORK FROM A DATABASE. The basic format for citing a work from a database appears in the source map on pp. 244–45.

For a periodical article that you access in an online database through a library subscription service such as Academic Search Premier, begin with the author's name (if given); the title of the work, in quotation marks; the title of the periodical, italicized; and the volume/issue and date of the print version of the work (see models 28–34). Include the page numbers from the print version. Then give the name of the online database, italicized, and the DOI or permalink for the article; if neither is available, give the URL of the database home page, omitting the protocol (*http://*).

Collins, Ross F. "Cattle Barons and Ink Slingers: How Cow Country Journalists Created a Great American Myth." *American Journalism*, vol. 24, no. 3, Summer 2007, pp. 7-29. *Communication and Mass Media Complete*, www.ebscohost.com/academic/communication-mass-media-complete.

MLA SOURCE MAP: Articles in Print Periodicals

1. **Author.** List the last name first. End with a period. For variations, see models 2–5.

2. **Article title.** Put the title and any subtitle in quotation marks; capitalize all major words. Place a period inside the closing quotation mark.

3. **Periodical title.** Italicize the title; capitalize all major words. End with a comma.

4. **Volume and issue/Date of publication.** Give the abbreviation *vol.* and the volume number, and the abbreviation *no.* and the issue number, if the periodical provides them. List day (if given), month (abbreviated except for May, June, and July), and year, or season and year, of publication. Put commas after the volume, issue, and date.

5. **Page numbers.** Give the abbreviation *p.* (for "page") or *pp.* (for "pages") and the inclusive page numbers. If the article skips pages, put the first page number and a plus sign. End with a period.

A citation for the article on p. 241 would look like this:

Quart, Alissa. "Lost Media, Found Media: Snapshots from the Future of Writing." *Columbia Journalism Review*, May/June 2008, pp. 30-34.

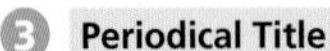

3 Periodical Title

COLUMBIA JOURNALISM REVIEW

May / June 2008 • cjr.org

4 Date of Publication

May/June 2008

The Fu

Wri

Nonfiction's

ALISSA QUA

Kindle isn't

EZRA KLEIN

UNDER TH

A reporter

that got hi

CAMERON M

LOVE THY

The religio

TIM TOWNS

Lost Media, Found Media

2 Article Title

Snapshots from the future of writing

BY ALISSA QUART

1 Author

ALISSA QUART

If there were an ashram for people who worship contemplative long-form journalism, it would be the Nieman Conference on Narrative Journalism. This March, at the Sheraton Boston Hotel, hundreds of journalists, authors, students, and aspirants came for the weekend event. Seated on metal chairs in large conference rooms, we learned about muscular storytelling (the Q-shaped narrative structure—who knew?). We sipped cups of coffee and ate bagels and heard about reporting history through letters and public documents and how to evoke empathy for our subjects, particularly our most marginal ones. As we listened to reporters discussing great feats—exposing Walter Reed's fetid living quarters for wounded soldiers, for instance—we also renewed our pride in our profession. In short, the conference exemplified the best of the older media models, the ones that have so recently fallen into economic turmoil.

Yet even at the weekend's strongest lectures on interview … we couldn't ignore the … ll knew as writers that … ssing require months … d, and that we were all … oney to do that. It was always hard for nonfiction writers, but something seems to have changed. For those of us who believed in the value of the journalism and literary nonfiction of the past, we had become like the people at the ashram after the guru has died.

5 Page Numbers

30–34

Right now, journalism is more or less divided into two camps, which I will call Lost Media and Found Media. I went to the Nieman conference partially because I wanted to see how the forces creating this new division are affecting and afflicting the Lost Media world that I love best, not on the institutional level, but for reporters and writers … des … spapers and magazines that are currently struggling with layoffs, speedups, hiring freezes, buyouts, the death or shrinkage of … ns, lim- its … rk, the er… he gen- er… bition. It … peting … competitors willing to write and publish online for free, the fade-out of established journalistic career paths, and, perhaps most crucially, a muddled sense of the meritorious, as blogs level and scramble the value and status of print publications, and of professional writers. The glamour and influence once associated with a magazine elite seem to have faded, becoming a sort of pastiche of winsome articles about yearning and boxers and dinners at Elaine's.

Found Media-ites, meanwhile, are the bloggers, the contributors to Huffington Post-type sites that aggregate blogs, as well as other work that somebody else paid for, and the new nonprofits and pay-per-article schemes that aim to save journalism from 20 percent profit-margin demands. Although these elements are often disparate, together they compose the new media landscape. In economic terms, I mean all the outlets for nonfiction writing that seem to be thriving in the new era or striving to fill niches that Lost Media is giving up in a new order. Stylistically, Found Media tends to feel spontaneous, almost accidental. It's a domain dominated by the young, where writers get points not for following traditions or burnishing them but for amateur and hybrid vigor, for creating their own venues and their own genres. It is about public expression and community—not quite John Dewey's Great Community, which the critic Eric Alterman alluded to in a recent *New Yorker* article on newspapers, but rather a fractured form of Dewey's ideal: call it Great Communities.

To be a Found Media journalist or pundit, one need not be elite, expert, or trained; one must simply produce punchy intellectual property that is in conversation with groups of

30 MAY/JUNE 2008

Illustration by Tomer Hanuka

 Checklist

Citing Works from Websites

When citing online sources, give as many of the following elements as you can find:

1. **Author.** Provide the author of the work, if you can find one. End with a period.
2. **Title.** Give the title of the work you are citing, ending with a period. If the work is part of a larger container (such as a video on YouTube), put the title in quotation marks.
3. **Website title.** If the title you identified is not the name of the website itself, list the website title, in italics, followed by a comma.
4. **Publisher or sponsor.** If the site's publisher or sponsor is different from the title of the site, identify the publisher or sponsor, followed by a comma. If the name is very similar to the site title, omit the publisher.
5. **Date of publication.** Give the date of publication or latest update, followed by a comma.
6. **Permalink or URL.** Give a permalink (if you can find one) or URL. End with a period.
7. **Date of access.** If the work does not include any date, add "Accessed" and the day, month (abbreviated, except for May, June, and July), and year you accessed the source. End with a period. If you provided a date before the URL, omit the access date.

36. ARTICLE FROM A JOURNAL ON THE WEB. Begin an entry for an online journal article as you would one for a print journal article (see model 28). End with the online location (permalink, DOI, or URL) and a period.

Clark, Msia Kibona. "Hip Hop as Social Commentary in Accra and Dar es Salaam." *African Studies Quarterly*, vol. 13, no. 3, Summer 2012, asq.africa.ufl.edu/files/Clark-V131s3.pdf.

37. ARTICLE IN A MAGAZINE ON THE WEB. List the author, article title, and name of the magazine. Then identify the date of publication, and provide a permalink or DOI, if one is available, or a URL.

Landhuis, Esther. "Is Dementia Risk Falling?" *Scientific American*, 25 Jan. 2016, www.scientificamerican.com/article/is-dementia-risk-falling/.

38. ARTICLE IN A NEWSPAPER ON THE WEB. After the name of the newspaper, give the publication date and the permalink (if you can find one) or URL.

Shyong, Frank. "Sriracha Showdown Intensifies as Irwindale Declares Public Nuisance." *Los Angeles Times*, 10 Apr. 2014, articles.latimes.com/2014/apr/10/local/la-me-in-sriracha-irwindale-public-nuisance-20140410.

39. DIGITAL BOOK. Provide information as for a print book (see models 6–27); then give the digital container title and any other relevant information, including the location.

Euripides. *The Trojan Women*. Translated by Gilbert Murray, Oxford UP, 1915. *Internet Sacred Text Archive*, 2011, www.sacred-texts.com/cla/eurip/trok_w.htm.

If you read the book on an e-reader such as a Kindle or Nook, specify the type of reader file you used.

Schaap, Rosie. *Drinking with Men: A Memoir*. Riverhead / Penguin, 2013. Kindle.

40. ONLINE POEM. Include the poet's name, the title of the poem, and the print publication information (if any) for the first container. For the second container, give the title, the date, and the DOI, permalink, or URL.

Geisel, Theodor. "Too Many Daves." *The Sneetches and Other Stories*, Random House, 1961. *Poetry Foundation*, 2015, www.poetryfoundation.org/poem/171612.

MLA SOURCE MAP: Articles from Databases

Library subscriptions—such as EBSCOhost and Academic Search Premier—provide access to huge databases of articles.

1. **Author.** List the last name first. End with a period. For variations, see models 2–5.
2. **Article title.** Enclose the title and any subtitle in quotation marks. End with a period.
3. **Periodical title.** Italicize it. Follow it with a comma.
4. **Volume and issue/Date of publication.** List the volume and issue number, if any, separated by commas. Use the abbreviations *vol.* and *no*. Then, add the date of publication, including the day (if given), month, and year, in that order. Last, add a comma.
5. **Page numbers.** Give the inclusive page numbers, using the abbreviations *p.* or *pp.* End with a period.
6. **Database name.** Italicize the name of the database. End with a period.
7. **Location.** Give the DOI or other permalink, if available. If not, give the URL for the home page of the database.

A citation for the article on p. 245 would look like this:

Arnett, Robert P. "*Casino Royale* and Franchise Remix: James Bond as Superhero." *Film Criticism*, vol. 33, no. 3, Spring 2009, pp. 1-16. *Academic Search Premier*, www.ebscohost.com/academic/academic-search-premier.

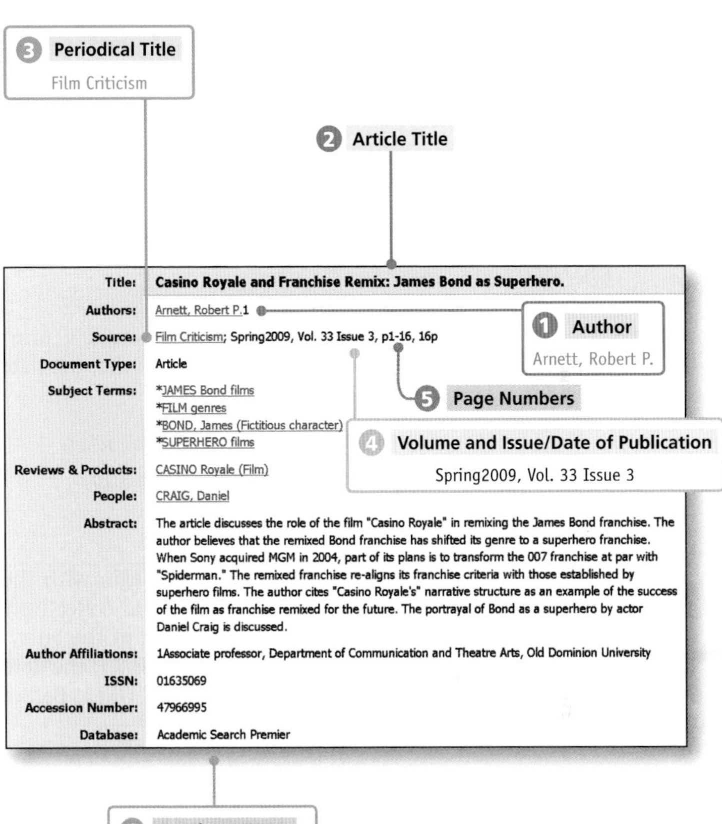

3 Periodical Title
Film Criticism
2 Article Title
Title: Casino Royale and Franchise Remix: James Bond as Superhero.
Authors: Arnett, Robert P.1
Source: Film Criticism; Spring2009, Vol. 33 Issue 3, p1-16, 16p
Document Type: Article
Subject Terms: *JAMES Bond films
*FILM genres
*BOND, James (Fictitious character)
*SUPERHERO films
Reviews & Products: CASINO Royale (Film)
People: CRAIG, Daniel
Abstract: The article discusses the role of the film "Casino Royale" in remixing the James Bond franchise. The author believes that the remixed Bond franchise has shifted its genre to a superhero franchise. When Sony acquired MGM in 2004, part of its plans is to transform the 007 franchise at par with "Spiderman." The remixed franchise re-aligns its franchise criteria with those established by superhero films. The author cites "Casino Royale's" narrative structure as an example of the success of the film as franchise remixed for the future. The portrayal of Bond as a superhero by actor Daniel Craig is discussed.
Author Affiliations: 1Associate professor, Department of Communication and Theatre Arts, Old Dominion University
ISSN: 01635069
Accession Number: 47966995
Database: Academic Search Premier
1 Author
Arnett, Robert P.
5 Page Numbers
4 Volume and Issue/Date of Publication
Spring2009, Vol. 33 Issue 3
6 Database Name
Academic Search Premier

41. ONLINE EDITORIAL OR LETTER TO THE EDITOR. Include the author's name (if given) and the title (if any). Follow the appropriate model for the type of source you are using. (Check the directory on pp. 227–28.) End with the label *Editorial* or *Letter*.

"Migrant Children Deserve a Voice in Court." *The New York Times*, 8 Mar. 2016, nyti.ms/1L08bKK. Editorial.

Starr, Evva. "Local Reporting Thrives in High Schools." *The Washington Post*, 4 Apr. 2014, wpo.st/7hmJ1. Letter.

42. ONLINE REVIEW. Cite an online review as you would a print review (see model 33). End with the name of the website, the date of publication, and the URL or permalink.

O'Hehir, Andrew. "Aronofsky's Deranged Biblical Action Flick." *Salon*, 27 May 2014, www.salon.com/2014/03/27/noah_aronofskys_deranged_biblical_action_flick/.

43. ENTRY IN AN ONLINE REFERENCE WORK OR WIKI. Begin with the title unless the author is named. (A wiki, which is collectively edited, will not include an author.) Include the title of the entry; the name of the work, italicized; the sponsor or publisher; the date of the latest update; and the location (permalink or URL). Before using a wiki as a source, check with your instructor.

Cartwright, Mark. "Apollo." *Ancient History Encyclopedia*, 18 May 2012, www.ancient.eu/apollo/.

"Gunpowder Plot." *Wikipedia*, 4 Mar. 2016, en.wikipedia.org/wiki/Gunpowder_Plot.

44. SHORT WORK FROM A WEBSITE. For basic information for citing a work on a website that is not part of a regularly published journal, magazine, or newspaper, see the source map on pp. 248–49. Treat a short work from a website as you would an online reference entry (see model 43). Include all of the following elements that are available: the author; the title of the document, in quotation marks; the name of the website, italicized; the name of the publisher or sponsor (if the name is different from the name of the site); the date of the publication; and the location. If the site gives no date, end with *Accessed* and your date of access.

Bali, Karan. "Kishore Kumar." *Upperstall.com,* upperstall.com/profile/kishore-kumar/. Accessed 2 Mar. 2016.

"Our Mission." *Trees for Life International,* 2011, www.treesforlife.org/our-work/our-mission.

45. ENTIRE WEBSITE. Follow the guidelines for a work from the web, beginning with the name of the author or editor (if any), followed by the title of the website, italicized; the name of the sponsor or publisher (if different from the name of the site); the date of publication or last update; and the location.

Glazier, Loss Pequeño, director. *Electronic Poetry Center.* State U of New York Buffalo, 1994-2016, epc.buffalo.edu/.

Weather.com. Weather Channel Interactive, 1995-2016, weather.com/.

For a personal website, include the name of the person who created the site as you would with a site's author or editor. If the site is undated, end with your date of access.

Enright, Mike. *Menright.com*. www.menright.com. Accessed 30 Mar. 2016.

46. BLOG. For an entire blog, give the author's name; the title of the blog, italicized; the date; and the URL. If the site is undated, end with your access date.

Levy, Carla Miriam. *Filmi Geek.* 2006-2015, www.filmigeek.com.

Little Green Footballs. littlegreenfootballs.com. Accessed 4 Mar. 2016.

Note: To cite a blogger who writes under a pseudonym, begin with the pseudonym and then put the writer's real name (if you know it) in parentheses.

Atrios (Duncan Black). *Eschaton.* www.eschatonblog.com. Accessed 8 Mar. 2016.

MLA SOURCE MAP: Works from Websites

You may need to browse other parts of a site to find some of the following elements, and some sites may omit elements. Uncover as much information as you can.

1. **Author.** List the last name first. End with a period. If no author is given, begin with the title. For variations, see models 2–5.
2. **Title of work.** Enclose the title and any subtitle of the work in quotation marks.
3. **Title of website.** Give the title of the entire website, italicized. Follow it with a comma.
4. **Publisher or sponsor.** Look for the sponsor's name at the bottom of the home page. If the sponsor's name is roughly the same as the site title, omit the sponsor. Follow it with a comma.
5. **Date of publication or latest update.** Give the most recent date, followed by a period.
6. **Location.** Give the permalink, if you can find one, or the site's URL, followed by a period.
7. **Date of access.** If the site is undated, end with *Accessed* and the date.

A citation for the work on p. 249 would look like this:

Tønnesson, Øyvind. "Mahatma Gandhi, the Missing Laureate." *Nobelprize.org*, 2015, www.nobelprize.org/nobel_prizes/themes/peace/gandhi/.

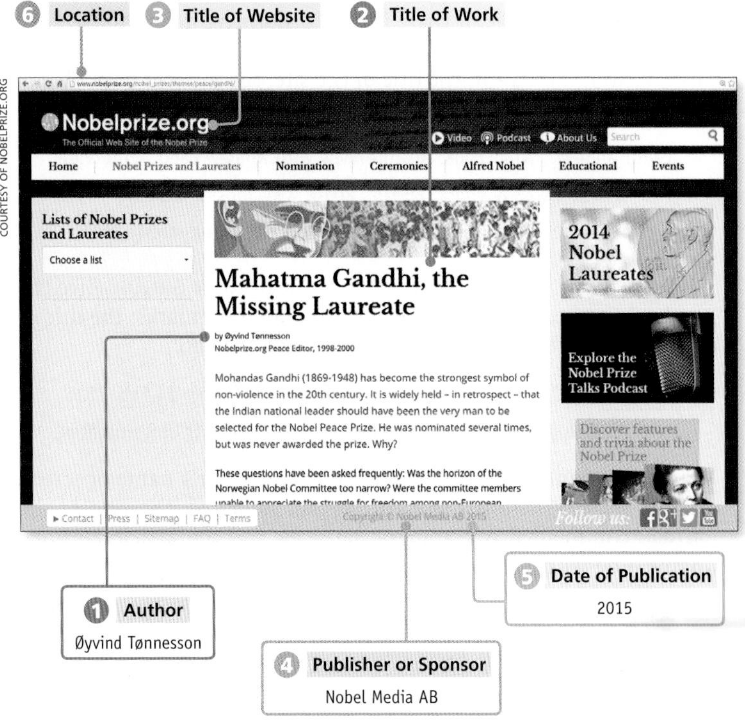

6 Location
3 Title of Website
2 Title of Work
Nobelprize.org
The Official Web Site of the Nobel Prize
Video
Podcast
About Us
Home
Nobel Prizes and Laureates
Nomination
Ceremonies
Alfred Nobel
Educational
Events
Lists of Nobel Prizes and Laureates
Choose a list
Mahatma Gandhi, the Missing Laureate
by Øyvind Tønnesson
Nobelprize.org Peace Editor, 1998-2000
Mohandas Gandhi (1869-1948) has become the strongest symbol of non-violence in the 20th century. It is widely held – in retrospect – that the Indian national leader should have been the very man to be selected for the Nobel Peace Prize. He was nominated several times, but was never awarded the prize. Why?
These questions have been asked frequently: Was the horizon of the Norwegian Nobel Committee too narrow? Were the committee members
2014 Nobel Laureates
Explore the Nobel Prize Talks Podcast
Discover features and trivia about the Nobel Prize
Contact | Press | Sitemap | FAQ | Terms
Follow us:
1 Author
Øyvind Tønnesson
4 Publisher or Sponsor
Nobel Media AB
5 Date of Publication
2015

47. ONLINE INTERVIEW. Start with the name of the person interviewed. Give the title, if there is one. If not, give a descriptive label such as *Interview*, neither italicized nor in quotation marks, and the interviewer, if relevant; the title of the site; the sponsor or publisher (if there is one); the date of publication; and the URL.

> Ladd, Andrew. "What Ends: An Interview with Andrew Ladd." Interview by Jill. *Looks & Books*, 25 Feb. 2014, www.looksandbooks.com/2014/02/25/what-ends-an-interview-with-andrew-ladd/.

48. POST OR COMMENT ON A BLOG OR DISCUSSION GROUP. Give the author's name; the title of the post, in quotation marks; the title of the site, italicized; the date of the post; and the URL.

> Edroso, Roy. "Going Down with the Flagship." *Alicublog*, 24 Feb. 2016, alicublog.blogspot.com/2016/02/going-down-with-flagship.html.

For a comment on an online post, give the writer's name or screen name; a label such as *Comment on*, not italicized; the title of the article commented on; and the label *by* and the article author's name. End with the citation information for the type of article.

> JennOfArk. Comment on "Going Down with the Flagship," by Roy Edroso. *Alicublog*, 24 Feb. 2016, alicublog.blogspot.com/2016/02/going-down-with-flagship.html#disqus_thread.

49. POSTING ON A SOCIAL NETWORKING SITE. To cite a posting on Facebook, Instagram, or another social networking site, include the writer's name; up to 140 characters of the posting, in quotation marks (or a description such as *Photograph*, not italicized and not in quotation marks, if there's no text); the name of the site, italicized; the date of the post; and the location of the post (URL).

> Cannon, Kevin. "Portrait of Norris Hall in #Savannah, GA—home (for a few months, anyway) of #SCAD's sequential art department." *Instagram*, Mar. 2014, www.instagram.com/p/lgmqk4i6DC/.

50. EMAIL OR MESSAGE. Include the writer's name; the subject line, in quotation marks, if one is provided, or a descriptive message such as *Text message*; *Received by* (not italicized or in quotation marks) followed by the recipient's name; and then the date of the message.

Carbone, Nick. "Screen vs. Print Reading." Received by Karita dos Santos, 17 Apr. 2016.

51. TWEET. Begin with the writer's Twitter handle, and put the real name, if known, in parentheses. Include the entire tweet, in quotation marks. Give the site name in italics (*Twitter*), the date and time of the message, and the tweet's URL.

@Lunsfordhandbks (Andrea A. Lunsford). "Technology & social media have changed the way we write. That doesn't mean literacy has declined https://community.macmillan.com/groups/macmillan-news/blog/2016/02/24/the-literacy-revolution... @MacmillanLearn." *Twitter*, 24 Feb. 2016, 10:17 a.m., twitter.com/LunsfordHandbks/status/702512638937460736.

Visual, audio, multimedia, and live sources

52. FILM (THEATRICAL, DVD, OR OTHER FORMAT). If you cite a particular person's work, start with that name. If not, start with the title of the film; then name the director, distributor, and year of release. Other contributors, such as writers or performers, may follow the director. If you cite a feature from a disc, treat the film as the first container and the disc as the second container.

Bale, Christian, performer. *The Big Short*. Directed by Adam McKay, Paramount Pictures, 2015.

Lasseter, John. Introduction. *Spirited Away*, directed by Hayao Miyazaki, 2001. Walt Disney Video, 2003, disc 1.

53. ONLINE VIDEO. Cite an online video as you would a short work from a website (see model 44).

Weber, Jan. "As We Sow, Part 1: Where Are the Farmers?" *YouTube*, 15 Mar. 2008, www.youtube.com/watch?v=_cdcDpMf6qE.

54. TELEVISION (BROADCAST OR ON THE WEB). For a show broadcast on television, begin with the title of the program, italicized (for an entire series), or the title of the episode, in quotation marks. Then list important contributors (writer, director, actor); season and episode number (for a specific episode); the network; the local station and city, if the show appeared on a local channel; and the broadcast date(s).

Breaking Bad. Created by Vince Gilligan, performances by Bryan Cranston, Aaron Paul, and Anna Gunn, AMC, 2008-2013.

"Time Zones." *Mad Men*, written by Matthew Weiner, directed by Scott Hornbacher, season 7, episode 1, AMC, 13 Apr. 2014.

For a show accessed on a network website, include the URL after the date of posting.

"Time Zones." *Mad Men*, written by Matthew Weiner, directed by Scott Hornbacher, season 7, episode 1, AMC, 13 Apr. 2014, www.amc.com/shows/mad-men/season-7/episode-01-time-zones.

55. RADIO (BROADCAST OR ON THE WEB). If you are citing a particular episode or segment, cite a radio broadcast as you would a television episode (see model 54).

"Tarred and Feathered." *This American Life*, narrated by Ira Glass, WNYC, 11 Apr. 2013.

For a show or segment accessed on the web, include the website title and URL after the date of posting.

"Obama's Failures Have Made Millennials Give Up Hope." *The Rush Limbaugh Show*, narrated by Rush Limbaugh, Premiere Radio Networks, 14 Apr. 2014, RushLimbaugh.com, www.rushlimbaugh.com/daily/2014/04/14/obama_s_failures_have_made_millennials_give_up_hope.

56. TELEVISION OR RADIO INTERVIEW. List the person interviewed and then the title, if any. If the interview has no title, use the label *Interview* and the name of the interviewer, if relevant. Then identify the source. End with information about the program and the interview date(s). (For an online interview, see model 47.)

Russell, David O. Interview by Terry Gross. *Fresh Air*, WNYC, 20 Feb. 2014.

57. PERSONAL INTERVIEW. List the person who was interviewed; the label *Telephone interview*, *Personal interview*, or *E-mail interview*; and the date the interview took place.

Freedman, Sasha. Personal interview. 10 Nov. 2015.

58. SOUND RECORDING. List the name of the person or group you wish to emphasize (such as the composer, conductor, or band); the title of the recording or composition; the artist, if appropriate; the manufacturer; and the year of issue. If you are citing a particular song or selection, include its title, in quotation marks.

Bach, Johann Sebastian. *Bach: Violin Concertos*. Performances by Itzhak Perlman and Pinchas Zukerman, English Chamber Orchestra, EMI, 2002.

Sonic Youth. "Incinerate." *Rather Ripped*, Geffen, 2006.

Note: If you are citing instrumental music that is identified only by form, number, and key, do not underline, italicize, or enclose it in quotation marks.

Grieg, Edvard. Concerto in A minor, op. 16. Conducted by Eugene Ormandy, Philadelphia Orchestra, RCA, 1989.

59. MUSICAL COMPOSITION. When you are not citing a specific published version, first give the composer's name, followed by the title.

Mozart, Wolfgang Amadeus. *Don Giovanni*, K527.

Mozart, Wolfgang Amadeus. Symphony no. 41 in C major, K551.

Note: Cite a published score as you would a book. If you include the date that the composition was written, do so immediately after the title.

Schoenberg, Arnold. *Chamber Symphony No. 1 for 15 Solo Instruments, Op. 9*. 1906. Dover, 2002.

60. VIDEO GAME. Start with the developer or author (if any). After the title, give the distributor and the date of publication.

Harmonix. *Rock Band Blitz*. MTV Games, 2012.

61. LECTURE OR SPEECH. For a live lecture or speech, list the speaker; the title (if any), in quotation marks; the sponsoring institution or group; the place; and the date. Add the label *Lecture* or *Speech* after the date if readers will not otherwise be able to identify the work.

> Eugenides, Jeffrey. Portland Arts and Lectures. Arlene Schnitzer Concert Hall, Portland, OR, 30 Sept. 2003.

For a lecture or speech on the web, cite as you would a short work from a website (see model 44).

> Burden, Amanda. "How Public Spaces Make Cities Work." *TED.com*, Mar. 2014, www.ted.com/talks/amanda_burden_how_public_spaces_make_cities_work.

62. LIVE PERFORMANCE. List the title, the appropriate names (such as the writer or performer), the place, and the date.

> *The Sea Ranch Songs.* By Aleksandra Vrebalov, performed by the Kronos Quartet, White Barn, The Sea Ranch, CA, 23 May 2015.

63. DIGITAL FILE OR PODCAST. A citation for a downloadable digital file—one that exists independently, not only on a website—begins with citation information required for the type of source (a photograph or sound recording, for example).

> "Return to the Giant Pool of Money." *This American Life*, narrated by Ira Glass, NPR, 25 Sept. 2009, www.thisamericanlife.org/radio-archives/episode/390/Return-To-The-Giant-Pool-of-Money.

Cite a podcast that you view or listen to online as you would a short work from a website (see model 44).

> Fogarty, Mignon. "Begs the Question: Update." *QuickandDirtyTips.com*, Macmillan, 6 Mar. 2014, www.quickanddirtytips.com/education/grammar/begs-the-question-update.

64. WORK OF ART OR PHOTOGRAPH. List the artist's or photographer's name; the work's title, italicized; and the date of composition. Then cite the name of the museum or other location and the city. To cite a reproduction in a book, add the publication information. To cite online artwork, add the title of the database or website, italicized, and the URL or permalink.

Bronzino, Agnolo. *Lodovico Capponi*. 1550-55, Frick Collection, New York.

General William Palmer in Old Age. 1810, National Army Museum, London. *White Mughals: Love and Betrayal in Eighteenth-Century India*, by William Dalrymple, Penguin Books, 2002, p. 270.

Hassam, Childe. *Isles of Shoals*, 1899, Minneapolis Institute of Arts, collections.artsmia.org/art/45/isles-of-shoals-childe-hassam.

65. MAP OR CHART. Cite a map or chart as you would a book or a short work within a longer work. For an online source, include the location. End with the label *Map* or *Chart* if needed for clarity.

"Australia." *Perry-Castaneda Library Map Collection*, U of Texas, 1999, www .lib.utexas.edu.maps.australia_pol99.jpg.

California. Rand McNally, 2002. Map.

66. CARTOON OR COMIC STRIP. List the artist's name; the title of the cartoon or comic strip, in quotation marks; and the usual publication information for a print periodical (see models 28–34) or a short work from a website (model 44). You may end with a label (*Cartoon* or *Comic strip*) for clarity.

Flake, Emily. *The New Yorker*, 13 Apr. 2015, p. 66. Cartoon.

Munroe, Randall. "Heartbleed Explanation." *xkcd.com*, xkcd.com/1354/. Comic strip.

67. ADVERTISEMENT. Include the label *Advertisement* at the end of the entry.

Ameritrade. *Wired*, Jan. 2014, p. 47. Advertisement.

Lufthansa. *The New York Times*, 16 Apr. 2014, www.nytimes.com. Advertisement.

Other sources (including digital versions)

If an online version is not shown in this section, use the appropriate model for the source and then end with a DOI, permalink, or URL.

68. REPORT OR PAMPHLET. Follow the guidelines for a print book (models 6–27) or a digital book (model 39).

Rainie, Lee, and Maeve Duggan. *Privacy and Information Sharing*. Pew Research Center, 14 Jan. 2016, www.pewinternet.org/files/2016/01/PI_2016.01.14_Privacy-and-Info-Sharing_FINAL.pdf.

69. GOVERNMENT PUBLICATION. Begin with the author, if identified. Otherwise, start with the name of the government, followed by the agency. For congressional documents, cite the number, session, and house of Congress; the type (*Report*, *Resolution*, *Document*); and the number. End with the publication information. For online versions, follow the models for a short work from a website (model 44), an entire website (model 45), or a digital file (model 63).

Gregg, Judd. *Report to Accompany the Genetic Information Act of 2003*. US 108th Congress, 1st session, Senate Report 108-22, Government Printing Office, 2003.

United States, Department of Health and Human Services, National Institutes of Health. *Keep the Beat Recipes: Deliciously Healthy Dinners*. Oct. 2009, healthyeating.nhlbi.nih.gov/pdfs/Dinners_Cookbook_508-compliant.pdf.

70. PUBLISHED PROCEEDINGS OF A CONFERENCE. Cite the proceedings as you would a book.

Cleary, John, and Gary Gurtler, editors. *Proceedings of the Boston Area Colloquium in Ancient Philosophy 2002*. Brill Academic Publishers, 2003.

71. DISSERTATION. Enclose the title in quotation marks. Add the label *Dissertation*, the school, and the year the work was accepted.

Thompson, Brian. "I'm Better Than You and I Can Prove It: Games, Expertise, and the Culture of Competition." Dissertation, Stanford U, 2015.

Note: Cite a published dissertation as a book, adding the identification *Dissertation* and the university after the title.

72. DISSERTATION ABSTRACT. Cite the abstract as you would an unpublished dissertation (model 71). For an abstract that uses *Dissertation Abstracts International*, include the volume, year, and page number.

Huang-Tiller, Gillian C. "The Power of the Meta-Genre: Cultural, Sexual, and Racial Politics of the American Modernist Sonnet." Dissertation, U of Notre Dame, 2000. Abstract. *Dissertation Abstracts International*, vol. 61, 2000, p. 1401.

Moore, Courtney L. "Stress and Oppression: Identifying Possible Protective Factors for African American Men." Dissertation, Chicago School of Professional Psychology, 2016. Abstract. *ProQuest Dissertations and Theses*, search.proquest.com/docview/1707351557.

73. UNPUBLISHED LETTER. Cite a published letter as a work in an anthology (see model 10). If the letter is unpublished, follow this form:

Anzaldúa, Gloria. Letter to the author. 10 Sept. 2002.

74. MANUSCRIPT OR OTHER UNPUBLISHED WORK. List the author's name; the title (if any) or a description of the material; any identifying numbers; and the name of the library or research institution housing the material, if applicable.

Woolf, Virginia. "The Searchlight." Papers of Virginia Woolf, 1902-1956, Series III, Box 4, Item 184, Smith College, Northampton.

75. LEGAL SOURCE. To cite a court case, give the names of the first plaintiff and defendant, the case number, the name of the court, and the date of the decision. To cite an act, give the name of the act followed by its Public Law (*Pub. L.*) number, its Statutes at Large (*Stat.*) cataloging number, and the date the act was enacted.

Citizens United vs. FEC. 558 US 310. Supreme Court of the US. 2010. Legal Information Institute, Cornell U Law School, www.law.cornell.edu/supct/pdf/08-205P.ZS.

Museum and Library Services Act of 2003. Pub. L. 108-81. Stat. 117.991. 25 Sept. 2003.

Note: You do not need an entry on the list of works cited when you cite articles of the U.S. Constitution and laws in the U.S. Code.

45f A sample student research project, MLA style

A brief research essay by David Craig appears on the following pages. David followed the MLA guidelines described in this chapter.

Documentation: MLA Style > Student Writing

STUDENT WRITING

1/2"

Craig 1

1"

David Craig

Professor Turkman

English 219

18 December 2014

Name, instructor, course, and date aligned at left

Messaging: The Language of Youth Literacy

Title centered

The English language is under attack. At least, that is what many people seem to believe. From concerned parents to local librarians, everyone seems to have a negative comment on the state of youth literacy today. They fear that the current generation of grade school students will graduate with an extremely low level of literacy, and they point out that although language education hasn't changed, kids are having more trouble reading and writing than in the past. When asked about the cause of this situation, many adults pin the blame on technologies such as texting and instant messaging, arguing that electronic shortcuts create and compound undesirable reading and writing habits and discourage students from learning conventionally correct ways to use language. But although the arguments against messaging are passionate, evidence suggests that they may not hold up.

Opens with attention-getting statement

Background on the problem of youth literacy

Explicit thesis statement concludes introductory paragraph

The disagreements about messaging shortcuts are profound, even among academics. John Briggs, an English professor at the University of California, Riverside, says, "Americans have always been informal, but now the informality of precollege culture is so ubiquitous that many students have no practice in using language in any formal setting at all" (qtd. in McCarroll). Such objections are not new; Sven Birkerts of Mount Holyoke College argued in 1999 that "[students] read more casually. They strip-mine what they read" online and consequently produce "quickly generated, casual prose" (qtd. in Leibowitz A67). However, academics are also among the defenders of texting and instant messaging (IM), with

Indirect quotation uses "qtd. in" and name of web source on list of works cited

Marginal annotations indicate effective choices or MLA-style formatting.

STUDENT WRITING

Craig 2

Writer's last name and page number at upper right corner of every page

some suggesting that messaging may be a beneficial force in the development of youth literacy because it promotes regular contact with words and the use of a written medium for communication.

Definition and example of messaging

Texting and instant messaging allow two individuals who are separated by any distance to engage in real-time, written communication. Although such communication relies on the written word, many messagers disregard standard writing conventions. For example, here is a snippet from an IM conversation between two teenage girls:[1]

> Teen One: sorry im talkinto like 10 ppl at a time
> Teen Two: u izzyful person
> Teen Two: kwel
> Teen One: hey i g2g

As this brief conversation shows, participants must use words to communicate via texting and messaging, but their words do not have to be in standard English.

Writer considers argument that youth literacy is in decline

Figure explained in text and cited in parenthetical reference

The issue of youth literacy does demand attention because standardized test scores for language assessments, such as the verbal and writing sections of the College Board's SAT, have declined in recent years. This trend is illustrated in a chart distributed by the College Board as part of its 2011 analysis of aggregate SAT data (see Fig. 1).

Discussion of Figure 1

The trend lines illustrate a significant pattern that may lead to the conclusion that youth literacy is on the decline. These lines display the ten-year paths (from 2001 to 2011) of reading and writing scores, respectively. Within this period, the average verbal score dropped a few points — and appears to be headed toward a further decline in the future.

Explanatory note adds information not found in list of works cited

1. This transcript of an IM conversation was collected on 20 Nov. 2014. The teenagers' names are concealed to protect privacy.

Craig 3

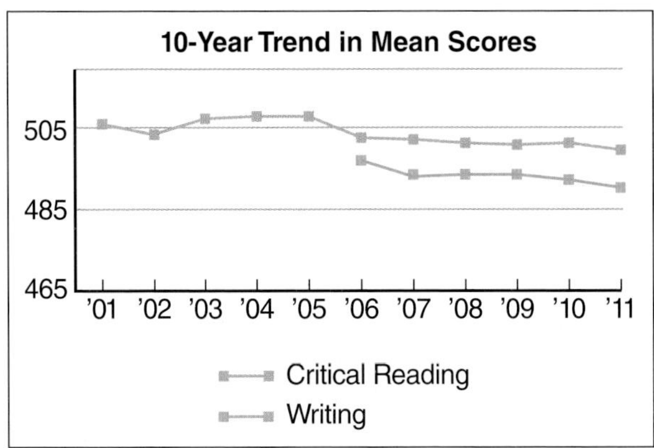

Fig. 1. Ten-year trend in mean SAT reading and writing scores (2001-2011). Data source: "2011 SAT Trends."

Figure labeled, titled, and credited to source; inserted at appropriate point in text

Based on the preceding statistics, parents and educators appear to be right about the decline in youth literacy. And this trend coincides with another phenomenon: digital communication is rising among the young. According to the Pew Internet & American Life Project, 85 percent of those aged twelve to seventeen at least occasionally write text messages, instant messages, or comments on social networking sites (Lenhart et al.). In 2001, the most conservative estimate based on Pew numbers showed that American youths spent, at a minimum, nearly three million hours per day on instant messaging services (Lenhart and Lewis 20). These numbers are now exploding thanks to texting, which was "the dominant daily mode of communication" for teens in 2012 (Lenhart), and messaging on popular social networking sites such as Facebook and Tumblr.

Writer accepts part of critics' argument; transition to next point

For a web source with no page numbers, only author names appear in parentheses

In the interest of establishing the existence of a messaging language, I analyzed 11,341 lines of text from IM conversations

Writer's field research described

STUDENT WRITING

Craig 4

between youths in my target demographic: U.S. residents aged twelve to seventeen. Young messagers voluntarily sent me chat logs, but they were unaware of the exact nature of my research. Once all of the logs had been gathered, I went through them, recording the number of times messaging language was used in place of conventional words and phrases. Then I generated graphs to display how often these replacements were used.

Findings of field research presented

During the course of my study, I identified four types of messaging language: phonetic replacements, acronyms, abbreviations, and inanities. An example of phonetic replacement is using *ur* for *you are*. Another popular type of messaging language is the acronym; for a majority of the people in my study, the most common acronym was *lol*, a construction that means *laughing out loud*. Abbreviations are also common in messaging, but I discovered that typical IM abbreviations, such as *etc.*, are not new to the English language. Finally, I found a class of words that I call "inanities." These words include completely new words or expressions, combinations of several slang categories, or simply nonsensical variations of other words. My favorite from this category is *lolz*, an inanity that translates directly to *lol* yet includes a terminating *z* for no obvious reason.

Figure introduced and explained

In the chat transcripts that I analyzed, the best display of typical messaging lingo came from the conversations between two thirteen-year-old Texan girls, who are avid IM users. Figure 2 is a graph showing how often they used certain phonetic replacements and abbreviations. On the *y*-axis, frequency of replacement is plotted, a calculation that compares the number of times a word or phrase is used in messaging language with the total number of times that it is communicated in any form. On the *x*-axis, specific messaging words and phrases are listed.

STUDENT WRITING

Craig 5

My research shows that the Texan girls use the first ten phonetic replacements or abbreviations at least 50 percent of the time in their normal messaging writing. For example, every time one of them writes *see*, there is a parallel time when *c* is used in its place. In light of this finding, it appears that the popular messaging culture contains at least some elements of its own language. It also seems that much of this language is new: no formal dictionary yet identifies the most common messaging words and phrases. Only in the heyday of the telegraph or on the rolls of a stenographer would you find a similar situation, but these "languages" were never a popular medium of youth communication. Texting and instant messaging, however, are very popular among young people and continue to generate attention and debate in academic circles.

Discussion of findings presented in Figure 2

My research shows that messaging is certainly widespread, and it does seem to have its own particular vocabulary, yet these two factors alone do not mean it has a damaging influence on youth literacy. As noted earlier, however, some people claim that

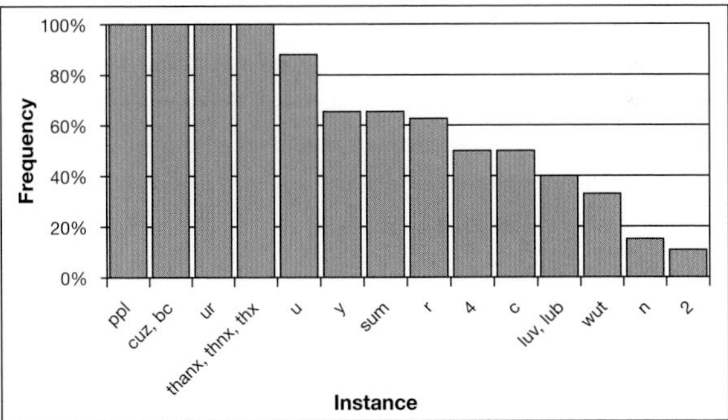

Fig. 2. Usage of phonetic replacements and abbreviations in messaging.

Figure labeled and titled

STUDENT WRITING

Craig 6

Writer returns to opposition argument

For author of web source named in signal phrase, no parenthetical citation needed

Transition to support of thesis and refutation of critics

Linguistic authority cited in support of thesis

Author of print source named in signal phrase, so parenthetical citation includes only page number

the new technology is a threat to the English language. In an article provocatively titled "Texting Makes U Stupid," historian Niall Ferguson argues, "The good news is that today's teenagers are avid readers and prolific writers. The bad news is that what they are reading and writing are text messages." He goes on to accuse texting of causing the United States to "[fall] behind more literate societies."

The critics of messaging are numerous. But if we look to the field of linguistics, a central concept — metalinguistics — challenges these criticisms and leads to a more reasonable conclusion — that messaging has no negative impact on a student's development of or proficiency with traditional literacy.

Scholars of metalinguistics offer support for the claim that messaging is not damaging to those who use it. As noted earlier, one of the most prominent components of messaging language is phonetic replacement, in which a word such as *everyone* becomes *every1*. This type of wordplay has a special importance in the development of an advanced literacy, and for good reason. According to David Crystal, an internationally recognized scholar of linguistics at the University of Wales, as young children develop and learn how words string together to express ideas, they go through many phases of language play. The singsong rhymes and nonsensical chants of preschoolers are vital to learning language, and a healthy appetite for wordplay leads to a better command of language later in life (182).

As justification for his view of the connection between language play and advanced literacy, Crystal presents an argument for metalinguistic awareness. According to Crystal, *metalinguistics* refers to the ability to "step back" and use words to analyze how language works:

STUDENT WRITING

Craig 7

> If we are good at stepping back, at thinking in a more abstract way about what we hear and what we say, then we are more likely to be good at acquiring those skills which depend on just such a stepping back in order to be successful — and this means, chiefly, reading and writing. . . . [T]he greater our ability to play with language, . . . the more advanced will be our command of language as a whole. (Crystal 181)

Block format for a quotation of more than four lines

Ellipses and brackets indicate omissions and changes in quotation

If we accept the findings of linguists such as Crystal that metalinguistic awareness leads to increased literacy, then it seems reasonable to argue that the phonetic language of messaging can also lead to increased metalinguistic awareness and, therefore, increases in overall literacy. As messagers develop proficiency with a variety of phonetic replacements and other types of texting and messaging words, they should increase their subconscious knowledge of metalinguistics.

Writer links Crystal's views to thesis

Metalinguistics also involves our ability to write in a variety of distinct styles and tones. Yet in the debate over messaging and literacy, many critics assume that either messaging or academic literacy will eventually win out in a person and that the two modes cannot exist side by side. This assumption is, however, false. Human beings ordinarily develop a large range of language abilities, from the formal to the relaxed and from the mainstream to the subcultural. Mark Twain, for example, had an understanding of local speech that he employed when writing dialogue for *Huckleberry Finn*. Yet few people would argue that Twain's knowledge of this form of English had a negative impact on his ability to write in standard English.

Another refutation of critics' assumptions

Example from well-known work of literature used as support

However, just as Mark Twain used dialects carefully in dialogue, writers must pay careful attention to the kind of language

STUDENT WRITING

Craig 8

they use in any setting. Composition specialist Andrea A. Lunsford backs up this idea in a blog post:

Email correspondence cited in support of claim

> [W]here English is concerned, there is never one solitary right way to proceed: everything depends on the rhetorical situation and the intended purpose.

The analytical ability that is necessary for writers to choose an appropriate tone and style in their writing is, of course, metalinguistic in nature because it involves the comparison of two or more language systems. Thus, youths who grasp multiple languages will have a greater natural understanding of metalinguistics.

Writer synthesizes evidence for claim

More specifically, young people who possess both messaging and traditional skills stand to be better off than their peers who have been trained only in traditional or conventional systems. Far from being hurt by their online pastime, instant messagers can be aided in standard writing by their experience with messaging language.

Transition to final point

Alternative explanation for decline in literacy

The fact remains, however, that youth literacy seems to be declining. What, if not messaging, is the main cause of this phenomenon? According to the College Board, which collects data on several questions from its test takers, course work in English composition classes has decreased by 14 percent between 1992 and 2002 (Carnahan and Coletti 11). The possibility of messaging causing a decline in literacy seems inadequate when statistics on English education for US youths provide other evidence of the possible causes. Simply put, students in the United States are not getting as much practice in academic writing as they used to. Rather than blaming texting and messaging language alone for the decline in literacy and test scores, we must also look toward our schools' lack of focus on the teaching of standard English skills.

STUDENT WRITING

Craig 9

My findings indicate that the use of messaging poses virtually no threat to the development or maintenance of formal language skills among American youths aged twelve to seventeen. Diverse language skills tend to increase a person's metalinguistic awareness and, thereby, his or her ability to use language effectively to achieve a desired purpose in a particular situation. The current decline in youth literacy is not due to the rise of texting and messaging. Rather, fewer young students seem to be receiving an adequate education in the use of conventional English. Unfortunately, it may always be fashionable to blame new tools for old problems, but in the case of messaging, that blame is not warranted. Although messaging may expose literacy problems, it does not create them.

Transition to conclusion

Concluding paragraph sums up argument and reiterates thesis

STUDENT WRITING

Craig 10

Heading centered

Works Cited

Report

Carnahan, Kristin, and Chiara Coletti. *Ten-Year Trend in SAT Scores Indicates Increased Emphasis on Math Is Yielding Results: Reading and Writing Are Causes for Concern*. College Board, 2002.

Print book

Crystal, David. *Language Play*. U of Chicago P, 1998.

Article from database

Ferguson, Niall. "Texting Makes U Stupid." *Newsweek,* vol. 158, no. 12, 19 Sept. 2011, p. 11. *EBSCOHost,* connection .ebscohost.com/c/articles/65454341/texting-makes-u-stupid.

Print newspaper article

Leibowitz, Wendy R. "Technology Transforms Writing and the Teaching of Writing." *Chronicle of Higher Education,* 26 Nov. 1999, pp. A67-A68.

Downloaded file

Lenhart, Amanda. *Teens, Smartphones, & Texting*. Pew Research Center, 19 Mar. 2012, www.pewinternet.org/files/old-media// Files/Reports/2012/PIP_Teens_Smartphones_and_Texting.pdf.

Online report

Lenhart, Amanda, et al. *Writing, Technology & Teens*. Pew Research Center, 24 Apr. 2008, www.pewinternet.org/2008/04/24/ writing-technology-and-teens/.

Subsequent lines of each entry indented

Lenhart, Amanda, and Oliver Lewis. *Teenage Life Online: The Rise of the Instant-Message Generation and the Internet's Impact on Friendships and Family Relationships*. Pew Research Center, 21 June 2001, www.pewinternet.org/2001/06/20/the-rise-of-the -instant-message-generation/.

Blog post

Lunsford, Andrea A. "Are You a 'Comma Queen'?" *Bedford Bits*, 9 Apr. 2015, community.macmillan.com/community/the-english -community/bedford-bits/blog/2015/04/09/are-you-a-comma -queen.

Online newspaper article

McCarroll, Christina. "Teens Ready to Prove Text-Messaging Skills Can Score SAT Points." *Christian Science Monitor,* 11 Mar. 2005, www.csmonitor.com/2005/0311/p01s02-ussc.html.

Graph source

"SAT Trends 2011." *Collegeboard.org,* 14 Sept. 2011, research .collegeboard.org/programs/sat/data/archived/cb-seniors -2011/tables.

46 APA Style

Chapter 46 discusses the basic formats prescribed by the American Psychological Association (APA), guidelines that are widely used for research in the social sciences. For further reference, consult the *Publication Manual of the American Psychological Association*, Sixth Edition (2010).

46a Understanding APA citation style

Why does academic work call for very careful citation practices when writing for the general public may not? The answer is that readers of academic work expect source citations for several reasons:

- Source citations demonstrate that you've done your homework on your topic and that you are a part of the conversation surrounding it.
- Source citations show that you understand the need to give credit when you make use of someone else's intellectual property. (See Chapter 15.)
- Source citations give explicit directions to guide readers who want to look for themselves at the works you're using.

The guidelines for APA style tell you exactly what information to include in your citation and how to format that information.

Types of sources. Look at the Directory to APA Style on pp. 278–79 for guidelines on citing various types of sources—print books (or parts of print books), print periodicals (journals, magazines, and newspapers), and digital written-word sources (an online article or a book on an e-reader). A digital version of a source may include updates or corrections that the print version lacks, so it's important to provide the correct information for readers. For sources that consist mainly of material other than written words—such as a film, song, or artwork—consult the "other sources" section of the directory. And if you can't find a model exactly like the source you've selected, see the box on p. 281.

ARTICLES FROM WEB AND DATABASE SOURCES. You need a subscription to look through most databases, so individual researchers almost always gain access to articles in databases through the computer system of a school or public library that pays to subscribe. The easiest way to tell whether a source comes from a database, then, is that its information is *not* generally available for free. Many databases are digital collections of articles that originally appeared in edited print periodicals, ensuring that an authority has vouched for the accuracy of the information. Such sources often have more credibility than free material available on the web.

Parts of citations. APA citations appear in two parts of your text—a brief in-text citation in the body of your written text and a full citation in the list of references, to which the in-text citation directs readers. The most straightforward in-text citations include the author's name, the publication year, and the page number, but many variations on this basic format are discussed in 46c.

In the text of her research essay (see 46e), Tawnya Redding includes a paraphrase of material from an online journal that she accessed through the publisher's website. She cites the authors' names and the year of publication in a parenthetical reference, pointing readers to the entry for "Baker, F., & Bor, W. (2008)" in her references list, shown on p. 309.

Content notes. APA style allows you to use content notes, either at the bottom of the page or on a separate page at the end of the text, to expand or supplement your text. Indicate such notes in the text by superscript numerals ([1]). Double-space all entries. Indent the first line of each note five spaces, but begin subsequent lines at the left margin.

SUPERSCRIPT NUMBER IN TEXT

The age of the children involved in the study was an important factor in the selection of items for the questionnaire.[1]

FOOTNOTE

[1]Marjorie Youngston Forman and William Cole of the Child Study Team provided great assistance in identifying appropriate items for the questionnaire.

MOOD MUSIC 9

References

Baker, F., & Bor, W. (2008). Can music preference indicate mental health status in young people? *Australasian Psychiatry, 16*(4), 284–288. Retrieved from http://www3.interscience.wiley.com/journal/118565538/home

George, D., Stickle, K., Rachid, F., & Wopnford, A. (2007). The

alter the mood of at-risk youth in a negative way. This view of the correlation between music and suicide risk is supported by a meta-analysis done by Baker and Bor (2008), in which the authors assert that most studies reject the notion that music is a causal factor and suggest that music preference is more indicative of emotional vulnerability. However, it is still unknown whether these genres can

n.

al music

lescence,

Taiwan. *Issues in Mental Health Nursing, 20,* 229–246. doi: 10.1080/016128499248637

46b Following APA manuscript format

The following formatting guidelines are adapted from the APA recommendations for preparing manuscripts for publication in journals. However, check with your instructor before preparing the final draft of a print text.

Title page. APA does not provide specific title-page guidelines. Center the title and include your name, the course name and number, the instructor's name, and the date. If your instructor wants you to include a running head, place it flush left on the first line. Write the words *Running head*, a colon, and a short version of the title (fifty characters or fewer, including spaces) using all capital letters. On the same line, flush with the right margin, type the number *1*.

Margins and spacing. Leave margins of at least one inch at the top and bottom and on both sides of the page. Do not justify the right margin. Double-space the entire text, including any headings, set-off quotations (39a), content notes, and the list of references. Indent one-half inch from the left margin for the first line of a paragraph and all lines of a quotation over forty words long.

Short title and page numbers. Place the running head and the short title in the upper left corner of each page. Place the page number in the upper right corner of each page, in the same position as on the title page.

Long quotations. For a long, set-off quotation (one having more than forty words), indent it one-half inch from the left margin, and do not use quotation marks. Place the page reference in parentheses one space after the final punctuation.

Abstract. If your instructor asks for an abstract, the abstract should go immediately after the title page, with the word *Abstract* centered about an inch from the top of the page. Double-space the text of the abstract. In most cases, a one-paragraph abstract of about one hundred words will be sufficient to introduce readers to your topic and provide a brief summary of your major thesis and supporting points.

Headings. Headings are frequently used within the text of APA-style projects. In a text with only one or two levels of headings, center the main headings; italicize the subheadings and position them flush with the left margin. Capitalize all major words; however, do not capitalize any **articles**, short **prepositions**, or **coordinating conjunctions** unless they are the first word or follow a colon.

Visuals. Tables should be labeled *Table*, numbered, and captioned. All other visuals (such as charts, graphs, photographs, and drawings) should be labeled *Figure*, numbered, and captioned with a description and the source information. Remember to refer to each visual in your text, stating how it contributes to the point(s) you are making. Tables and figures should generally appear near the relevant text; check with your instructor for guidelines on the placement of visuals.

46c Creating APA in-text citations

An in-text citation in APA style always indicates which source on the references page the writer is referring to, and it explains in what year the material was published; for quoted material, the in-text citation also indicates where in the source the quotation can be found.

Note that APA style generally calls for using the past tense or present perfect tense for signal verbs: *Baker (2003) showed* or *Baker (2003) has shown.* Use the present tense only to discuss results (*the experiment demonstrates*) or widely accepted information (*researchers agree*).

1. BASIC FORMAT FOR A QUOTATION. Generally, use the author's name in a signal phrase to introduce the cited material, and place the date, in parentheses, immediately after the author's name. The page number, preceded by *p.*, appears in parentheses after the quotation.

> Gitlin (2001) pointed out that "political critics, convinced that the media are rigged against them, are often blind to other substantial reasons why their causes are unpersuasive" (p. 141).

DIRECTORY TO APA STYLE

APA style for in-text citations

If the author is not named in a signal phrase, place the author's name, the year, and the page number in parentheses after the quotation: (Gitlin, 2001, p. 141). For a long, set-off quotation (more than forty words), place the page reference in parentheses one space after the final quotation.

For quotations from works without page numbers, you may use paragraph numbers, if the source includes them, preceded by the abbreviation *para.*

> Driver (2007) has noticed "an increasing focus on the role of land" in policy debates over the past decade (para. 1).

2. BASIC FORMAT FOR A PARAPHRASE OR SUMMARY. Include the author's last name and the year as in model 1, but omit the page or paragraph number unless the reader will need it to find the material in a long work.

> Gitlin (2001) has argued that critics sometimes overestimate the influence of the media on modern life.

3. TWO AUTHORS. Use both names in all citations. Use *and* in a signal phrase, but use an ampersand (&) in parentheses.

> Babcock and Laschever (2003) have suggested that many women do not negotiate their salaries and pay raises as vigorously as their male counterparts do.

> A recent study has suggested that many women do not negotiate their salaries and pay raises as vigorously as their male counterparts do (Babcock & Laschever, 2003).

4. THREE TO FIVE AUTHORS. List all the authors' names for the first reference.

> Safer, Voccola, Hurd, and Goodwin (2003) reached somewhat different conclusions by designing a study that was less dependent on subjective judgment than were previous studies.

In subsequent references, use just the first author's name followed by *et al.*

Based on the results, Safer et al. (2003) determined that the apes took significant steps toward self-expression.

5. SIX OR MORE AUTHORS. Use only the first author's name and *et al.* in every citation.

As Soleim et al. (2002) demonstrated, advertising holds the potential for manipulating "free-willed" consumers.

6. CORPORATE OR GROUP AUTHOR. If the name of the organization or corporation is long, spell it out the first time you use it, followed by an abbreviation in brackets. In later references, use the abbreviation only.

FIRST CITATION	(Centers for Disease Control and Prevention [CDC], 2006)
LATER CITATIONS	(CDC, 2006)

7. UNKNOWN AUTHOR. Use the title or its first few words in a signal phrase or in parentheses. A book's title is italicized, as in the following example; an article's title is placed in quotation marks.

The employment profiles for this time period substantiated this trend (*Federal Employment*, 2001).

8. TWO OR MORE AUTHORS WITH THE SAME LAST NAME. Include the authors' initials in each citation.

S. Bartolomeo (2000) conducted the groundbreaking study on teenage childbearing.

9. TWO OR MORE WORKS BY AN AUTHOR IN A SINGLE YEAR. Assign lowercase letters (*a*, *b*, and so on) alphabetically by title, and include the letters after the year.

Gordon (2004b) examined this trend in more detail.

10. TWO OR MORE SOURCES IN ONE PARENTHETICAL REFERENCE. List any sources by different authors in alphabetical order by the authors' last names, separated by semicolons: (Cardone, 1998; Lal, 2002).

List works by the same author in chronological order, separated by commas: (Lai, 2000, 2002).

11. SOURCE REPORTED IN ANOTHER SOURCE. Use the phrase *as cited in* to indicate that you are reporting information from a secondary source. Name the original source in a signal phrase, but list the secondary source in your list of references.

> Amartya Sen developed the influential concept that land reform was necessary for "promoting opportunity" among the poor (as cited in Driver, 2007, para. 2).

12. PERSONAL COMMUNICATION. Cite any personal letters, email messages, electronic postings, telephone conversations, or interviews as shown. Do not include personal communications in the reference list.

> R. Tobin (personal communication, November 4, 2006) supported his claims about music therapy with new evidence.

13. ELECTRONIC DOCUMENT. Cite a web or electronic document as you would a print source, using the author's name and date.

> Link and Phelan (2005) argued for broader interventions in public health that would be accessible to anyone, regardless of individual wealth.

The APA recommends the following for electronic sources without names, dates, or page numbers:

AUTHOR UNKNOWN

Use a shortened form of the title in a signal phrase or in parentheses (see model 7). If an organization is the author, see model 6.

DATE UNKNOWN

Use the abbreviation *n.d.* (for "no date") in place of the year: (*Hopkins, n.d.*).

NO PAGE NUMBERS

Many works found online or in electronic databases lack stable page numbers. (Use the page numbers for an electronic work in a format, such as PDF, that has stable pagination.) If paragraph numbers are included in such a source, use the abbreviation *para.*: (*Giambetti, 2006, para. 7*). If no paragraph numbers are included but the source includes headings, give the heading and identify the paragraph in the section:

> Jacobs and Johnson (2007) have argued that "the South African media is still highly concentrated and not very diverse in terms of race and class" (South African Media after Apartheid, para. 3).

14. TABLE OR FIGURE REPRODUCED IN THE TEXT. Number figures (graphs, charts, illustrations, and photographs) and tables separately.

For a table, place the label (*Table 1*) and an informative heading (*Hartman's Key Personality Traits*) above the table; below, provide information about its source.

Table 1

Hartman's Key Personality Traits

Trait category	Color			
	Red	Blue	White	Yellow
Motive	Power	Intimacy	Peace	Fun
Strengths	Loyal to tasks	Loyal to people	Tolerant	Positive
Limitations	Arrogant	Self-righteous	Timid	Uncommitted

Note: Adapted from *The Hartman Personality Profile*, by N. Hayden. Retrieved February 24, 2016, from http://students.cs.byu.edu/~nhayden/Code/index.php

For a figure, place the label (*Figure 3*) and a caption indicating the source below the image. If you do not cite the source of the table or figure elsewhere in your text, you do not need to include the source on your list of references.

46d Creating an APA list of references

The alphabetical list of the sources cited in your document is called *References*. If your instructor asks that you list everything you have read—not just the sources you cite—call the list *Bibliography*.

Documentation: APA Style > Tutorials (2)

DIRECTORY TO APA STYLE

APA style for references

DIRECTORY TO APA STYLE

APA style for references, *continued*

All the entries in this section of the book use hanging indent format, in which the first line aligns on the left and the subsequent lines indent one-half inch or five spaces. This is the customary APA format.

Guidelines for author listings

List authors' last names first, and use only initials for first and middle names. The in-text citations in your text point readers toward particular sources in your list of references (see 46c).

NAME CITED IN SIGNAL PHRASE IN TEXT

Driver (2007) has noted . . .

NAME IN PARENTHETICAL CITATION IN TEXT

. . . (Driver, 2007).

BEGINNING OF ENTRY IN LIST OF REFERENCES

Driver, T. (2007).

Models 1–5 below explain how to arrange author names. The information that follows the name of the author depends on the type of work you are citing—a book (models 6–15), a print periodical (models 16–23), a digital written-word source (models 24–34), or another kind of source (models 35–48).

Checklist

Formatting a List of References

- Start your list on a new page after the text of your document but before appendices or notes. Continue consecutive page numbers.
- Center the heading *References* one inch from the top of the page.
- Begin each entry flush with the left margin, but indent subsequent lines one-half inch or five spaces. Double-space the entire list.
- List sources alphabetically by author's last name. If no author is given, alphabetize the source by the first word of the title other than *A*, *An*, or *The*. If the list includes two or more works by the same author, list them in chronological order.
- Italicize titles and subtitles of books and periodicals. Do not italicize titles of articles, and do not enclose them in quotation marks.
- For titles of books and articles, capitalize only the first word of the title and the subtitle and any proper nouns or proper adjectives.
- For titles of periodicals, capitalize all major words.

1. ONE AUTHOR. Give the last name, a comma, the initial(s), and the date in parentheses.

Zimbardo, P. G. (2009).

2. MULTIPLE AUTHORS. List up to seven authors, last name first, with commas separating authors' names and an ampersand (&) before the last author's name.

Walsh, M. E., & Murphy, J. A. (2003).

Note: For a work with more than seven authors, list the first six, then an ellipsis (. . .), and then the final author's name.

3. CORPORATE OR GROUP AUTHOR

Resources for Rehabilitation. (2003).

 Checklist

Combining Parts of Models

What should you do if your source doesn't match the model exactly? Suppose, for instance, that your source is a translation of a republished book with an editor.

- Identify a basic model to follow. If you decide that your source looks most like a republished book, for example, start with a citation that looks like model 13.
- Look for models that show additional elements in your source. For this example, you would need elements of model 9 (for the translation) and model 7 (for the editor).
- Add new elements from other models to your basic model in the order that makes the most sense to you.
- If you still aren't sure how to arrange the pieces to create a combination model, ask your instructor.

4. UNKNOWN AUTHOR. Begin with the work's title. Italicize book titles, but do not italicize article titles or enclose them in quotation marks. Capitalize only the first word of the title and subtitle (if any) and proper nouns and proper adjectives.

Safe youth, safe schools. (2009).

5. TWO OR MORE WORKS BY THE SAME AUTHOR. List works by the same author in chronological order. Repeat the author's name in each entry.

Goodall, J. (1999).

Goodall, J. (2002).

If the works appeared in the same year, list them alphabetically by title, and assign lowercase letters (*a*, *b*, etc.) after the dates.

Shermer, M. (2002a). On estimating the lifetime of civilizations. *Scientific American, 287*(2), 33.

Shermer, M. (2002b). Readers who question evolution. *Scientific American, 287*(1), 37.

Print books

6. BASIC FORMAT FOR A BOOK. Begin with the author name(s). (See models 1–5.) Then include the publication year, title and subtitle, city of publication, country or state abbreviation, and publisher. The source map on pp. 284–85 shows where to find this information in a typical book.

Levick, S. E. (2003). *Clone being: Exploring the psychological and social dimensions*. Lanham, MD: Rowman & Littlefield.

7. EDITOR. For a book with an editor but no author, list the source under the editor's name.

Dickens, J. (Ed.). (1995). *Family outing: A guide for parents of gays, lesbians and bisexuals*. London, England: Peter Owen.

To cite a book with an author and an editor, place the editor's name, with a comma and the abbreviation *Ed.*, in parentheses after the title.

Austin, J. (1995). *The province of jurisprudence determined.* (W. E. Rumble, Ed.). Cambridge, England: Cambridge University Press.

8. SELECTION IN A BOOK WITH AN EDITOR

Burke, W. W., & Nourmair, D. A. (2001). The role of personality assessment in organization development. In J. Waclawski & A. H. Church (Eds.), *Organization development: A data-driven approach to organizational change* (pp. 55–77). San Francisco, CA: Jossey-Bass.

9. TRANSLATION

Al-Farabi, A. N. (1998). *On the perfect state* (R. Walzer, Trans.). Chicago, IL: Kazi.

10. EDITION OTHER THAN THE FIRST

Moore, G. S. (2002). *Living with the earth: Concepts in environmental health science* (2nd ed.). New York, NY: Lewis.

11. MULTIVOLUME WORK WITH AN EDITOR

Barnes, J. (Ed.). (1995). *Complete works of Aristotle* (Vols. 1–2). Princeton, NJ: Princeton University Press.

Note: If you are citing just one volume of a multivolume work, list that volume, not the complete span of volumes, in parentheses after the title.

12. ARTICLE IN A REFERENCE WORK

Dean, C. (1994). Jaws and teeth. In *The Cambridge encyclopedia of human evolution* (pp. 56–59). Cambridge, England: Cambridge University Press.

If no author is listed, begin with the title.

13. REPUBLISHED BOOK

Piaget, J. (1952). *The language and thought of the child.* London, England: Routledge & Kegan Paul. (Original work published 1932)

14. INTRODUCTION, PREFACE, FOREWORD, OR AFTERWORD

Klosterman, C. (2007). Introduction. In P. Shirley, *Can I keep my jersey?: 11 teams, 5 countries, and 4 years in my life as a basketball vagabond* (pp. v–vii). New York, NY: Villard-Random House.

15. BOOK WITH A TITLE WITHIN THE TITLE. Do not italicize or enclose in quotation marks a title within a book title.

Klarman, M. J. (2007). Brown v. Board of Education *and the civil rights movement*. New York, NY: Oxford University Press.

Print periodicals

Begin with the author name(s). (See models 1–5.) Then include the publication date (year only for journals, and year, month, and day for all other periodicals); the article title; the periodical title; the volume number and issue number, if any; and the page numbers. The source map on pp. 288–89 shows where to find this information in a sample periodical.

APA SOURCE MAP: Books

Take information from the book's title page and copyright page (on the reverse side of the title page), not from the book's cover or a library catalog.

1. **Author.** List all authors' last names first, and use only initials for first and middle names. For more about citing authors, see models 1–5.
2. **Publication year.** Enclose the year of publication in parentheses.
3. **Title.** Italicize the title and any subtitle. Capitalize only the first word of the title and the subtitle and any proper nouns or proper adjectives.
4. **City and state of publication, and publisher.** List the city of publication and the country or state abbreviation, a colon, and the publisher's name, dropping any *Inc.*, *Co.*, or *Publishers*.

A citation for the book on p. 285 would look like this:

Tsutsui, W. (2004). *Godzilla on my mind: Fifty years of the king of monsters.* New York, NY: Palgrave Macmillan.

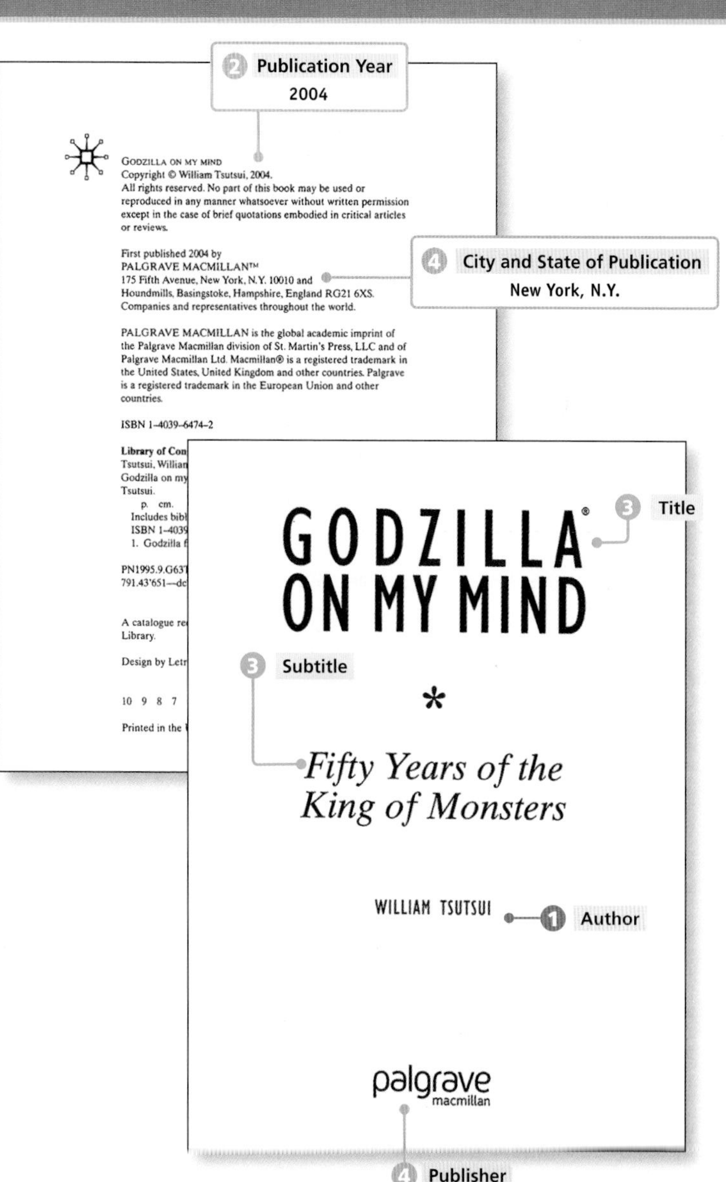

Publication Year
2004
GODZILLA ON MY MIND
Copyright © William Tsutsui, 2004.
All rights reserved. No part of this book may be used or reproduced in any manner whatsoever without written permission except in the case of brief quotations embodied in critical articles or reviews.
First published 2004 by
PALGRAVE MACMILLAN™
175 Fifth Avenue, New York, N.Y. 10010 and
Houndmills, Basingstoke, Hampshire, England RG21 6XS.
Companies and representatives throughout the world.
City and State of Publication
New York, N.Y.
PALGRAVE MACMILLAN is the global academic imprint of the Palgrave Macmillan division of St. Martin's Press, LLC and of Palgrave Macmillan Ltd. Macmillan® is a registered trademark in the United States, United Kingdom and other countries. Palgrave is a registered trademark in the European Union and other countries.
ISBN 1-4039-6474-2
GODZILLA®
ON MY MIND
Title
Subtitle
*
Fifty Years of the
King of Monsters
WILLIAM TSUTSUI
Author
palgrave
macmillan
Publisher

16. ARTICLE IN A JOURNAL PAGINATED BY VOLUME

Banks, A. (2015). Ain't no walls behind the sky, baby! Funk, flight, freedom. *College Composition and Communication, 67*, 267–279.

17. ARTICLE IN A JOURNAL PAGINATED BY ISSUE. If each issue begins with page 1, include the issue number (in parentheses and not italicized) after the volume number (italicized).

Hall, R. E. (2000). Marriage as vehicle of racism among women of color. *Psychology: A Journal of Human Behavior, 37*(2), 29–40.

18. ARTICLE IN A MAGAZINE. Include the month (and day, if given).

Solomon, A. (2014, March 17). The reckoning. *The New Yorker,* (*90*)4, 36-45.

19. ARTICLE IN A NEWSPAPER. Use *p.* or *pp.* for the page number(s) of a newspaper article.

Reynolds Lewis, K. (2011, December 22). Why some business owners think now is the time to sell. *The New York Times,* p. B5.

20. EDITORIAL OR LETTER TO THE EDITOR. Add an identifying label.

Zelneck, B. (2003, July 18). Serving the public at public universities [Letter to the editor]. *The Chronicle Review,* p. B18.

21. UNSIGNED ARTICLE

Annual meeting announcement. (2003, March). *Cognitive Psychology, 46*, 227.

22. REVIEW. Identify the work reviewed.

Ringel, S. (2003). [Review of the book *Multiculturalism and the therapeutic process*]. *Clinical Social Work Journal, 31*, 212–213.

23. PUBLISHED INTERVIEW. Identify the person interviewed.

Smith, H. (2002, October). [Interview with A. Thompson]. *The Sun,* pp. 4–7.

Digital written-word sources

Updated guidelines for citing digital resources are maintained at the APA's website (www.apa.org).

24. ARTICLE FROM AN ONLINE PERIODICAL. Give the author, date, title, and publication information as you would for a print document. Include both the volume and issue numbers for all journal articles. If the article has a digital object identifier (DOI), include it. If there is no DOI, write *Retrieved from* and the URL for the periodical's home page or for the article (if the article is difficult to find from the home page). For newspaper articles accessible from a searchable website, give the site URL only.

Barringer, F. (2008, February 7). In many communities, it's not easy going green. *The New York Times.* Retrieved from http://www.nytimes.com

Cleary, J. M., & Crafti, N. (2007). Basic need satisfaction, emotional eating, and dietary restraint as risk factors for recurrent overeating in a community sample. *E-Journal of Applied Psychology, 2*(3), 27–39. Retrieved from http://ojs.lib.swin.edu.au/index.php/ejap/article /view/90/116

25. ARTICLE FROM A DATABASE. Give the author, date, title, and publication information as you would for a print document. Include both the volume and issue numbers for all journal articles. If the article has a DOI, include it. If there is no DOI, write *Retrieved from* and the URL of the journal's home page (not the URL of the database). The source map on pp. 292–93 shows where to find this information for a typical article from a database.

Hazleden, R. (2003, December). Love yourself: The relationship of the self with itself in popular self-help texts. *Journal of Sociology, 39*(4), 413–428. Retrieved from http://jos.sagepub.com

Morley, N. J., Ball, L. J., & Ormerod, T. C. (2006). How the detection of insurance fraud succeeds and fails. *Psychology, Crime, & Law, 12*(2), 163–180. doi:10.1080/10683160512331316325

APA SOURCE MAP: Articles from Print Periodicals

1. **Author.** List all authors' last names first, and use only initials for first and middle names. For more about citing authors, see models 1–5.

2. **Publication date.** Enclose the date in parentheses. For journals, use only the year. For magazines and newspapers, use the year, a comma, the month (spelled out), and the day, if given.

3. **Article title.** Do not italicize or enclose article titles in quotation marks. Capitalize only the first word of the article title and subtitle and any proper nouns or proper adjectives.

4. **Periodical title.** Italicize the periodical title (and subtitle, if any), and capitalize all major words. Follow the periodical title with a comma.

5. **Volume and issue numbers.** Give the volume number (italicized) and, without a space in between, the issue number (if given) in parentheses. Follow with a comma.

6. **Page numbers.** Give the inclusive page numbers of the article. For newspapers only, include the abbreviation *p.* ("page") or *pp.* ("pages") before the page numbers. End the citation with a period.

A citation for the periodical article on p. 289 would look like this:

Etzioni, A. (2006). Leaving race behind: Our growing Hispanic population creates a golden opportunity. *The American Scholar, 75*(2), 20–30.

The AMERICAN SCHOLAR

4 Periodical Title

Spring 2006 | Vol. 75, No. 2

5 Volume and Issue Numbers

2 Publication Date

The AMERICAN SCHOLAR

3 Article Title

Leaving Race Behind

Our growing Hispanic population creates a golden opportunity

AMITAI ETZIONI

1 Author

Some years ago the United States government asked me what my race was. I was reluctant to respond because my 50 years of practicing sociology—and some powerful personal experiences—have underscored for me what we all know to one degree or another, that racial divisions bedevil America, just as they do many other societies across the world. Not wanting to encourage these divisions, I refused to check off one of the specific racial options on the U.S. Census form and instead marked a box labeled "Other." I later found out that the federal government did not accept such an attempt to de-emphasize race, by me or by some 6.75 million other Americans who tried it. Instead the government assigned me to a racial category, one it chose for me. Learning this made me conjure up what I admit is a far-fetched association. I was in this place once before. When I was a Jewish child in Nazi Germany in the early 1930s, many Jews who saw themselves as good Germans wanted to "pass" as Aryans. But the Nazi regime would have none of it. Never mind, they told these Jews, *we determine* who is Jewish and who is not. A similar practice prevailed in the Old South, where if you had one drop of African blood you were a Negro, disregarding all other facts and considerations, including how you saw yourself.

You might suppose that in the years since my little Census-form protest

Amitai Etzioni is University Professor at George Washington University and the author of *The Monochrome Society*.

20

6 Page Numbers

Checklist

Citing Digital Sources

When citing sources accessed online or from an electronic database, include as many of the following elements as you can find:

- **Author.** Give the author's name, if available.
- **Publication date.** Include the date of electronic publication or of the latest update, if available. When no publication date is available, use *n.d.* ("no date").
- **Title.** If the source is not from a larger work, italicize the title.
- **Print publication information.** For articles from online journals, magazines, or reference databases, give the publication title and other publishing information as you would for a print periodical (see models 16–23).
- **Retrieval information.** For a work from a database, do the following: if the article has a DOI (digital object identifier), include that number after the publication information; do not include the name of the database. If there is no DOI, write *Retrieved from* followed by the URL for the journal's home page (not the database URL). For a work found on a website, write *Retrieved from* and include the URL. If the work seems likely to be updated, include the retrieval date. If the URL is longer than one line, break it only before a punctuation mark; do not break *http://*.

26. ABSTRACT FOR AN ONLINE ARTICLE. Include a label.

Gudjonsson, G. H., & Young, S. (2010). Does confabulation in memory predict suggestibility beyond IQ and memory? [Abstract]. *Personality & Individual Differences, 49*(1), 65–67. doi: 10.1016/j.paid.2010.03.014

27. COMMENT ON AN ONLINE ARTICLE. Give the writer's real name (if known) or screen name. Use *Re:* before the title of the article, and add the label *[Comment]*.

Checklist

Citing Sources without Models in APA Style

You may need to cite a source for which you cannot find a model in APA style. If so, collect as much information as you can find about the creator, title, sponsor, date, and so on, with the goal of helping readers find the source for themselves. Then look at the models in this section to see which one most closely matches the type of source you are using.

In an academic writing project, before citing an electronic source for which you have no model, also be sure to ask your instructor's advice.

The Lone Ranger. (2014, April 22). Re: The American middle class is no longer the world's richest [Comment]. *The New York Times*. Retrieved from http://www.nytimes.com/

28. REPORT OR LONG DOCUMENT FROM A WEBSITE. Include all of the following information that you can find: the author's name; the publication date (or *n.d.* if no date is available); the title of the document, italicized; and *Retrieved from* and the URL. Provide your date of access only if an update seems likely. The source map on pp. 296–97 shows where to find this information for a report from a website.

Nice, M. L., & Katzev, R. (n.d.). *Internet romances: The frequency and nature of romantic on-line relationships.* Retrieved from http://www .publicpolicyresearch.net/papers.html

29. SHORT WORK FROM A WEBSITE. Include the name of the work (with no italics) and the name of the site, italicized.

Zimbardo, P. G. (2013). Constructing the experiment. *Stanford Prison Experiment.* Retrieved from http://www.prisonexp.org /psychology/5

APA SOURCE MAP: Articles from Databases

1. **Author.** Include the author's name as you would for a print source. List all authors' last names first, and use initials for first and middle names. For more about citing authors, see models 1–5.
2. **Publication date.** Enclose the date in parentheses. For journals, use only the year. For magazines and newspapers, use the year, a comma, the month, and the day if given.
3. **Article title.** Capitalize only the first word of the article title and the subtitle and any proper nouns or proper adjectives.
4. **Periodical title.** Italicize the periodical title.
5. **Volume and issue number.** For journals and magazines, give the volume number (italicized) and the issue number (in parentheses).
6. **Page numbers.** For journals only, give inclusive page numbers.
7. **Retrieval information.** If the article has a DOI (digital object identifier), include that number after the publication information; do not include the name of the database. If there is no DOI, write *Retrieved from* followed by the URL of the journal's home page (not the database URL).

A citation for the article on p. 293 would look like this:

Knobloch-Westerwick, S., & Crane, J. (2012). A losing battle: Effects of prolonged exposure to thin-ideal images on dieting and body satisfaction. *Communication Research, 39*(1), 79–102. doi:10.1177/0093650211400596

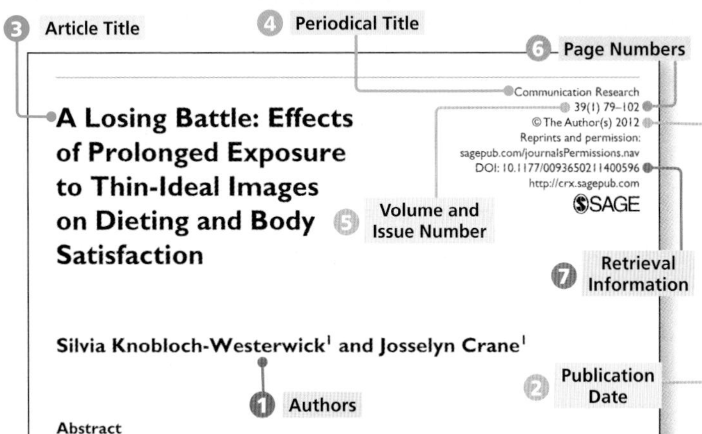

Communication Research
39(1) 79–102

DOI: 10.1177/0093650211400596
http://crx.sagepub.com
SAGE

A Losing Battle: Effects of Prolonged Exposure to Thin-Ideal Images on Dieting and Body Satisfaction

Silvia Knobloch-Westerwick[1] and Josselyn Crane[1]

Abstract

The present study examined prolonged exposure effects of thin-ideal media messages. College-aged females participated in seven online sessions over 10 days including a baseline measures session, five daily measures, and a posttest. Two experimental groups viewed magazine pages with thin-ideal imagery. One of those groups was induced to engage in social comparisons with the thin-ideal models. The control group viewed messages with body-neutral images of women. Prolonged exposure to thin-ideal messages led to greater body satisfaction. This finding was attributed to the fact that the experimental groups reported more dieting behaviors. A mediation analysis showed that the impact of thin-ideal message exposure on body satisfaction was mediated by dieting.

Keywords

body dissatisfaction, body image, dieting, prolonged exposure, social comparison

Idealized body images in the media have been linked to unrealistic body shape aspirations and body dissatisfaction (see meta-analysis by Grabe, Ward, & Hyde, 2008), which, in turn, have been linked to numerous pathological problems, including depression, obesity, dieting, and eating disorders (e.g., Johnson & Wardle, 2005; Neumark-Sztainer, Paxton, Hannan, Haines, & Story, 2006; Ricciardelli & McCabe, 2001). However, another meta-analysis by Holmstrom (2004) found that the longer the media exposure, the *better* the individuals felt about their body. This inconsistency indicates that the factors and processes at work have not yet been fully understood and captured by the research at hand and deserve further investigation. Social comparison theory is the theoretical framework that has guided much

[1]The Ohio State University

Corresponding Author:
Silvia Knobloch-Westerwick, The Ohio State University, 154 N Oval Mall, Columbus, OH 43210
Email: knobloch-westerwick.1@osu.edu

30. ONLINE BOOK. Give the original print publication date, if different, in parentheses at the end of the entry.

Russell, B. (2008). *The analysis of mind.* Retrieved from http://onlinebooks.library.upenn.edu/webbin/gutbook/lookup?num=2529 (Original work published 1921)

31. EMAIL OR PRIVATE MESSAGE. The APA stresses that any sources cited in your list of references be retrievable by your readers, so do not include entries for email messages or any postings that are not archived. Instead, cite these sources in your text as forms of personal communication (see p. 276).

32. POSTING ON PUBLIC SOCIAL MEDIA. List an online posting in the references list only if you are able to retrieve the message from an archive. Provide the author's name, the date of posting, and a few words from the post. (If you are citing Twitter, include the entire tweet.) Include other identifying information, such as *[Tweet]* or *[Facebook post]*. Then end with the date you retrieved the post and the URL of the public page.

HeForShe. (2016, May 17). "Dads are stepping up in the fight for caregiver rights" #HeForShe @TIMEIdeas [Tweet]. Retrieved May 17, 2016, from https://twitter.com/HeforShe/status/732629285756932096

33. BLOG POST OR COMMENT. For a blog post, give the author's real name (if known) or screen name; the date (or *n.d.* if no date is given); the title, followed by the label *[Blog post]*; and the URL.

Black, D. (2016, May 14). How to succeed [Blog post]. Retrieved from http://www.eschatonblog.com/2016/05/how-to-succeed.html

For a comment, put *Re:* before the title of the post commented on, and use the label *[Blog comment]*.

34. WIKI ENTRY. Use the date of posting, if there is one, or *n.d.* for "no date" if there is none. Include the retrieval date because wiki content can change frequently.

Happiness. (2007, June 14). Retrieved March 24, 2016, from PsychWiki: http://www.psychwiki.com/wiki/Happiness

Other sources (including online versions)

35. GOVERNMENT PUBLICATION

Office of the Federal Register. (2003). *The United States government manual 2003/2004.* Washington, DC: U.S. Government Printing Office.

Cite an online government document as you would a printed government work, adding the URL. If there is no date, use *n.d.*

U.S. Public Health Service. (1999). *The surgeon general's call to action to prevent suicide.* Retrieved from http://www.mentalhealth.org/suicideprevention/calltoaction.asp

36. DATA SET

U.S. Department of Education, Institute of Education Sciences. (2009). *NAEP state comparisons* [Data set]. Retrieved from http://nces.ed.gov/nationsreportcard/statecomparisons/

37. DISSERTATION. If you retrieved the dissertation from a database, give the database name and the accession number, if one is assigned.

Lengel, L. L. (1968). *The righteous cause: Some religious aspects of Kansas populism.* Retrieved from ProQuest Digital Dissertations (6900033)

If you retrieve a dissertation from a website, give the type of dissertation and the institution after the title, and provide a retrieval statement.

Meeks, M. G. (2006). *Between abolition and reform: First-year writing programs, e-literacies, and institutional change* (Doctoral dissertation, University of North Carolina). Retrieved from http://dc.lib.unc.edu/etd/

38. TECHNICAL OR RESEARCH REPORT. Give the report number, if available, in parentheses after the title.

McCool, R., Fikes, R., & McGuinness, D. (2003). *Semantic web tools for enhanced authoring* (Report No. KSL-03-07). Retrieved from www.ksl.stanford.edu/KSL_Abstracts/KSL-03-07.html

APA SOURCE MAP: Reports and Long Works from Websites

1. **Author.** If one is given, include the author's name (see models 1–5). List last names first, and use only initials for first names. The site's sponsor may be the author. If no author is identified, begin the citation with the title of the document.

2. **Publication date.** Enclose the date of publication or latest update in parentheses. Use *n.d.* ("no date") when no publication date is available.

3. **Title of work.** Italicize the title. Capitalize only the first word of the title and subtitle and any proper nouns or proper adjectives.

4. **Retrieval information.** Write *Retrieved from* and include the URL. For a report from an organization's website, identify the organization in the retrieval statement. If the work seems likely to be updated, include the retrieval date.

A citation for the web document on p. 297 would look like this:

Parker, K., & Wang, W. (2013, March 14). *Modern parenthood: Roles of moms and dads converge as they balance work and family.* Retrieved from the Pew Research Center website: http://www.pewsocialtrends.org/2013/03/14/modern-parenthood-roles-of-moms-and-dads-converge-as-they-balance-work-and-family/

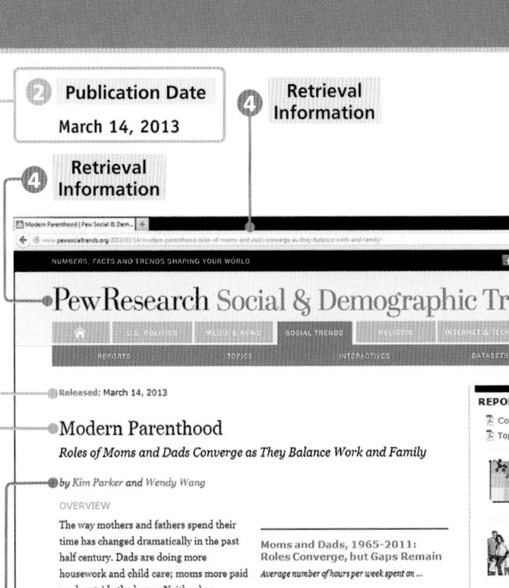

Publication Date

March 14, 2013

Retrieval Information

Retrieval Information

Modern Parenthood | Pew Social & Dem...

www.pewsocialtrends.org/2013/03/14/modern-parenthood-roles-of-moms-and-dads-converge-as-they-balance-work-and-family/

NUMBERS, FACTS AND TRENDS SHAPING YOUR WORLD

Search

PewResearch Social & Demographic Trends

U.S. POLITICS | MEDIA & NEWS | SOCIAL TRENDS | RELIGION | INTERNET & TECH | HISPANICS | GLOBAL

REPORTS | TOPICS | INTERACTIVES | DATASETS | ABOUT

Released: March 14, 2013

Modern Parenthood

Roles of Moms and Dads Converge as They Balance Work and Family

by Kim Parker and Wendy Wang

OVERVIEW

The way mothers and fathers spend their time has changed dramatically in the past half century. Dads are doing more housework and child care; moms more paid work outside the home. Neither has overtaken the other in their "traditional" realms, but their roles are converging, according to a new Pew Research Center analysis of long-term data on time use.

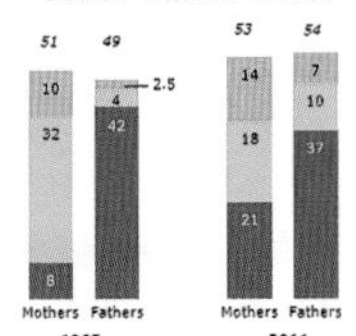

At the same time, roughly equal shares of working mothers and fathers report in a new Pew Research Center survey feeling stressed about juggling work and family life: 56% of working moms and 50% of working dads say they find it very or somewhat difficult to balance these responsibilities.

Still, there are important gender role differences. While a nearly equal share of mothers and fathers say they wish they could be at home raising their children rather than working, dads are much more likely than moms to say they want to work full time. And when it comes to what they value most in a job, working fathers place more importance on having a high-paying job, while working mothers are more concerned with having a flexible schedule.[1]

REPORT MATERIALS

Complete Report

Topline Questionnaire

Quiz: Which Parent Does More in Your Home?

Slideshow: Key Findings from the Survey

Data Trends: Parental Time Use Since 1965

TABLE OF CONTENTS

Author

Kim Parker and Wendy Wang

Title of Work

39. CONFERENCE PROCEEDINGS

Robertson, S. P., Vatrapu, R. K., & Medina, R. (2009). YouTube and Facebook: Online video "friends" social networking. In *Conference proceedings: YouTube and the 2008 election cycle* (pp. 159–176). Amherst, MA: University of Massachusetts. Retrieved from http://scholarworks.umass.edu/jitpc2009

40. PAPER PRESENTED AT A MEETING OR SYMPOSIUM, UNPUBLISHED. Cite the month of the meeting if it is available.

Jones, J. G. (1999, February). *Mental health intervention in mass casualty disasters*. Paper presented at the Rocky Mountain Region Disaster Mental Health Conference, Laramie, WY.

41. POSTER SESSION

Barnes Young, L. L. (2003, August). *Cognition, aging, and dementia*. Poster session presented at the 2003 Division 40 APA Convention, Toronto, Ontario, Canada.

42. PRESENTATION SLIDES

Mader, S. (2007, March 27). *The Zen aesthetic* [Presentation slides]. Retrieved from http://www.slideshare.net/slmader/the-zen-aesthetic

43. FILM, VIDEO, DVD, OR BLU-RAY. Begin with the director, the producer, and other relevant contributors.

Bigelow, K. (Director, Producer), Boal, M. (Producer), & Ellison, M. (Producer). (2012). *Zero dark thirty* [Motion picture]. United States: Annapurna.

If you watched the film in another medium, such as on a DVD or Blu-ray disc, indicate the medium in brackets. If the DVD or Blu-ray and the film were not released in the same year, put *Original release* and the year in parentheses at the end of the entry.

Hitchcock, A. (Director, Producer). (2010). *Psycho* [Blu-ray]. United States: Universal. (Original release 1960.)

44. ONLINE (STREAMING) AUDIO OR VIDEO FILE

Klusman, P. (2008, February 13). An engineer's guide to cats [Video file]. Retrieved from http://www.youtube.com/watch?v=mHXBL6bzAR4

Koenig, S. (2013, January 25). Petticoats in a twist [Audio file]. Retrieved from http://www.thisamericanlife.org/radio-archives/episode/485/surrogates

45. TELEVISION PROGRAM, SINGLE EPISODE

Imperioli, M. (Writer), & Buscemi, S. (Director). (2002). Everybody hurts [Television series episode]. In D. Chase (Executive Producer), *The Sopranos*. New York, NY: Home Box Office.

46. TELEVISION SERIES

Gilligan, V. (2008-2013). *Breaking Bad* [Television series]. New York, NY: AMC.

47. PODCAST (DOWNLOADED AUDIO FILE)

Noguchi, Yugi. (2010, 24 May). BP hard to pin down on oil spill claims [Audio podcast]. *NPR Morning Edition.* Retrieved from http://www.npr.org

48. RECORDING

The Avalanches. (2001). Frontier psychiatrist. On *Since I left you* [CD]. Los Angeles, CA: Elektra/Asylum Records.

46e A sample student writing project, APA style

On the following pages is a paper by Tawnya Redding that conforms to the APA guidelines described in this chapter.

STUDENT WRITING

Running head (fifty characters or fewer, all capital letters) appears flush left on first line of every page, preceded on title page only by *Running head* and colon

Page number appears flush right on first line of every page

Title, name, and affiliation centered and double-spaced

Running head: MOOD MUSIC 1

Mood Music: Music Preference and the Risk for Depression and Suicide in Adolescents

Tawnya Redding

University of Oregon

Annotations indicate effective choices or APA-style formatting.

STUDENT WRITING

MOOD MUSIC 2

Abstract

Heading centered and not boldface

No indentation

There has long been concern for the effects that certain genres of music (such as heavy metal and country) have on youth. While a correlational link between these genres and increased risk for depression and suicide in adolescents has been established, researchers have been unable to pinpoint what is responsible for this link, and a causal relationship has not been determined. This paper will begin by discussing correlational literature concerning music preference and increased risk for depression and suicide, as well as the possible reasons for this link. Finally, studies concerning the effects of music on mood will be discussed. This examination of the literature on music and increased risk for depression and suicide points out the limitations of previous research and suggests the need for new research establishing a causal relationship for this link as well as research into the specific factors that may contribute to an increased risk for depression and suicide in adolescents.

Use of passive voice appropriate for social sciences

Double-spaced text

Clear, straightforward description of literature under review

Conclusions indicated

STUDENT WRITING

Full title, centered and not boldface

Paragraphs indented

Background information about review supplied

Questions focus reader's attention

Boldface headings help organize review

Multiple sources in one parenthetical citation separated by semicolons

Mood Music: Music Preference and the Risk for Depression and Suicide in Adolescents

Music is a significant part of American culture. Since the explosion of rock and roll in the 1950s there has been a concern for the effects that music may have on listeners, and especially on young people. The genres most likely to come under suspicion in recent decades have included heavy metal, country, and blues. These genres have been suspected of having adverse effects on the mood and behavior of young listeners. But can music really alter the disposition and create self-destructive behaviors in listeners? And if so, which genres and aspects of those genres are responsible? The following review of the literature will establish the correlation between potentially problematic genres of music such as heavy metal and country and depression and suicide risk. First, correlational studies concerning music preference and suicide risk will be discussed, followed by a discussion of the literature concerning the possible reasons for this link. Finally, studies concerning the effects of music on mood will be discussed. Despite the link between genres such as heavy metal and country and suicide risk, previous research has been unable to establish the causal nature of this link.

The Correlation Between Music and Depression and Suicide Risk

Studies over the past two decades have set out to answer this question by examining the correlation between youth music preference and risk for depression and suicide. A large portion of these studies have focused on heavy metal and country music as the main genre culprits associated with youth suicidality and depression (Lacourse, Claes, & Villeneuve, 2001; Scheel &

STUDENT WRITING

Westefeld, 1999; Stack & Gundlach, 1992). Stack and Gundlach (1992) examined the radio airtime devoted to country music in 49 metropolitan areas and found that the higher the percentages of country music airtime, the higher the incidence of suicides among whites. The researchers hypothesized that themes in country music (such as alcohol abuse) promoted audience identification and reinforced a preexisting suicidal mood, and that the themes associated with country music were responsible for elevated suicide rates. Similarly, Scheel and Westefeld (1999) found a correlation between heavy metal music listeners and an increased risk for suicide, as did Lacourse et al. (2001).

In parentheses, two author names joined with *&*; in text, names joined with *and*

Reasons for the Link: Characteristics of Those Who Listen to Problematic Music

Unfortunately, previous studies concerning music preference and suicide risk have been unable to determine a causal relationship and have focused mainly on establishing a correlation between suicide risk and music preference. This leaves the question open as to whether an individual at risk for depression and suicide is attracted to certain genres of music or whether the music helps induce the mood — or both. Some studies have suggested that music preference may simply be a reflection of other underlying problems associated with increased risk for suicide (Lacourse et al., 2001; Scheel & Westefeld, 1999). For example, in research done by Scheel and Westefeld (1999), adolescents who listened to heavy metal were found to have lower scores on the Reason for Living Inventory and several of its subscales, a self-report measure designed to assess potential reasons for not committing suicide. These adolescents were also found to have lower scores on several subscales of the Reason for Living Inventory, including

Discussion of correlation vs. causation points out limitations of previous studies

STUDENT WRITING

Alternative explanations considered

After first mention of source with more than two authors, first author name and *et al.* used

responsibility to family along with survival and coping beliefs. Other risk factors associated with suicide and suicidal behaviors include poor family relationships, depression, alienation, anomie, and drug and alcohol abuse (Lacourse et al., 2001). Lacourse et al. (2001) examined 275 adolescents in the Montreal region with a preference for heavy metal and found that this preference was not significantly related to suicide risk when other risk factors were controlled for. This was also the conclusion of Scheel and Westefeld (1999), in which music preference for heavy metal was thought to be a red flag for suicide vulnerability, suggesting that the source of the problem may lie more in personal and familial characteristics.

George, Stickle, Rachid, and Wopnford (2007) further explored the correlation between suicide risk and music preference by attempting to identify the personality characteristics of those with a preference for different genres of music. A sample of 358 individuals was assessed for preference of thirty different styles of music along with a number of personality characteristics, including self-esteem, intelligence, spirituality, social skills, locus of control, openness, conscientiousness, extraversion, agreeableness, emotional stability, hostility, and depression (George et al., 2007). The thirty styles of music were then categorized into eight factors: rebellious (for example, punk and heavy metal), classical, rhythmic and intense (including hip-hop, rap, and pop), easy listening, fringe (for example, techno), contemporary Christian, jazz and blues, and traditional Christian. The results revealed an almost comprehensively negative personality profile for those who preferred to listen to the rebellious and rhythmic and intense categories, while those who preferred classical music tended to have a comprehensively positive profile. Like Scheel and Westefeld (1999) and

MOOD MUSIC 6

Lacourse et al. (2001), this study also supports the theory that youth are drawn to certain genres of music based on already existing factors, whether they be related to personality or situational variables.

Reasons for the Link: Characteristics of Problematic Music

Another possible explanation is that the lyrics and themes of the music have an effect on listeners. In this scenario, music is thought to exacerbate an already depressed mood and hence contribute to an increased risk for suicide. This was the proposed reasoning behind higher suicide rates in whites in Stack and Gundlach's (1992) study linking country music to suicide risk. In this case, the themes associated with country music were thought to promote audience identification and reinforce preexisting self-destructive behaviors (such as excessive alcohol consumption). Stack (2000) also studied individuals with a musical preference for blues to determine whether the genre's themes could increase the level of suicide acceptability. The results demonstrated that blues fans were no more accepting of suicide than nonfans, but that blues listeners were found to have low religiosity levels, an important factor for suicide acceptability (Stack, 2000). Despite this link between possible suicidal behavior and a preference for blues music, the actual suicide behavior of blues fans has not been explored, and thus no concrete associations can be made.

Transition links paragraphs

Need for more research indicated

The Effect of Music on Mood

While studies examining the relationship between music genres such as heavy metal, country, and blues have been able to establish a correlation between music preference and suicide risk, it is still unclear from these studies what effect music has

Discussion of previous research

STUDENT WRITING

on the mood of the listener. Previous research has suggested that some forms of music can both improve and depress mood (Lai, 1999; Siedliecki & Good, 2006; Smith & Noon, 1998). Lai (1999) found that changes in mood were more likely to be found in an experimental group of depressed women versus a control group. It was also found that both the experimental and control groups showed significant increases in the tranquil mood state, but the amount of change was not significant between the groups (Lai, 1999). This study suggests that music can have a positive effect on depressed individuals when they are allowed to choose the music they are listening to. In a similar study, Siedliecki and Good (2006) found that music can increase a listener's sense of power and decrease depression, pain, and disability. Researchers randomly assigned sixty African American and Caucasian participants with chronic nonmalignant pain to a standard music group (offering them a choice of instrumental music types — piano, jazz, orchestra, harp, and synthesizer), a patterning music group (asking them to choose music to ease muscle tension, to facilitate sleep, or to decrease anxiety), or a control group. There were no statistically significant differences between the two music groups. However, the music groups had significantly less pain, depression, and disability than the control group (Siedliecki & Good, 2006). On the other hand, Martin, Clark, and Pearce (1993) identified a subgroup of heavy metal fans who reported feeling worse after listening to their music of choice. Although this subgroup did exist, there was also evidence that listening to heavy metal results in more positive affect, and it was hypothesized that those who experience negative effects after listening to their preferred genre of heavy metal may be most at risk for suicidal behaviors (Martin et al., 1993).

Smith and Noon (1998) also determined that music can have a negative effect on mood. Six songs were selected for the particular theme they embodied: (1) vigorous, (2) fatigued, (3) angry, (4) depressed, (5) tense, and (6) all moods. The results indicated that selections 3 – 6 had significant effects on the mood of participants, with selection 6 (all moods) resulting in the greatest positive change in the mood and selection 5 (tense) resulting in the greatest negative change in mood. Selection 4 (depressed) was found to sap the vigor and increase anger / hostility in participants, while selection 5 (tense) significantly depressed participants and made them more anxious. Although this study did not specifically comment on the effects of different genres on mood, the results do indicate that certain themes can indeed depress mood. The participants for this study were undergraduate students who were not depressed, and thus it seems that certain types of music can have a negative effect on the mood of healthy individuals.

Is There Evidence for a Causal Relationship?

Despite the correlation between certain music genres (especially heavy metal) and increased risk for depression and suicidal behaviors in adolescents, it remains unclear whether these types of music can alter the mood of at-risk youth in a negative way. This view of the correlation between music and suicide risk is supported by a meta-analysis done by Baker and Bor (2008), in which the authors assert that most studies reject the notion that music is a causal factor and suggest that music preference is more indicative of emotional vulnerability. However, it is still unknown whether these genres can negatively alter mood at all, and if they can, whether the themes and lyrics associated with the music are responsible. Clearly, more research is needed to further examine

Conclusion indicates need for further research

this correlation, as a causal link between these genres of music and adolescent suicide risk has yet to be shown. However, even if the theory put forth by Baker and Bon and other researchers is true, it is still important to investigate the effects that music can have on those who may be at risk for suicide and depression. Even if music genres are not the ultimate cause of suicidal behavior, they may act as a catalyst that further pushes adolescents into a state of depression and increased risk for suicidal behavior.

STUDENT WRITING

MOOD MUSIC 10

References

References begin on new page

Baker, F., & Bor, W. (2008). Can music preference indicate mental health status in young people? *Australasian Psychiatry, 16*(4), 284–288. Retrieved from http://www3.interscience.wiley.com /journal/118565538/home

George, D., Stickle, K., Rachid, F., & Wopnford, A. (2007). The association between types of music enjoyed and cognitive, behavioral, and personality factors of those who listen. *Psychomusicology, 19*(2), 32–56.

Lacourse, E., Claes, M., & Villeneuve, M. (2001). Heavy metal music and adolescent suicidal risk. *Journal of Youth and Adolescence, 30*(3), 321–332.

Lai, Y. (1999). Effects of music listening on depressed women in Taiwan. *Issues in Mental Health Nursing, 20*, 229–246. doi: 10.1080/016128499248637

Martin, G., Clark, M., & Pearce, C. (1993). Adolescent suicide: Music preference as an indicator of vulnerability. *Journal of the American Academy of Child and Adolescent Psychiatry, 32*, 530–535.

Scheel, K., & Westefeld, J. (1999). Heavy metal music and adolescent suicidality: An empirical investigation. *Adolescence, 34*(134), 253–273.

Siedliecki, S., & Good, M. (2006). Effect of music on power, pain, depression and disability. *Journal of Advanced Nursing, 54*(5), 553–562. doi: 10.1111/j.1365-2648.2006.03860.x

Smith, J. L., & Noon, J. (1998). Objective measurement of mood change induced by contemporary music. *Journal of Psychiatric & Mental Health Nursing, 5*, 403–408.

Stack, S. (2000). Blues fans and suicide acceptability. *Death Studies, 24*, 223–231.

Stack, S., & Gundlach, J. (1992). The effect of country music on suicide. *Social Forces, 71*(1), 211–218. Retrieved from http:// socialforces.unc.edu/

Journal article from a database, no DOI

Print journal article

Journal article from a database with DOI

47 Chicago Style

The style guide of the University of Chicago Press has long been used in history as well as in other areas of the arts and humanities. The Sixteenth Edition of *The Chicago Manual of Style* (2010) provides a complete guide to *Chicago* style, including two systems for citing sources. This chapter presents the notes and bibliography system.

47a Understanding *Chicago* citation style

Why does academic work call for very careful citation practices when writing for the general public may not? The answer is that readers of academic work expect source citations for several reasons:

- Source citations demonstrate that you've done your homework on your topic and that you are a part of the conversation surrounding it.
- Source citations show that you understand the need to give credit when you make use of someone else's intellectual property. (See Chapter 15.)
- Source citations give explicit directions to guide readers who want to look for themselves at the works you're using.

Guidelines from *The Chicago Manual of Style* will tell you exactly what information to include in your citation and how to format that information.

Types of sources. Look at the Directory to *Chicago* Style on p. 314. You will need to be careful to tell your readers whether you read a print version or a digital version of a source that consists mainly of written words. Digital magazine and newspaper articles may include updates or corrections that the print version lacks; digital books may not number pages or screens the same way the print book does. If you are citing a source with media elements—such as a film, song, or artwork—consult the "other sources" section of the directory. And if you can't find a model exactly like the source you've selected, see the box on p. 319.

ARTICLES FROM WEB AND DATABASE SOURCES. You need a subscription to look through most databases, so individual researchers almost always gain access to articles in databases through the computer system of a school or public library that pays to subscribe. The easiest way to tell whether a source comes from a database, then, is that its information is *not* generally available free to anyone with an Internet connection. Many databases are digital collections of articles that originally appeared in edited print periodicals, ensuring that an authority has vouched for the accuracy of the information. Such sources may have more credibility than free material available on the web.

Parts of citations. Citations in *Chicago* style will appear in three places in your text—a note number in the text marks the material from the source, a footnote or an endnote includes information to identify the source (or information about supplemental material), and the bibliography provides the full citation.

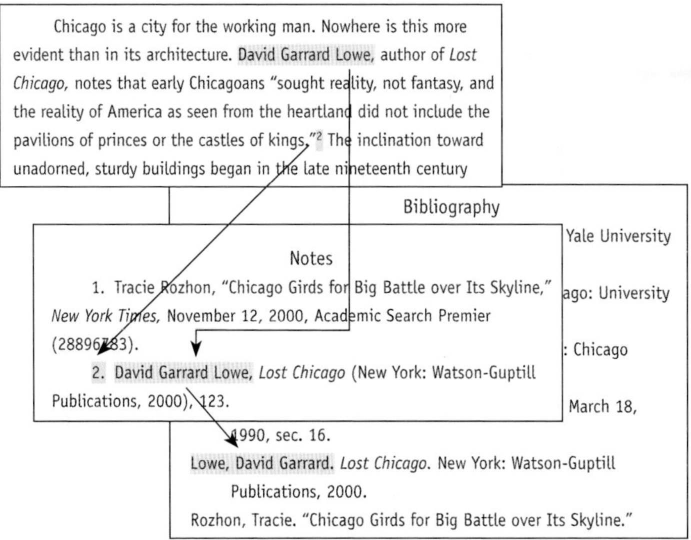

47b Following *Chicago* manuscript format

Title page. About halfway down the title page, center the full title of your project and your name. Unless otherwise instructed, at the bottom of the page also list the course name, the instructor's name, and the date submitted. Do not type a number on this page. Check to see if your instructor has a preference on whether to count the title page as part of the text (if so, the first text page will be page 2) or as part of the frontmatter (if so, the first text page will be page 1).

Margins and spacing. Leave one-inch margins at the top, bottom, and sides of your pages. Double-space the entire text, including block quotations, notes, and bibliography.

Page numbers. Number all pages (except the title page) in the upper right-hand corner. Also use a short title or your name before page numbers.

Long quotations. For a long quotation, indent one-half inch (or five spaces) from the left margin and do not use quotation marks. *Chicago* defines a long quotation as one hundred words or eight lines, though you may set off shorter quotes for emphasis (39a).

Headings. *Chicago* style allows, but does not require, headings. Many students and instructors find them helpful.

Visuals. Visuals (photographs, drawings, charts, graphs, and tables) should be placed as near as possible to the relevant text. (See 15b for guidelines on incorporating visuals into your text.) Tables should be labeled *Table*, numbered, and captioned. All other visuals should be labeled *Figure* (abbreviated *Fig.*), numbered, and captioned. Remember to refer to each visual in your text, pointing out how it contributes to the point(s) you are making.

Notes. Notes can be footnotes (each one appearing at the bottom of the page on which its citation appears) or endnotes (in a list on a separate page at the end of the text). (Check your instructor's preference.) Indent the first line of each note one-half inch and begin with a number, a period, and one space before the first word. All remaining lines of the entry are flush with the left margin. Single-space footnotes and endnotes, with a double space between each entry.

Use superscript numbers (1) to mark citations in the text. Place the superscript number for each note just after the relevant quotation, sentence, clause, or phrase. Type the number after any punctuation mark except the dash, and do not leave a space before the superscript. Number citations sequentially throughout the text. When you use signal phrases to introduce source material, note that *Chicago* style requires you to use the present tense (*citing Bebout's studies, Meier points out . . .*).

IN THE TEXT

Sweig argues that Castro and Che Guevara were not the only key players in the Cuban Revolution of the late 1950s.[19]

IN THE FIRST NOTE REFERRING TO THE SOURCE

19. Julia Sweig, *Inside the Cuban Revolution* (Cambridge, MA: Harvard University Press, 2002), 9.

After giving complete information the first time you cite a work, shorten additional references to that work: list only the author's last name, a comma, a short version of the title, a comma, and the page number. If you refer to the same source cited in the previous note, you can use the Latin abbreviation *Ibid.* ("in the same place") instead of the name and title.

IN FIRST AND SUBSEQUENT NOTES

19. Julia Sweig, *Inside the Cuban Revolution* (Cambridge, MA: Harvard University Press, 2002), 9.

20. Ibid., 13.

21. Ferguson, "Comfort of Being Sad," 63.

22. Sweig, *Cuban Revolution*, 21.

Bibliography. Begin the list of sources on a separate page after the main text and any endnotes. Continue numbering the pages consecutively. Center the title *Bibliography* (without underlining,

DIRECTORY TO *CHICAGO* STYLE

Chicago style for notes and bibliographic entries

italics, or quotation marks) one inch below the top of the page. Double-space, and then begin each entry at the left margin. Indent the second and subsequent lines of each entry one-half inch, or five spaces.

List sources alphabetically by authors' last names or by the first major word in the title if the author is unknown. See p. 332 for an example of a *Chicago*-style bibliography.

In the bibliographic entry, include the same information as in the first note for that source, but omit the page reference. Give the first author's last name first, followed by a comma and the first name; separate the main elements of the entry with periods rather than commas; and do not enclose the publication information for books in parentheses.

IN THE BIBLIOGRAPHY

Sweig, Julia. *Inside the Cuban Revolution*. Cambridge, MA: Harvard University Press, 2002.

47c Creating *Chicago* notes and bibliographic entries

The following examples demonstrate how to format both notes and bibliographic entries according to *Chicago* style. The note, which is numbered, appears first; the bibliographic entry, which is not numbered, appears below the note.

Print and digital books

The note for a book typically includes five elements: author's name, title and subtitle, city of publication and publisher, year, and page number(s) or electronic locator information for the information in the note. The bibliographic entry usually includes all these elements but the page number (and does include a URL or other locator if the book is digitally published), but it is styled differently: commas separate major elements of a note, but a bibliographic entry uses periods.

1. ONE AUTHOR

1. Nell Irvin Painter, *The History of White People* (New York: W. W. Norton, 2010), 119.

Painter, Nell Irvin. *The History of White People*. New York: W. W. Norton, 2010.

2. MULTIPLE AUTHORS

2. Margaret Macmillan and Richard Holbrooke, *Paris 1919: Six Months That Changed the World* (New York: Random House, 2003), 384.

Macmillan, Margaret, and Richard Holbrooke. *Paris 1919: Six Months That Changed the World*. New York: Random House, 2003.

With more than three authors, you may give the first-listed author followed by *et al.* in the note. In the bibliography, list all the authors' names.

2. Stephen J. Blank et al., *Conflict, Culture, and History: Regional Dimensions* (Miami: University Press of the Pacific, 2002), 276.

Blank, Stephen J., Lawrence E. Grinter, Karl P. Magyar, Lewis B. Ware, and Bynum E. Weathers. *Conflict, Culture, and History: Regional Dimensions*. Miami: University Press of the Pacific, 2002.

3. ORGANIZATION AS AUTHOR

3. World Intellectual Property Organization, *Intellectual Property Profile of the Least Developed Countries* (Geneva: World Intellectual Property Organization, 2002), 43.

World Intellectual Property Organization. *Intellectual Property Profile of the Least Developed Countries*. Geneva: World Intellectual Property Organization, 2002.

4. UNKNOWN AUTHOR

4. *Broad Stripes and Bright Stars* (Kansas City, MO: Andrews McMeel, 2002), 10.

Broad Stripes and Bright Stars. Kansas City, MO: Andrews McMeel, 2002.

5. ONLINE BOOK

5. Dorothy Richardson, *Long Day: The Story of a New York Working Girl, as Told by Herself* (1906; UMDL Texts, 2010), 159, http://quod.lib.umich.edu/cgi/t/text/text-idx?c=moa;idno=AFS7156.0001.001.

Richardson, Dorothy. *Long Day: The Story of a New York Working Girl, as Told by Herself*. 1906. UMDL Texts, 2010. http://quod.lib.umich.edu/cgi/t/text/text-idx?c=moa;idno=AFS7156.0001.001.

6. ELECTRONIC BOOK (E-BOOK)

6. Manal M. Omar, *Barefoot in Baghdad* (Naperville, IL: Sourcebooks, 2010), Kindle edition, ch. 4.

Omar, Manal M. *Barefoot in Baghdad*. Naperville, IL: Sourcebooks, 2010. Kindle edition.

7. EDITED BOOK WITH NO AUTHOR

7. James H. Fetzer, ed., *The Great Zapruder Film Hoax: Deceit and Deception in the Death of JFK* (Chicago: Open Court, 2003), 56.

Fetzer, James H., ed. *The Great Zapruder Film Hoax: Deceit and Deception in the Death of JFK*. Chicago: Open Court, 2003.

8. EDITED BOOK WITH AUTHOR

8. Leopold von Ranke, *The Theory and Practice of History*, ed. Georg G. Iggers (New York: Routledge, 2010), 135.

von Ranke, Leopold. *The Theory and Practice of History*. Edited by Georg G. Iggers. New York: Routledge, 2010.

9. SELECTION IN AN ANTHOLOGY OR CHAPTER IN A BOOK WITH AN EDITOR

9. Denise Little, "Born in Blood," in *Alternate Gettysburgs*, ed. Brian Thomsen and Martin H. Greenberg (New York: Berkley Publishing Group, 2002), 245.

Give the inclusive page numbers of the selection or chapter in the bibliographic entry.

Little, Denise. "Born in Blood." In *Alternate Gettysburgs*. Edited by Brian Thomsen and Martin H. Greenberg, 242–55. New York: Berkley Publishing Group, 2002.

10. INTRODUCTION, PREFACE, FOREWORD, OR AFTERWORD

10. Robert B. Reich, introduction to *Making Work Pay: America after Welfare*, ed. Robert Kuttner (New York: New Press, 2002), xvi.

Reich, Robert B. Introduction to *Making Work Pay: America after Welfare*, vii–xvii. Edited by Robert Kuttner. New York: New Press, 2002.

11. TRANSLATION

11. Suetonius, *The Twelve Caesars*, trans. Robert Graves (London: Penguin Classics, 1989), 202.

Suetonius. *The Twelve Caesars.* Translated by Robert Graves. London: Penguin Classics, 1989.

12. EDITION OTHER THAN THE FIRST

12. Dee Brown, *Bury My Heart at Wounded Knee: An Indian History of the American West*, 4th ed. (New York: Owl Books, 2007), 12.

Brown, Dee. *Bury My Heart at Wounded Knee: An Indian History of the American West*, 4th ed. New York: Owl Books, 2007.

13. MULTIVOLUME WORK

13. John Watson, *Annals of Philadelphia and Pennsylvania in the Olden Time*, vol. 2 (Washington, DC: Ross & Perry, 2003), 514.

Watson, John. *Annals of Philadelphia and Pennsylvania in the Olden Time.* Vol. 2. Washington, DC: Ross & Perry, 2003.

14. REFERENCE WORK. In a note, use *s.v.*, the abbreviation for the Latin *sub verbo* ("under the word") to help your reader find the entry. Do not list reference works such as encyclopedias or dictionaries in your bibliography.

14. *Encyclopedia Britannica*, s.v. "carpetbagger."

15. WORK WITH A TITLE WITHIN THE TITLE. Use quotation marks around any title within a book title.

15. John A. Alford, *A Companion to "Piers Plowman"* (Berkeley: University of California Press, 1988), 195.

Alford, John A. *A Companion to "Piers Plowman."* Berkeley: University of California Press, 1988.

16. SACRED TEXT. Do not include sacred texts in the bibliography.

16. Luke 18:24–25 (New International Version).

16. Qur'an 7:40–41.

17. SOURCE QUOTED IN ANOTHER SOURCE. Identify both the original and the secondary source.

17. Frank D. Millet, "The Filipino Leaders," *Harper's Weekly*, March 11, 1899, quoted in Richard Slotkin, *Gunfighter Nation: The Myth of the Frontier in Twentieth-Century America* (New York: HarperCollins, 1992), 110.

Millet, Frank D. "The Filipino Leaders." *Harper's Weekly*, March 11, 1899. Quoted in Richard Slotkin, *Gunfighter Nation: The Myth of the Frontier in Twentieth-Century America* (New York: HarperCollins, 1992), 110.

Print and digital periodicals

The note for an article in a periodical typically includes the author's name, the article title, and the periodical title. The format for other information, including the volume and issue numbers (if any) and the date of publication, as well as the page number(s) to which the note refers, varies according to the type of periodical and whether you consulted it in print, on the web, or in a database. In a bibliographic entry for a journal or magazine article from a database or a print periodical, also give the inclusive page numbers.

Checklist

Citing Sources without Models in *Chicago* Style

To cite a source for which you cannot find a model, collect as much information as you can find—about the creator, title, date of creation or update, and location of the source—with the goal of helping your readers find the source for themselves, if possible. Then look at the models in this section to see which one most closely matches the type of source you are using.

In an academic writing project, before citing an electronic source for which you have no model, also be sure to ask your instructor's advice.

18. ARTICLE IN A PRINT JOURNAL

18. Karin Lützen, "The Female World: Viewed from Denmark," *Journal of Women's History* 12, no. 3 (2000): 36.

Lützen, Karin. "The Female World: Viewed from Denmark." *Journal of Women's History* 12, no. 3 (2000): 34–38.

19. ARTICLE IN AN ONLINE JOURNAL. Give the DOI if there is one. If not, include the article URL. If page numbers are provided, include them as well.

19. Jeffrey J. Schott, "America, Europe, and the New Trade Order," *Business and Politics* 11, no. 3 (2009), doi:10.2202/1469-3569.1263.

Schott, Jeffrey J. "America, Europe, and the New Trade Order." *Business and Politics* 11, no. 3 (2009). doi:10.2202/1469-3569.1263.

20. JOURNAL ARTICLE FROM A DATABASE. For basic information on citing a periodical article from a database in *Chicago* style, see the source map on pp. 322–23.

20. W. Trent Foley and Nicholas J. Higham, "Bede on the Britons," *Early Medieval Europe* 17, no. 2 (2009), 157, doi:10.1111/j.1468-0254.2009.00258.x.

Foley, W. Trent, and Nicholas J. Higham. "Bede on the Britons." *Early Medieval Europe* 17, no. 2 (2009). 154–85. doi:10.1111/j.1468-0254.2009.00258.x.

21. ARTICLE IN A PRINT MAGAZINE

21. Terry McDermott, "The Mastermind: Khalid Sheikh Mohammed and the Making of 9/11," *New Yorker*, September 13, 2010, 42.

McDermott, Terry. "The Mastermind: Khalid Sheikh Mohammed and the Making of 9/11." *New Yorker*, September 13, 2010, 38–51.

22. ARTICLE IN AN ONLINE MAGAZINE

22. Tracy Clark-Flory, "Educating Women Saves Kids' Lives," *Salon*, September 17, 2010, http://www.salon.com/life/broadsheet/2010/09/17/education_women/index.html.

Clark-Flory, Tracy. "Educating Women Saves Kids' Lives." *Salon*, September 17, 2010. http://www.salon.com/life/broadsheet/2010/09/17/education_women/index.html.

23. MAGAZINE ARTICLE FROM A DATABASE

23. Sami Yousafzai and Ron Moreau, "Twisting Arms in Afghanistan," *Newsweek*, November 9, 2009, 8, Academic Search Premier (44962900).

Yousafzai, Sami, and Ron Moreau. "Twisting Arms in Afghanistan." *Newsweek*, November 9, 2009. 8. Academic Search Premier (44962900).

24. ARTICLE IN A NEWSPAPER. Do not include page numbers for a newspaper article, but you may include the section, if any.

24. Caroline E. Mayer, "Wireless Industry to Adopt Voluntary Standards," *Washington Post*, September 9, 2003, sec. E.

Mayer, Caroline E. "Wireless Industry to Adopt Voluntary Standards." *Washington Post*, September 9, 2003, sec. E.

If you provide complete documentation of a newspaper article in a note, you may not need to include it in the bibliography. Check your instructor's preference.

25. ARTICLE IN AN ONLINE NEWSPAPER. If the URL for the article is very long, use the URL for the newspaper's home page.

25. Andrew C. Revkin, "Arctic Melt Unnerves the Experts," *New York Times*, October 2, 2007, http://www.nytimes.com.

Revkin, Andrew C. "Arctic Melt Unnerves the Experts." *New York Times*, October 2, 2007. http://www.nytimes.com.

26. NEWSPAPER ARTICLE FROM A DATABASE

26. Demetria Irwin, "A Hatchet, Not a Scalpel, for NYC Budget Cuts," *New York Amsterdam News*, November 13, 2008, Academic Search Premier (35778153).

Irwin, Demetria. "A Hatchet, Not a Scalpel, for NYC Budget Cuts." *New York Amsterdam News*, November 13, 2008. Academic Search Premier (35778153).

CHICAGO SOURCE MAP: Articles from Databases

1 **Author.** In a note, list the author(s) first name first. In the bibliographic entry, list the first author last name first, comma, first name; list other authors first name first.

2 **Article title.** Enclose the title and subtitle (if any) in quotation marks, and capitalize major words. In the notes section, put a comma before and after the title. In the bibliography, put a period before and after.

3 **Periodical title.** Italicize the title and subtitle, and capitalize all major words. For a magazine or newspaper, follow with a comma.

4 **Volume and issue numbers (for journals) and date.** For journals, follow the title with the volume number, a comma, the abbreviation *no.*, and the issue number; enclose the publication year in parentheses and follow with a comma (in a note) or with a period (in a bibliography). For other periodicals, give the month and year or month, day, and year, not in parentheses, followed by a comma.

5 **Page numbers.** In a note, give the page where the information is found. In the bibliographic entry, give the page range.

6 **Retrieval information.** Provide the article's DOI, if one is given, the name of the database and an accession number, or a "stable or persistent" URL for the article in the database. Because you provide stable retrieval information, you do not need to identify the electronic format of the work (i.e., PDF, as in the example shown here). End with a period.

Citations for the journal article on p. 323 would look like this:

ENDNOTE

1. Elizabeth Tucker, "Changing Concepts of Childhood: Children's Folklore Scholarship since the Late Nineteenth Century," *Journal of American Folklore* 125, no. 498 (2012), 399, http://www.jstor.org/stable/10.5406/jamerfolk.125.498.0389.

BIBLIOGRAPHIC ENTRY

Tucker Elizabeth. "Changing Concepts of Childhood: Children's Folklore Scholarship since the Late Nineteenth Century." *Journal of American Folklore* 125, no. 498 (2012), 389–410. http://www.jstor.org/stable/10.5406/jamerfolk.125.498.0389.

3 Periodical Title

4 Volume and Issue Numbers and Date

Changing Concepts of Childhood: Children's Folklore Scholarship since the Late Nineteenth Century
Author(s): Elizabeth Tucker
Source: *The Journal of American Folklore*, Vol. 125, No. 498 (Fall 2012), pp. 389-410
Published by: University of Illinois Press on behalf of American Folklore Society
Stable URL: http://www.jstor.org/stable/10.5406/jamerfolk.125.498.0389

6 Retrieval Information

5 Page Numbers

ELIZABETH TUCKER

1 Author

Changing Concepts of Childhood: Children's Folklore Scholarship since the Late Nineteenth Century

This essay examines children's folklore scholarship from the late nineteenth century to the present, tracing key concepts from the Gilded Age to the contemporary era. These concepts reflect significant social, cultural, political, and scientific changes. From the "savage child" to the "secret-keeping child," the "magic-making child," the "cerebral child," the "taboo-breaking child," the "monstrous child," and others, scholarly representations of young people have close connections to the eras in which they developed. Nineteenth-century children's folklore scholarship relied on evolutionism; now evolutionary biology provides a basis for children's folklore research, so we have re-entered fam

2 Article Title and Subtitle

SINCE 1977, WHEN THE American Folklore Society decided to form a new section for scholars interested in young people's traditions, I have belonged to the Children's Folklore Section. It has been a joy to contribute to this dynamic organization, which has significantly influenced children's folklore scholarship and children's book authors' focus on folk tradition. This essay examines children's folklore scholarship from the late nineteenth century to the present, tracing key concepts from the Gilded Age to the contemporary era in the English language. These concepts reflect significant social, cultural, political, and scientific changes that have occurred since William Wells Newell, the first secretary of the American Folklore Society and the first editor of the *Journal of American Folklore*, published *Games and Songs of American Children* in 1883. They also reveal some very interesting commonalities. Those of us who pursue children's folklore scholarship today may consider ourselves to be light years away from nineteenth-century scholars' research but may find, when reading nineteenth-century works, that we have stayed fairly close to our scholarly "home base."

Before examining concepts of childhood that folklorists have developed, I will offer a working definition of this life stage and briefly explain the beginning of childhood studies. I will also summarize the Children's Folklore Section's work during the past thirty-four years. According to the *Oxford English Dictionary*, childhood consists of "the state or stage of life of a child; the time during which one is a child; the time from birth to puberty" (2011). Scholars of childhood tend to draw a line between childhood and adolescence, which begins at puberty and follows pre-adolescence. The folklore

ELIZABETH TUCKER is Professor of English at Binghamton University

Journal of American Folklore 125(498):389–410

27. BOOK REVIEW. After the information about the book under review, give publication information for the appropriate kind of source (see models 18–26).

27. Arnold Relman, "Health Care: The Disquieting Truth," review of *Tracking Medicine: A Researcher's Quest to Understand Health Care*, by John E. Wennberg, *New York Review of Books* 57, no. 14 (2010), 45.

Relman, Arnold. "Health Care: The Disquieting Truth." Review of *Tracking Medicine: A Researcher's Quest to Understand Health Care*, by John E. Wennberg. *New York Review of Books* 57, no. 14 (2010), 45–48.

Online sources

In general, include the author (if given); the title of a work from a website (in quotation marks); the name of the site (in italics, if the site is an online publication, but otherwise neither italicized nor in quotation marks); the sponsor of the site, if different from the name of the site or name of the author; the date of publication or most recent update; and a URL. If the online source does not indicate when it was published or last modified, or if your instructor requests an access date, place it before the URL.

For basic information on citing works from websites in *Chicago* style, see the source map on pp. 326–27.

28. WEBSITE

28. Rutgers School of Arts and Sciences, *The Rutgers Oral History Archive*, 2010, http://oralhistory.rutgers.edu/.

Rutgers School of Arts and Sciences. *The Rutgers Oral History Archive.* 2010. http://oralhistory.rutgers.edu/.

29. WORK FROM A WEBSITE

29. Rose Cohen, "My First Job," *The Triangle Factory Fire*, Cornell University School of Industrial and Labor Relations, 2005, http://www.ilr.cornell.edu/trianglefire/texts/.

Cohen, Rose. "My First Job." *The Triangle Factory Fire.* Cornell University School of Industrial and Labor Relations. 2005. http://www.ilr.cornell.edu/trianglefire/texts/.

30. BLOG (WEB LOG) POST. Treat a blog post as a short work from a website (see model 29).

30. Jai Arjun Singh, "On the Road in the USSR," *Jabberwock* (blog), November 29, 2007, http://jaiarjun.blogspot.com/2007/11/on-road-in-ussr.html.

Chicago recommends that blog posts appear in the notes section only, not in the bibliography, unless the blog is cited frequently. Check your instructor's preference. A bibliography reference to an entire blog would look like this:

Singh, Jai Arjun. *Jabberwock* (blog). http://jaiarjun.blogspot.com/.

31. EMAIL AND OTHER PERSONAL COMMUNICATIONS. Cite email messages and other personal communications, such as letters and telephone calls, in the text or in a note only, not in the bibliography. (*Chicago* style recommends hyphenating *e-mail.*)

31. Kareem Adas, e-mail message to author, February 11, 2013.

32. PODCAST. Treat a podcast as a short work from a website (see model 29) and give as much of the following information as you can find: the author or speaker, the title or a description of the podcast, the title of the site, the site sponsor (if different from the author or site name), the type of podcast or file format, the date of posting or access, and the URL.

32. Barack Obama, "Weekly Address: A Solar Recovery," *The White House*, podcast video, July 3, 2010, http://www.whitehouse.gov/photos-and-video/video/weekly-address-a-solar-recovery.

Obama, Barack. "Weekly Address: A Solar Recovery." *The White House.* Podcast video. July 3, 2010. http://www.whitehouse.gov/photos-and-video/video/weekly-address-a-solar-recovery.

33. ONLINE AUDIO OR VIDEO. Treat an online audio or video source as a short work from a website (see model 29). If the source is downloadable, give the medium or file format before the URL (see model 32).

33. Alyssa Katz, "Did the Mortgage Crisis Kill the American Dream?" YouTube video, 4:32, posted by NYCRadio, June 24, 2009, http://www.youtube.com/watch?v=uivtwjwd_Qw.

Katz, Alyssa. "Did the Mortgage Crisis Kill the American Dream?" YouTube video, 4:32. Posted by NYCRadio. June 24, 2009. http://www.youtube.com/watch?v=uivtwjwd_Qw.

CHICAGO SOURCE MAP: Works from Websites

1. **Author.** In a note, list the author(s) first name first. In a bibliographic entry, list the first author last name first, comma, first name; list additional authors first name first. Note that the host may serve as the author.
2. **Document title.** Enclose the title in quotation marks, and capitalize all major words. In a note, put a comma before and after the title. In the bibliography, put a period before and after.
3. **Title of website.** Capitalize all major words. If the site's title is analogous to a book or periodical title, italicize it. In the notes section, put a comma after the title. In the bibliography, put a period after the title.
4. **Sponsor of site.** If the sponsor is the same as the author or site title, you may omit it. End with a comma (in the note) or a period (in the bibliographic entry).
5. **Date of publication or last modification.** If no date is available, or if your instructor requests it, include your date of access (with the word *accessed*).
6. **Retrieval information.** Give the URL for the website. If you are required to include a date of access, put the word *accessed* and the date in parentheses after the URL. End with a period.

Citations for the website on p. 327 would look like this:

ENDNOTE

1. Rebecca Edwards, "The Populist Party," *1896: The Presidential Campaign: Cartoons & Commentary*, Vassar College, 2000, http://projects.vassar.edu/1896/populists.html.

BIBLIOGRAPHIC ENTRY

Edwards, Rebecca. "The Populist Party." *1896: The Presidential Campaign: Cartoons & Commentary.* Vassar College. 2000. http://projects.vassar.edu/1896/populists.html.

6 Retrieval Information
projects.vassar.edu/1896/populists.html

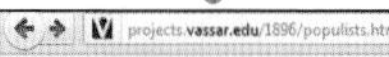

The Populist Party — 2 Document Title

The Rise of Populism
The People's Party (or Populist Party, as it was widely known) was much younger than the Democratic and Republican Parties, which had been founded before the Civil War. Agricultural areas in the West and South had been hit by economic depression years before industrial areas. In the 1880s, as drought hit the wheat-growing areas of the Great Plains and prices for Southern cotton sunk to new lows, many tenant farmers fell into deep debt. This exacerbated long-held grievances against railroads, lenders, grain-elevator owners, and others with whom farmers did business. By the early 1890s, as the depression worsened, some industrial workers shared these farm families' views on labor andthe trusts.

In 1890 Populists won control of the Kansas state legislature, and Kansan **William Peffer** became the party's first U.S. Senator. Peffer, with his long white beard, was a humorous figure to many Eastern journalists and politicians, who saw little evidence of Populism in their states and often treated the party as a joke. Nonetheless, Western and Southern Populists gained support rapidly. In 1892 the national party was officially founded through a merger of the Farmers' Alliance and the Knights of Labor. In that year the Populist presidential candidate, James B. Weaver, won over one million votes. Between 1892 and 1896, however, the party failed to make further gains, in part because of fraud, intimidation, and violence by Southern Democrats.

By 1896 the Populist organization was in even more turmoil than that of Democrats. Two main factions had appear…
organi…
"fused…
third p…

3 Title of Website

Homepage

© 2000, Rebecca Edwards, Vassar College

4 Sponsor of Site

5 Date of Publication

1 Author

Other sources

34. PUBLISHED OR BROADCAST INTERVIEW

34. Nina Totenberg, interview by Charlie Rose, *The Charlie Rose Show*, PBS, June 29, 2010.

Totenberg, Nina. Interview by Charlie Rose. *The Charlie Rose Show*. PBS, June 29, 2010.

Interviews you conduct are considered personal communications (see model 31).

35. VIDEO OR DVD

35. Edward Norton and Edward Furlong, *American History X*, directed by Tony Kaye (1998; Los Angeles: New Line Studios, 2002), DVD.

Norton, Edward, and Edward Furlong. *American History X*. Directed by Tony Kaye, 1998. Los Angeles: New Line Studios, 2002. DVD.

36. SOUND RECORDING

36. Paul Robeson, *The Collector's Paul Robeson*, recorded 1959, Monitor MCD-61580, 1989, compact disc.

Robeson, Paul. *The Collector's Paul Robeson*. Recorded 1959. Monitor MCD-61580, 1989, compact disc.

37. WORK OF ART. Begin with the artist's name and the title of the work. If you viewed the work in person, give the medium, the date, and the name of the place where you saw it.

37. Mary Cassatt, *The Child's Bath*, oil on canvas, 1893, The Art Institute of Chicago, Chicago, IL.

Cassatt, Mary. *The Child's Bath*. Oil on canvas, 1893. The Art Institute of Chicago, Chicago, IL.

If you refer to a reproduction, give the publication information.

37. Mary Cassatt, *The Child's Bath*, oil on canvas, 1893, on *Art Access*, The Art Institute of Chicago, August 2004, http://www.artic.edu/artaccess/AA_Impressionist/pages/IMP_6.shtml#.

Cassatt, Mary. *The Child's Bath*. Oil on canvas, 1893. On *Art Access*, The Art Institute of Chicago. August 2004. http://www.artic.edu/artaccess /AA_Impressionist/pages/IMP_6.shtml#.

38. PAMPHLET, REPORT, OR BROCHURE. Information about the author or publisher may not be readily available, but give enough information to identify your source.

38. Jamie McCarthy, *Who Is David Irving?* (San Antonio, TX: Holocaust History Project, 1998).

McCarthy, Jamie. *Who Is David Irving?* San Antonio, TX: Holocaust History Project, 1998.

39. GOVERNMENT DOCUMENT

39. U.S. House Committee on Ways and Means, *Report on Trade Mission to Sub-Saharan Africa*, 108th Cong., 1st sess. (Washington, DC: Government Printing Office, 2003), 28.

U.S. House Committee on Ways and Means. *Report on Trade Mission to Sub-Saharan Africa*. 108th Cong., 1st sess. Washington, DC: Government Printing Office, 2003.

47d A sample student research essay, *Chicago* style

On the following pages are excerpts from an essay by Amanda Rinder that conforms to the *Chicago* guidelines described in this chapter. The digital resources for this book include her complete project. (See the inside back cover for more details.)

Documentation: *Chicago* Style > Student Writing

STUDENT WRITING

First page of body text is p. 2

Paper refers to each figure by number

Thesis introduced

Double-spaced text

Source cited using superscript numeral

Figure caption includes number, short title, and source

Rinder 2

Only one city has the "Big Shoulders" described by Carl Sandburg: Chicago (fig. 1). So renowned are its skyscrapers and celebrated building style that an entire school of architecture is named for Chicago. Presently, however, the place that Frank Sinatra called "my kind of town" is beginning to lose sight of exactly what kind of town it is. Many of the buildings that give Chicago its distinctive character are being torn down in order to make room for new growth. Both preserving the classics and encouraging new creation are important; the combination of these elements gives Chicago architecture its unique flavor. Witold Rybczynski, a professor of urbanism, told Tracie Rozhon of the *New York Times*, "Of all the cities we can think of . . . we associate Chicago with new things, with building new. Combining that with preservation is a difficult task, a tricky thing. It's hard to find the middle ground in Chicago."[1] Yet finding a middle ground is essential if the city is to retain the original character that sets it apart from the rest. In order to

Fig. 1. Chicago skyline, circa 1940s. (Postcard courtesy of Minnie Dangburg.)

Annotations indicate effective choices or *Chicago*-style formatting.

STUDENT WRITING

Rinder 9

Notes

1. Tracie Rozhon, "Chicago Girds for Big Battle over Its Skyline," *New York Times*, November 12, 2000, Academic Search Premier (28896783).

Newspaper article in database

2. David Garrard Lowe, *Lost Chicago* (New York: Watson-Guptill Publications, 2000), 123.

Print book

3. *Columbia Encyclopedia*, Sixth Ed., s.v. "Louis Sullivan."

4. Daniel Bluestone, *Constructing Chicago* (New Haven: Yale University Press, 1991), 105.

5. Alan J. Shannon, "When Will It End?" *Chicago Tribune*, September 11, 1987, quoted in Karen J. Dilibert, *From Landmark to Landfill* (Chicago: Chicago Architectural Foundation, 2000), 11.

Indirect source

6. Steve Kerch, "Landmark Decisions," *Chicago Tribune*, March 18, 1990, sec. 16.

7. John W. Stamper, *Chicago's North Michigan Avenue* (Chicago: University of Chicago Press, 1991), 215.

8. Alf Siewers, "Success Spoiling the Magnificent Mile?" *Chicago Sun-Times*, April 9, 1995, http://www.sun-times.com/.

Newspaper article online

9. Paul Gapp, "McCarthy Building Puts Landmark Law on a Collision Course with Developers," *Chicago Tribune*, April 20, 1986, quoted in Karen J. Dilibert, *From Landmark to Landfill* (Chicago: Chicago Architectural Foundation, 2000), 4.

10. Ibid.

Reference to previous source

11. Rozhon, "Chicago Girds for Big Battle."

12. Kerch, "Landmark Decisions."

Second reference to source

13. Robert Bruegmann, *The Architects and the City* (Chicago: University of Chicago Press, 1997), 443.

STUDENT WRITING

Rinder 10

Bibliography starts on new page

Bibliography

Bluestone, Daniel. *Constructing Chicago.* New Haven: Yale University Press, 1991.

Print book

Bruegmann, Robert. *The Architects and the City.* Chicago: University of Chicago Press, 1997.

Pamphlet

Dilibert, Karen J. *From Landmark to Landfill.* Chicago: Chicago Architectural Foundation, 2000.

Newspaper article

Kerch, Steve. "Landmark Decisions." *Chicago Tribune*, March 18, 1990, sec. 16.

Lowe, David Garrard. *Lost Chicago.* New York: Watson-Guptill Publications, 2000.

Article from database

Rozhon, Tracie. "Chicago Girds for Big Battle over Its Skyline." *New York Times*, November 12, 2000. Academic Search Premier (28896783).

Bibliography entries use hanging indent and are not numbered

Siewers, Alf. "Success Spoiling the Magnificent Mile?" *Chicago Sun-Times*, April 9, 1995. http://www.sun-times.com/.

Stamper, John W. *Chicago's North Michigan Avenue.* Chicago: University of Chicago Press, 1991.

48 CSE Style

Writers in the physical sciences, the life sciences, and mathematics often use the documentation style set forth by the Council of Science Editors (CSE). Guidelines for citing print sources can be found in *Scientific Style and Format: The CSE Manual for Authors, Editors, and Publishers*, Seventh Edition (2006).

48a Following CSE manuscript format

Title page. Center the title of your paper. Beneath it, center your name. Include other relevant information, such as the course name and number, the instructor's name, and the date submitted.

Margins and spacing. Leave standard margins at the top and bottom and on both sides of each page. Double-space the text and the references list.

Page numbers. Type a short version of the paper's title and the page number in the upper right-hand corner of each page.

Abstract. CSE style frequently calls for a one-paragraph abstract (about one hundred words). The abstract should be on a separate page, right after the title page, with the title *Abstract* centered one inch from the top of the page.

Headings. CSE style does not require headings, but it notes that they can help readers quickly find the contents of a section of the paper.

Tables and figures. Tables and figures must be labeled *Table* or *Figure* and numbered separately, one sequence for tables and one for figures. Give each table and figure a short, informative title. Be sure to introduce each table and figure in your text, and comment on its significance.

List of references. Start the list of references on a new page at the end of the essay, and continue to number the pages consecutively. Center the title *References* one inch from the top of the page, and double-space before beginning the first entry.

48b Creating CSE in-text citations

In CSE style, citations within an essay follow one of three formats.

- The *citation-sequence format* calls for a superscript number or a number in parentheses after any mention of a source. The sources are numbered in the order they appear. Each number refers to the same source every time it is used. The first source mentioned in the paper is numbered *1*, the second source is numbered *2*, and so on.
- The *citation-name format* also calls for a superscript number or a number in parentheses after any mention of a source. The numbers are added after the list of references is completed and alphabetized, so that the source numbered *1* is alphabetically first in the list of references, *2* is alphabetically second, and so on.
- The *name-year format* calls for the last name of the author and the year of publication in parentheses after any mention of a source. If the last name appears in a signal phrase, the name-year format allows for giving only the year of publication in parentheses.

Before deciding which system to use, ask your instructor's preference.

1. IN-TEXT CITATION USING CITATION-SEQUENCE OR CITATION-NAME FORMAT

VonBergen[12] provides the most complete discussion of this phenomenon.

For the citation-sequence and citation-name formats, you would use the same superscript ([12]) for each subsequent citation of this work by VonBergen.

2. IN-TEXT CITATION USING NAME-YEAR FORMAT

VonBergen (2003) provides the most complete discussion of this phenomenon.

Hussar's two earlier studies of juvenile obesity (1995, 1999) examined only children with diabetes.

The classic examples of such investigations (Morrow 1968; Bridger et al. 1971; Franklin and Wayson 1972) still shape the assumptions of current studies.

48c Creating a CSE list of references

The citations in the text of an essay correspond to items on a list titled *References*, which starts on a new page at the end of the essay. Continue to number the pages consecutively, center the title *References* one inch from the top of the page, and double-space before beginning the first entry.

The order of the entries depends on which format you follow:

- **Citation-sequence format:** number and list the references in the order the references are first cited in the text.
- **Citation-name format:** list and number the references in alphabetical order.
- **Name-year format:** list the references, unnumbered, in alphabetical order.

In the following examples, you will see that both the citation-sequence and citation-name formats call for listing the date after the publisher's name in references for books and after the periodical name in references for articles. The name-year format calls for listing the date immediately after the author's name in any kind of reference.

CSE style also specifies the treatment and placement of the following basic elements in the list of references:

- **Author.** List all authors last name first, and use only initials for first and middle names. Do not place a comma after the author's last name, and do not place periods after or spaces between the initials. Use a period after the last initial of the last author listed.
- **Title.** Do not italicize titles and subtitles of books and titles of periodicals. Do not enclose titles of articles in quotation marks. For books and articles, capitalize only the first word of the title and any proper nouns or proper adjectives. Abbreviate and capitalize all major words in a periodical title.

As you refer to these examples, pay attention to how publication information (publishers for books, details about periodicals for articles) and other specific elements are styled and punctuated.

Books

1. ONE AUTHOR

CITATION-SEQUENCE AND CITATION-NAME

1. Buchanan M. Nexus: small worlds and the groundbreaking theory of networks. New York: Norton; 2003.

NAME-YEAR

Buchanan M. 2003. Nexus: small worlds and the groundbreaking theory of networks. New York: Norton.

2. TWO OR MORE AUTHORS

CITATION-SEQUENCE AND CITATION-NAME

2. Wojciechowski BW, Rice NM. Experimental methods in kinetic studies. 2nd ed. St. Louis (MO): Elsevier Science; 2003.

DIRECTORY TO CSE STYLE

CSE style for references

NAME-YEAR

Wojciechowski BW, Rice NM. 2003. Experimental methods in kinetic studies. 2nd ed. St. Louis (MO): Elsevier Science.

3. ORGANIZATION AS AUTHOR

CITATION-SEQUENCE AND CITATION-NAME

3. World Health Organization. The world health report 2002: reducing risks, promoting healthy life. Geneva (Switzerland): The Organization; 2002.

Place the organization's abbreviation at the beginning of the name-year entry, and use the abbreviation in the corresponding in-text citation. Alphabetize the entry by the first word of the full name, not by the abbreviation.

NAME-YEAR

[WHO] World Health Organization. 2002. The world health report 2002: reducing risks, promoting healthy life. Geneva (Switzerland): The Organization.

4. BOOK PREPARED BY EDITOR(S)

CITATION-SEQUENCE AND CITATION-NAME

4. Torrence ME, Isaacson RE, editors. Microbial food safety in animal agriculture: current topics. Ames: Iowa State University Press; 2003.

NAME-YEAR

Torrence ME, Isaacson RE, editors. 2003. Microbial safety in animal agriculture: current topics. Ames: Iowa State University Press.

5. SECTION OF A BOOK WITH AN EDITOR

CITATION-SEQUENCE AND CITATION-NAME

5. Kawamura A. Plankton. In: Perrin MF, Wursig B, Thewissen JGM, editors. Encyclopedia of marine mammals. San Diego: Academic Press; 2002. p. 939–942.

NAME-YEAR

Kawamura A. 2002. Plankton. In: Perrin MF, Wursig B, Thewissen JGM, editors. Encyclopedia of marine mammals. San Diego: Academic Press. p. 939–942.

6. CHAPTER OF A BOOK

CITATION-SEQUENCE AND CITATION-NAME

6. Honigsbaum M. The fever trail: in search of the cure for malaria. New York: Picador; 2003. Chapter 2, The cure; p. 19–38.

NAME-YEAR

Honigsbaum M. 2003. The fever trail: in search of the cure for malaria. New York: Picador. Chapter 2, The cure; p. 19–38.

7. PAPER OR ABSTRACT IN CONFERENCE PROCEEDINGS

CITATION-SEQUENCE AND CITATION-NAME

7. Gutierrez AP. Integrating biological and environmental factors in crop system models [abstract]. In: Integrated Biological Systems Conference; 2003 Apr 14–16; San Antonio, TX. Beaumont (TX): Agroeconomics Research Group; 2003. p. 14–15.

NAME-YEAR

Gutierrez AP. 2003. Integrating biological and environmental factors in crop system models [abstract]. In: Integrated Biological Systems Conference; 2003 Apr 14–16; San Antonio, TX. Beaumont (TX): Agroeconomics Research Group. p. 14–15.

Periodicals

Provide volume and issue numbers for journals. For newspaper and magazine articles, include the section designation and column number, if any, and the date. For all periodicals, give inclusive page numbers. For rules on abbreviating journal titles, consult the CSE manual or ask an instructor.

8. ARTICLE IN A JOURNAL

CITATION-SEQUENCE AND CITATION-NAME

8. Mahmud K, Vance ML. Human growth hormone and aging. New Engl J Med. 2003;348(2):2256–2257.

NAME-YEAR

Mahmud K, Vance ML. 2003. Human growth hormone and aging. New Engl J Med. 348(2):2256–2257.

9. ARTICLE IN A WEEKLY JOURNAL

CITATION-SEQUENCE AND CITATION-NAME

9. Holden C. Future brightening for depression treatments. Science. 2003 Oct 31:810–813.

NAME-YEAR

Holden C. 2003. Future brightening for depression treatments. Science. Oct 31:810–813.

10. ARTICLE IN A MAGAZINE

CITATION-SEQUENCE AND CITATION-NAME

10. Livio M. Moving right along: the accelerating universe holds secrets to dark energy, the Big Bang, and the ultimate beauty of nature. Astronomy. 2002 Jul:34–39.

NAME-YEAR

Livio M. 2002 Jul. Moving right along: the accelerating universe holds secrets to dark energy, the Big Bang, and the ultimate beauty of nature. Astronomy. 34–39.

11. ARTICLE IN A NEWSPAPER

CITATION-SEQUENCE AND CITATION-NAME

11. Kolata G. Bone diagnosis gives new data but no answers. New York Times (National Ed.). 2003 Sep 28;Sect. 1:1 (col. 1).

NAME-YEAR

Kolata G. 2003 Sep 28. Bone diagnosis gives new data but no answers. New York Times (National Ed.). Sect. 1:1 (col. 1).

Digital sources

These examples use the citation-sequence or citation-name system. To adapt them to the name-year system, delete the note number and place the update date immediately after the author's name.

The basic entry for most sources accessed through the Internet should include the following elements:

- **Author.** Give the author's name, if available, last name first, followed by the initial(s) and a period.
- **Title.** For book, journal, and article titles, follow the style for print materials. For all other types of electronic material, reproduce the title that appears on the screen.
- **Medium.** Indicate, in brackets, that the source is not in print format by using a designation such as *[Internet]*.
- **Place of publication.** The city usually should be followed by the two-letter abbreviation for the state. No state abbreviation is necessary for well-known cities such as New York, Chicago, Boston, and London or for a publisher whose location is part of its name (for example, University of Oklahoma Press). If the city is implied, put the city and state in brackets. If the city cannot be inferred, use the words *place unknown* in brackets.
- **Publisher.** For material other than journal articles from websites and online databases, include the individual or organization that produces or sponsors the site. If no publisher can be determined, use the words *publisher unknown* in brackets.
- **Dates.** Cite three important dates if possible: the date that the publication was placed on the Internet or the copyright date; the latest date of any update or revision; and the date the publication was accessed by you.
- **Page, document, volume, and issue numbers.** When citing a portion of a larger work or site, list the inclusive page numbers or document numbers of the specific item being cited. For journals or journal articles, include volume and issue numbers. If exact page

numbers are not available, include in brackets the approximate length in computer screens, paragraphs, or bytes: [2 screens], [10 paragraphs], [332K bytes].

- **Address.** Include the URL or other electronic address; use the phrase *Available from:* to introduce the address. Only URLs that end with a slash are followed by a period.

12. MATERIAL FROM AN ONLINE DATABASE

12. Shilts E. Water wanderers. Can Geographic [Internet]. 2002 [cited 2010 Jan 27];122(3):72–77. Academic Search Premier. Ipswich (MA): EBSCO. Available from: http://www.ebscohost.com/ Document No.: 6626534.

13. ARTICLE IN AN ONLINE JOURNAL

13. Perez P, Calonge TM. Yeast protein kinase C. J Biochem [Internet]. 2002 Oct [cited 2008 Nov 3];132(4):513–517. Available from: http://edpex104.bcasj.or.jp/jb-pdf/132-4/jb132-4-513.pdf

14. ARTICLE IN AN ONLINE NEWSPAPER

14. Brody JE. Reasons, and remedies, for morning sickness. New York Times Online [Internet]. 2004 Apr 27 [cited 2009 Apr 30]. Available from: http://www.nytimes.com/2009/04/27/health /27BROD.html

15. ONLINE BOOK

15. Patrick TS, Allison JR, Krakow GA. Protected plants of Georgia [Internet]. Social Circle (GA): Georgia Department of Natural Resources; c1995 [cited 2010 Dec 3]. Available from: http://www.georgiawildlife .com/content/displaycontent.asp?txtDocument=89&txtPage=9

To cite a portion of an online book, give the name of the part after the publication information: *Chapter 6, Encouraging germination.* See model 6.

16. WEBSITE

16. Geology and public policy [Internet]. Boulder (CO): Geological Society of America; c2010 [updated 2010 Jun 3; cited 2010 Sep 19]. Available from: http://www.geosociety.org/geopolicy.htm

17. GOVERNMENT WEBSITE

17. Health disparities: reducing health disparities in cancer [Internet]. Atlanta (GA): Centers for Disease Control and Prevention (US); 2010 [updated 2010 Apr 5; cited 2010 May 1]. Available from: http://www.cdc.gov/cancer/healthdisparities/basic_info/disparities.htm

48d A sample student writing project, CSE style

The following excerpt from a literature review by Joanna Hays conforms to the name-year format in the CSE guidelines described in this chapter. The digital resources for this book include her complete project. (See the inside back cover for more details.)

STUDENT WRITING

Niemann-Pick Disease 2

Running head has short title, page number

Overview

Niemann-Pick Disease (NP) occurs in patients with deficient acid sphingomyelinase (ASM) activity as well as with the lysosomal accumulation of sphingomyelin. It is an autosomal recessive disorder (Levran et al. 1991). As recently as 1991, researchers had classified two major phenotypes: Type A and Type B (Levran et al. 1991). In more recent studies several more phenotypes have been identified, including Types C and D. Each type of NP has distinct characteristics and effects on the patient. NP is distributed worldwide, but is closely associated with Ashkenazi Jewish descendants. Niemann-Pick Disease is relevant to the molecular world today because of advances being made in the ability to identify mutations, to trace ancestry where the mutation may have originated, and to counsel patients with a high potential of carrying the disease. Genetic counseling primarily consists of confirmation of the particular disease and calculation of the possible future reappearance in the same gene line (Brock 1974). The following discussion will summarize the identification of mutations causing the various forms of NP, the distribution of NP, as well as new genotypes and phenotypes that are correlated with NP.

Mutations Causing NP

Headings organize project

Levran et al. (1991) inform readers of the frequent identification of missense mutations in the gene associated with Ashkenazi Jewish persons afflicted by Type A and Type B NP. This paper identifies the mutations associated with NP and the beginning of many molecular techniques to develop diagnoses. Greer et al. (1998) identify a new mutation that is specifically identified to be the cause of Type D. NP in various forms is closely associated with the founder effect caused by a couple married in the early 1700s in what is now Nova Scotia. Simonaro et al. (2002) discusses the distribution of Type B NP as well as new phenotypes and genotypes. All three of these papers identify

Annotations indicate CSE-style formatting.

STUDENT WRITING

Niemann-Pick Disease 9

References

Alphabetical by name

Brock DJH. 1974. Prenatal diagnosis and genetic counseling. J Clin Pathol Suppl. (R Coll Path.) 8:150–155.

Greer WL, Ridell DC, Gillan TL, Girouard GS, Sparrow SM, Byers DM, Dobson MJ, Neumann PE. 1998. The Nova Scotia (type D) form of Niemann-Pick disease is caused by a $G_{3097} \rightarrow T$ transversion in NPC1. Am J Hum Genet 63:52–54.

Levran O, Desnick RJ, Schuchman EH. 1991. Niemann-Pick disease: a frequent missense mutation in the acid sphingomyelinase gene of Ashkenazi Jewish type A and B patients. P Natl Acad Sci USA 88:3748–3752.

Simonaro CM, Desnick RJ, McGovern MM, Wasserstein MP, Schuchman EH. 2002. The demographics and distribution of type B Niemann-Pick disease: novel mutations lead to new genotype/phenotype correlations. Am J Hum Genet 71:1413–1419.

Glossary of Usage

Conventions of usage might be called the "good manners" of discourse. And just as manners vary from culture to culture and time to time, so do conventions of usage. Matters of usage, like other language choices you must make, depend on what your purpose is and on what is appropriate for a particular audience at a particular time.

a, an Use *a* with a word that begins with a consonant (*a book*), a consonant sound such as "y" or "w" (*a euphoric moment, a one-sided match*), or a sounded *h* (*a hemisphere*). Use *an* with a word that begins with a vowel (*an umbrella*), a vowel sound (*an X-ray*), or a silent *h* (*an honor*).

accept, except The verb *accept* means "receive" or "agree to." *Except* is usually a preposition that means "aside from" or "excluding." *All the plaintiffs except Mr. Kim decided to accept the settlement.*

advice, advise The noun *advice* means "opinion" or "suggestion"; the verb *advise* means "offer advice." *Doctors advise everyone not to smoke, but many people ignore the advice.*

affect, effect As a verb, *affect* means "influence" or "move the emotions of"; as a noun, it means "emotions" or "feelings." *Effect* is a noun meaning "result"; less commonly, it is a verb meaning "bring about." *The storm affected a large area. Its effects included widespread power failures. The drug effected a major change in the patient's affect.*

aggravate The formal meaning is "make worse." *Having another mouth to feed aggravated their poverty*. In academic and professional writing, avoid using *aggravate* to mean "irritate" or "annoy."

all ready, already *All ready* means "fully prepared." *Already* means "previously." *We were all ready for Lucy's party when we learned that she had already left.*

all right, alright Avoid the spelling *alright.*

all together, altogether *All together* means "all in a group" or "gathered in one place." *Altogether* means "completely" or "everything considered." *When the board members were all together, their mutual distrust was altogether obvious.*

allude, elude *Allude* means "refer indirectly." *Elude* means "avoid" or "escape from." *The candidate did not even allude to her opponent. The suspect eluded the police for several days.*

allusion, illusion An *allusion* is an indirect reference. An *illusion* is a false or misleading appearance. *The speaker's allusion to the Bible created an illusion of piety.*

a lot Avoid the spelling *alot*.

already See *all ready, already*.

alright See *all right, alright*.

altogether See *all together, altogether*.

among, between In referring to two things or people, use *between*. In referring to three or more, use *among*. *The relationship between the twins is different from that among the other three children.*

amount, number Use *amount* with quantities you cannot count; use *number* for quantities you can count. *A small number of volunteers cleared a large amount of brush.*

an See *a, an*.

and/or Avoid this term except in business or legal writing. Instead of *fat and/or protein*, write *fat, protein, or both*.

any body, anybody, any one, anyone *Anybody* and *anyone* are pronouns meaning "any person." *Anyone* [or *anybody*] *would enjoy this film. Any body* is an adjective modifying a noun. *Any body of water has its own ecology. Any one* is two adjectives or a pronoun modified by an adjective. *Customers could buy only two sale items at any one time. The winner could choose any one of the prizes.*

anyplace In academic and professional discourse, use *anywhere* instead.

anyway, anyways In writing, use *anyway*, not *anyways*.

apt, liable, likely *Likely to* means "probably will," and *apt to* means "inclines or tends to." In many instances, they are interchangeable. *Liable* often carries a more negative sense and is also a legal term meaning "obligated" or "responsible."

as Avoid sentences in which it is not clear if *as* means "when" or "because." For example, does *Carl left town as his father was* *arriving* mean "at the same time as his father was arriving" or "because his father was arriving"?

as, as if, like In academic and professional writing, use *as* or *as if* instead of *like* to introduce a clause. *The dog howled as if* [not *like*] *it were in pain. She did as* [not *like*] *I suggested.*

assure, ensure, insure *Assure* means "convince" or "promise"; its direct object is usually a person or persons. *She assured voters she would not raise taxes. Ensure* and *insure* both mean "make certain," but *insure* usually refers specifically to protection against financial loss. *When the city rationed water to ensure that the supply would last, the Browns could no longer afford to insure their car-wash business.*

as to Do not use *as to* as a substitute for *about*. *Karen was unsure about* [not *as to*] *Bruce's intentions.*

at, where See *where*.

awhile, a while Always use *a while* after a preposition such as *for*, *in*, or *after*. *We drove awhile and then stopped for a while*.

bad, badly Use *bad* after a linking verb such as *be*, *feel*, or *seem*. Use *badly* to modify an action verb, an adjective, or another verb. *The hostess felt bad because the dinner was badly prepared.*

bare, bear Use *bare* to mean "uncovered" and *bear* to refer to the animal or to mean "carry" or "endure": *The walls were bare. The emptiness was hard to bear*.

because of, due to Use *due to* when the effect, stated as a noun, appears before the verb *be*. *His illness was due to malnutrition*. (*Illness*, a noun, is the effect.) Use *because of* when the effect is stated as a clause. *He was sick because of malnutrition*. (*He was sick*, a clause, is the effect.)

being as, being that In academic or professional writing, use *because* or *since* instead of these expressions. *Because* [not *being as*] *Romeo killed Tybalt, he was banished to Padua.*

beside, besides *Beside* is a preposition meaning "next to." *Besides* can be a preposition meaning "other than" or an adverb meaning "in addition." *No one besides Francesca would sit beside him.*

between See *among, between*.

brake, break *Brake* means "to stop" and also refers to a stopping mechanism: *Check the brakes*. *Break* means "fracture" or an interruption. *The coffee break was too short.*

breath, breathe *Breath* is a noun; *breathe*, a verb. "*Breathe*," *said the nurse, so June took a deep breath*.

bring, take Use *bring* when an object is moved from a farther to a nearer place; use *take* when the opposite is true. *Take the box to the post office; bring back my mail.*

but that, but what Avoid using these as substitutes for *that* in expressions of doubt. *Hercule Poirot never doubted that* [not *but that*] *he would solve the case.*

but yet Do not use these words together. *He is strong but* [not *but yet*] *gentle.*

can, may *Can* refers to ability and *may* to possibility or permission. *Since I can ski the slalom well, I may win the race.*

can't hardly *Hardly* has a negative meaning; therefore, *can't hardly* is a double negative. This expression is commonly used in some varieties of English but is not used in academic English. *Tim can* [not *can't*] *hardly wait.*

can't help but This expression is not used in academic English. Use *I can't help going* rather than *I can't help but go.*

censor, censure *Censor* means "remove that which is considered offensive." *Censure* means "formally reprimand." *The newspaper censored stories that offended advertisers. The legislature censured the official for misconduct.*

compare to, compare with *Compare to* means "regard as similar." *Jamie compared the loss to a kick in the head. Compare with* means "examine to find differences or similarities." *Compare Tim Burton's films with David Lynch's.*

complement, compliment *Complement* means "go well with." *Compliment* means "praise." *Guests complimented her on how her earrings complemented her gown.*

comprise, compose *Comprise* means "contain." *Compose* means "make up." *The class comprises twenty students. Twenty students compose the class.*

conscience, conscious *Conscience* means "a sense of right and wrong." *Conscious* means "awake" or "aware." *Lisa was conscious of a guilty conscience.*

consensus of opinion Use *consensus* instead of this redundant phrase. *The family consensus was to sell the old house.*

consequently, subsequently *Consequently* means "as a result"; *subsequently* means "then." *He quit, and subsequently his wife lost her job; consequently, they had to sell their house.*

continual, continuous *Continual* means "repeated at regular or frequent intervals." *Continuous* means "continuing or connected without a break." *The damage done by continuous erosion was increased by the continual storms.*

could of *Have*, not *of*, should follow *could, would, should*, or *might*. *We could have* [not *of*] *invited them.*

criteria, criterion *Criterion* means "standard of judgment" or "necessary qualification." *Criteria* is the plural form. *Image is the wrong criterion for choosing a president.*

data *Data* is the plural form of the Latin word *datum*, meaning "fact." Although *data* is used informally as either singular or plural, in academic or professional writing, treat *data* as plural. *These data indicate that fewer people are smoking.*

different from, different than *Different from* is generally preferred in academic and professional writing, although both of these phrases are widely used. *Her lab results were no different from* [not *than*] *his.*

discreet, discrete *Discreet* means "tactful" or "prudent." *Discrete* means "separate" or "distinct." *The leader's discreet efforts kept all the discrete factions unified.*

disinterested, uninterested *Disinterested* means "unbiased." *Uninterested* means "indifferent." *Finding disinterested jurors was difficult. She was uninterested in the verdict.*

distinct, distinctive *Distinct* means "separate" or "well defined." *Distinctive* means "characteristic." *Germany includes many distinct regions, each with a distinctive accent.*

doesn't, don't *Doesn't* is the contraction for *does not*. Use it with *he, she, it*, and singular nouns. *Don't* stands for *do not*; use it with *I, you, we, they*, and plural nouns.

due to See *because of, due to*.

each other, one another Use *each other* in sentences involving two subjects and *one another* in sentences involving more than two.

effect See *affect, effect.*

elicit, illicit The verb *elicit* means "draw out." The adjective *illicit* means "illegal." *The police elicited from the criminal the names of others involved in illicit activities.*

elude See *allude, elude.*

emigrate from, immigrate to *Emigrate from* means "move away from one's country." *Immigrate to* means "move to another country." *We emigrated from Norway in 1999. We immigrated to the United States.*

ensure See *assure, ensure, insure.*

enthused, enthusiastic Use *enthusiastic* rather than *enthused* in academic and professional writing.

equally as good Replace this redundant phrase with *equally good* or *as good.*

every day, everyday *Everyday* is an adjective meaning "ordinary." *Every day* is an adjective and a noun, meaning "each day." *I wore everyday clothes almost every day.*

every one, everyone *Everyone* is a pronoun. *Every one* is an adjective and a pronoun, referring to each member of a group. *Because he began after everyone else, David could not finish every one of the problems.*

except See *accept, except.*

explicit, implicit *Explicit* means "directly or openly expressed." *Implicit* means "indirectly expressed or implied." *The explicit message of the ad urged consumers to buy the product, while the implicit message promised popularity if they did so.*

farther, further *Farther* refers to physical distance. *How much farther is it to Munich? Further* refers to time or degree. *I want to avoid further delays.*

fewer, less Use *fewer* with nouns that can be counted. Use *less* with general amounts that you cannot count. *The world needs fewer bombs and less hostility.*

finalize *Finalize* is a pretentious way of saying "end" or "make final." *We <u>closed</u>* [not *finalized*] *the deal.*

firstly, secondly, etc. *First, second,* etc., are more common in U.S. English.

flaunt, flout *Flaunt* means to "show off." *Flout* means to "mock" or "scorn." *The drug dealers <u>flouted</u> authority by <u>flaunting</u> their wealth.*

former, latter *Former* refers to the first and *latter* to the second of two things previously mentioned. *Kathy and Anna are athletes; the <u>former</u> plays tennis, and the <u>latter</u> runs.*

further See *farther, further.*

good, well *Good* is an adjective and should not be used as a substitute for the adverb *well. Gabriel is a <u>good</u> host who cooks <u>well</u>.*

good and *Good and* is colloquial for "very"; avoid it in academic and professional writing.

hanged, hung *Hanged* refers to executions; *hung* is used for all other meanings.

hardly See *can't hardly.*

herself, himself, myself, yourself Do not use these reflexive pronouns as subjects or as objects unless they are necessary. *Jane and I* [not *myself*] *agree. They invited John and me* [not *myself*].

he/she, his/her Better solutions for avoiding sexist language are to write out *he or she,* to eliminate pronouns entirely, or to make the subject plural. Instead of writing *Everyone should carry his/her driver's license,* try *<u>Drivers</u> should carry <u>their</u> licenses* or *<u>People</u> should carry <u>their</u> driver's licenses.*

himself See *herself, himself, myself, yourself.*

hisself Use *himself* instead in academic or professional writing.

hopefully *Hopefully* is often used informally to mean "it is hoped," but its formal meaning is "with hope." *Sam watched the roulette wheel <u>hopefully</u>* [not *Hopefully, Sam will win*].

hung See *hanged, hung.*

illicit See *elicit, illicit.*

illusion See *allusion, illusion.*

immigrate to See *emigrate from, immigrate to.*

impact Some readers object to the colloquial use of *impact* or *impact on* as a verb meaning "affect." *Population control may reduce* [not *impact*] *world hunger.*

implicit See *explicit, implicit.*

imply, infer To *imply* is to suggest indirectly. To *infer* is to guess or conclude on the basis of indirect suggestion. *The note implied they were planning a small wedding; we inferred we would not be invited.*

inside of, outside of Use *inside* and *outside* instead. *The class regularly met outside* [not *outside of*] *the building.*

insure See *assure, ensure, insure.*

interact, interface *Interact* is a vague word meaning "do something that somehow involves another person." *Interface* is computer jargon; when used as a verb, it means "discuss" or "communicate." Avoid both verbs in academic and professional writing.

irregardless, regardless *Irregardless* is a double negative. Use *regardless.*

is when, is where These vague expressions are often incorrectly used in definitions. *Schizophrenia is a psychotic condition in which* [not *is when* or *is where*] *a person withdraws from reality.*

its, it's *Its* is the possessive form of *it*. *It's* is a contraction for *it is* or *it has*. *It's important to observe the rat before it eats its meal.*

kind, sort, type These singular nouns should be modified with *this* or *that*, not *these* or *those*, and followed by other singular nouns, not plural nouns. *Wear this kind of dress* [not *those kind of dresses*].

kind of, sort of In formal writing, avoid these colloquialisms. *Amy was somewhat* [not *kind of*] *tired.*

know, no Use *know* to mean "understand." *No* is the opposite of *yes.*

later, latter *Later* means "after some time." *Latter* refers to the second of two items named. *Juan and Chad won all their early matches, but the latter was injured later in the season.*

latter See *former, latter* and *later, latter.*

lay, lie *Lay* means "place" or "put." Its main forms are *lay, laid, laid*. It generally has a direct object, specifying what has been placed. *She laid her books on the desk. Lie* means "recline" or "be positioned" and does not take a direct object. Its main forms are *lie, lay, lain. She lay awake until two.*

leave, let *Leave* means "go away." *Let* means "allow." *Leave alone* and *let alone* are interchangeable. *Let me leave now, and leave* [or *let*] *me alone from now on!*

lend, loan In academic and professional writing, do not use *loan* as a verb; use *lend* instead. *Please lend me your pen so that I may fill out this application for a loan.*

less See *fewer, less.*

let See *leave, let.*

liable See *apt, liable, likely.*

lie See *lay, lie.*

like See *as, as if, like.*

likely See *apt, liable, likely.*

literally *Literally* means "actually" or "exactly as stated." Use it to stress the truth of a statement that might otherwise be understood as figurative. Do not use *literally* as an intensifier in a figurative statement. *Mirna was literally at the edge of her seat* may be accurate, but *Mirna is so hungry that she could literally eat a horse* is not.

loan See *lend, loan.*

loose, lose *Lose* is a verb meaning "misplace." *Loose* is an adjective that means "not securely attached." *Sew on that loose button before you lose it.*

lots, lots of Avoid these informal expressions meaning "much" or "many" in academic or professional discourse.

man, mankind Replace these terms with *people, humans, humankind, men and women*, or similar wording.

may See *can, may.*

may be, maybe *May be* is a verb phrase. *Maybe* is an adverb that means "perhaps." *He may be the head of the organization, but maybe someone else would handle a crisis better.*

media *Media* is the plural form of the noun *medium* and takes a plural verb in formal contexts. *The media are* [not *is*] *obsessed with scandals.*

might of See *could of.*

moral, morale A *moral* is a succinct lesson. *The moral of the story is that generosity is rewarded. Morale* means "spirit" or "mood." *Office morale was low.*

myself See *herself, himself, myself, yourself.*

no See *know, no.*

nor, or Use *either* with *or* and *neither* with *nor.*

number See *amount, number.*

off, of Use *off* without *of. The spaghetti slipped off* [not *off of*] *the plate.*

OK, O.K., okay All are acceptable spellings, but avoid the term in academic and professional discourse.

on account of Use this substitute for *because of* sparingly or not at all.

one another See *each other, one another.*

or See *nor, or.*

outside of See *inside of, outside of.*

owing to the fact that Avoid this and other wordy expressions for *because.*

passed, past Use *passed* to mean "went by" or "received a passing grade": *The marching band passed the reviewing stand.* Use *past* to refer to a time before the present: *Historians study the past.*

per In formal writing, use the Latin *per* only in standard technical phrases such as *miles per hour.* Otherwise, find English equivalents. *As mentioned in* [not *As per*] *the latest report, the country's average daily food consumption is only 2,000 calories.*

percent, percentage Use *percent* with a specific number; use *percentage* with an adjective such as *large* or *small. Last year, 80 percent of the members were female. A large percentage of the members are women.*

plenty *Plenty* means "enough" or "a great abundance." *They told us America was a land of plenty.* Colloquially, it is used to mean "very," a usage you should avoid in academic and professional writing. *He was very* [not *plenty*] *tired.*

plus *Plus* means "in addition to." *Your salary plus mine will cover our expenses.* In academic writing, do not use *plus* to mean "besides" or "moreover." *That dress does not fit me. Besides* [not *Plus*], *it is the wrong color.*

precede, proceed *Precede* means "come before"; *proceed* means "go forward." *Despite the storm that preceded the ceremony, the wedding proceeded on schedule.*

pretty Except in informal situations, avoid using *pretty* as a substitute for "rather," "somewhat," or "quite." *Bill was quite* [not *pretty*] *disagreeable.*

principal, principle When used as a noun, *principal* refers to a head official or an amount of money; when used as an adjective, it means "most significant." *Principle* means "fundamental law or belief." *Albert went to the principal and defended himself with the principle of free speech.*

proceed See *precede, proceed.*

quotation, quote *Quote* is a verb, and *quotation* is a noun. *He quoted the president, and the quotation* [not *quote*] *was preserved in history books.*

raise, rise *Raise* means "lift" or "move upward." (Referring to children, it means "bring up.") It takes a direct object; someone raises something. *The guests raised their glasses to toast. Rise* means "go upward." It does not take a direct object; something rises by itself. *She saw the steam rise from the pan.*

rarely ever Use *rarely* by itself, or use *hardly ever. When we were poor, we rarely went to the movies.*

real, really *Real* is an adjective, and *really* is an adverb. Do not substitute *real* for *really*. In academic and professional writing, do not use *real* or *really* to mean "very." *The old man walked very* [not *real* or *really*] *slowly.*

reason is because Use either *the reason is that* or *because*—not both. *The reason the copier stopped is that* [not *is because*] *the paper jammed.*

reason why Avoid this expression in formal writing. *The reason* [not *reason why*] *this book is short is market demand.*

regardless See *irregardless, regardless.*

respectfully, respectively *Respectfully* means "with respect." *Respectively* means "in the order given." *Karen and David are, respectively, a juggler and an acrobat. The children treated their grandparents respectfully.*

rise See *raise, rise.*

set, sit *Set* usually means "put" or "place" and takes a direct object. *Sit* refers to taking a seat and does not take an object. *Set your cup on the table, and sit down.*

should of See *could of.*

since Be careful not to use *since* ambiguously. In *Since I broke my leg, I've stayed home*, the word *since* might be understood to mean either "because" or "ever since."

sit See *set, sit.*

so In academic and professional writing, avoid using *so* alone to mean "very." Instead, follow *so* with *that* to show how the intensified condition leads to a result. *Aaron was so tired that he fell asleep at the wheel.*

someplace Use *somewhere* instead in academic and professional writing.

some time, sometime, sometimes *Some time* refers to a length of time. *Please leave me some time to dress. Sometime* means "at some indefinite later time." *Sometime I will take you to London. Sometimes* means "occasionally." *Sometimes I eat sushi.*

sort See *kind, sort, type.*

sort of See *kind of, sort of.*

stationary, stationery *Stationary* means "standing still"; *stationery* means "writing paper." *When the bus was stationary, Pat took out stationery and wrote a note.*

subsequently See *consequently, subsequently.*

supposed to, used to Be careful to include the final *-d* in these expressions. *He is supposed to attend.*

sure, surely Avoid using *sure* as an intensifier. Instead, use *certainly. I was certainly glad to see you.*

take See *bring, take.*

than, then Use *than* in comparative statements. *The cat was bigger than the dog.* Use *then* when referring to a sequence of events. *I won, and then I cried.*

that, which A clause beginning with *that* singles out the item being described. *The book that is on the table is a good one* specifies the book on the table as opposed to some other book. A clause beginning with *which* may or may not single out the item, although some writers use *which* clauses only to add more information about an item being described. *The book, which is on the table, is a good one* contains a *which* clause between the commas. The clause simply adds extra, nonessential information about the book; it does not specify which book.

theirselves Use *themselves* instead in academic and professional writing.

then See *than, then.*

thorough, threw, through *Thorough* means "complete": *After a thorough inspection, the restaurant reopened. Threw* is the past tense of *throw*, and *through* means "in one side and out the other": *He threw the ball through a window.*

to, too, two *To* generally shows direction. *Too* means "also." *Two* is the number. *We, too, are going to the meeting in two hours.* Avoid using *to* after *where. Where are you flying* [not *flying to*]?

two See *to, too, two.*

type See *kind, sort, type.*

uninterested See *disinterested, uninterested.*

unique Some people argue that *unique* means "one and only" and object to usage that suggests it means merely "unusual." In formal writing, avoid constructions such as *quite unique.*

used to See *supposed to, used to.*

very Avoid using *very* to intensify a weak adjective or adverb; instead, replace the adjective or adverb with a stronger, more precise, or more colorful word. Instead of *very nice*, for example, use *kind, warm, sensitive, endearing*, or *friendly.*

way, ways When referring to distance, use *way. Graduation was a long way* [not *ways*] *off.*

well See *good, well.*

where In formal writing, use *where* alone, not with words such as *at* and *to. Where are you going* [not *going to*]?

which See *that, which.*

who, whom In formal writing, use *who* if the word is the subject of the clause and *whom* if the word is the object of the clause. *Monica, who smokes incessantly, is my godmother.* (*Who* is the subject of the clause; the verb is *smokes.*) *Monica, whom I saw last winter, lives in Tucson.* (*Whom* is the object of the verb *saw.*) Because *whom* can seem excessively formal, some writers rephrase sentences to avoid it.

who's, whose *Who's* is a contraction for *who is* or *who has. Who's on the patio? Whose* is a possessive form. *Whose sculpture is in the garden? Whose is on the patio?*

would of See *could of.*

yet See *but yet.*

your, you're *Your* shows possession. *Bring your sleeping bag along. You're* is the contraction for *you are. You're in the wrong sleeping bag.*

yourself See *herself, himself, myself, yourself.*

Index

with Glossary of Terms

Words in blue are followed by a definition. **Boldface** terms in definitions are themselves defined elsewhere in this index.

E

Q

R

regular verb, 118 A **verb** that forms the **past tense** and past **participle** by adding *-d* or *-ed* to the **base form** (*care, cared, cared; look, looked, looked*).

subject The **noun** or **pronoun** and related words that indicate who or what a **sentence** is about. The simple subject is the noun or pronoun:

W

Look for the "Multilingual" icon to find advice of special interest to international students and others whose home language is not English.

Boxed Tips for Multilingual Writers

Revision Symbols

Numbers in bold refer to sections of this book.

abbr	abbreviation **42a**
ad	adjective/adverb **24**
agr	agreement **23, 26b**
awk	awkward
cap	capitalization **41**
case	case **26a**
cliché	cliché **20d**
com	incomplete comparison **30d**
concl	weak conclusion
cs	comma splice **28**
def	define
dm	dangling modifier **25c**
doc	documentation **45–48**
emph	emphasis unclear
ex	example needed
frag	sentence fragment **29**
fs	fused sentence **28**
hyph	hyphen **44**
inc	incomplete construction **30**
it	italics **43**
jarg	jargon **20a**
lc	lower case **41**
lv	language variety **19**
mix	mixed construction **30, 34**
mm	misplaced modifier **25a**
ms	manuscript form **45c, 46b, 47b, 48a**
no ,	no comma **35i**
num	number **42b**
¶	paragraph
//	faulty parallelism **33**
para	paraphrase **15a**
pass	inappropriate passive **21g, 34b**
ref	unclear pronoun reference **26c**
run-on	run-on (fused) sentence **28**
sexist	sexist language **18b, 26b**
shift	shift **34**
slang	slang **20a**
sp	spelling
sum	summarize **15a**
trans	transition
verb	verb form **21**
vs	verb sequence **21f**
vt	verb tense **21e–f**
wc	word choice **20**
wrdy	wordy **32**
wv	weak verb **32d**
ww	wrong word **20b**
. ? !	period, question mark, exclamation point **37**
,	comma **35**
;	semicolon **36**
'	apostrophe **38**
" "	quotation marks **39**
( ) [ ] —	parentheses, brackets, dash **40a–c**
: / . . .	colon, slash, ellipses **40d–f**
^	insert
∼	transpose
⁀	close up
X	delete